WITH PERRY TO JAPAN

William Heine, brigadier general (brevet), 1865.
(U.S. Army Military History Institute)

With Perry to Japan

A MEMOIR BY WILLIAM HEINE

TRANSLATED,

WITH AN INTRODUCTION AND ANNOTATIONS,

BY FREDERIC TRAUTMANN

UNIVERSITY OF HAWAII PRESS

HONOLULU

The portion of Heine's text presented here was
first published as part of *Reise um die Erde
nach Japan an Bord der Expeditions-Escadre unter
Commodore M. C. Perry.* 2 vols. Leipzig: Hermann
Costenoble; New York: Carl F. Günther, 1856.

Library of Congress Cataloging-in-Publication Data

Heine, Wilhelm, 1827–1885.

[Reise um die Erde nach Japan. English. Selections]

With Perry to Japan : a memoir / by William Heine ; translated,

with an introduction and annotations

by Frederic Trautmann.

p.   cm.

Translation of: Reise um die Erde nach Japan.

Includes bibliographical references.

ISBN 0–8248–1258–1 (alk. paper)

1. United States Naval Expedition to Japan, 1852–1854. 2. Heine,
Wilhelm, 1827–1885—Journeys—Japan. 3. Japan—Description and
travel—1801–1900. I. Trautmann, Frederic. II. Title.

DS881.8.H452513 1990   89–20495

915.204'25—dc20   CIP

University of Hawaii Press books are printed
on acid-free paper and meet the guidelines
for permanence and durability of the Council
on Library Resources.

To

Alexander von Humboldt

(W. H.)

To

Oskar

(F. T.)

CONTENTS

I N T H E S E pages I bring home to my country the most important part of William Heine's account of his journey with Commodore Perry around the world to Japan. Thus I put into English and return to the United States a memoir of an American enterprise. I remake it into the language it belongs in, I refer it to the audience most interested in it, and I restore it to the nation entitled to it. Heine drew navy pay and received a grant from Congress, and I hand his work to readers whose ancestors paid for it.

Heine earned his pay. For in Perry's report of the expedition, in those hundreds upon hundreds of pages, one fact recurs: *Mr. Heine took a sketch of it.* He went everywhere, up a tree or a cliff, for a look at the view, the thing, or the event. He studied, painted, and drew, and he produced the biggest and finest part of the visual record. He also wrote the longest, liveliest, and most-detailed memoir, better in literary quality than anything else by eyewitnesses and second only to Perry's report in descriptive value. Henry F. Graff, in *Bluejackets with Perry to Japan,* lists Heine's among the significant books on the expedition.

Yet Heine has received little notice and less credit. He has been not only slighted but also wronged. In *Black Ships off Japan* Arthur Walworth refers but three times to Heine and once to his memoir. The references are brief and treat a translation of the memoir as if it were the original. In *"Old Bruin"* Samuel Eliot Morison calls the memoir "a partial German translation" of Perry's report, although it appeared at the same time and does not resemble it. Worse he suggests that before the expedition Heine did nothing but become an artist, and that afterward he merely returned to Germany to write "a brief history of Japan in German" and died "a private teacher of landscape painting."

Before he joined Perry, Heine was an artist and illustrator, a teacher of painting in Europe and the United States, a consular aide in Central America, and an author. After Perry's expedition he returned to Japan as an artist with the Prussian Far-Eastern Expedition, held three commands and finished as a brigadier general in the

Civil War, and served as a member of the diplomatic corps in Paris and Liverpool. Yet Heine's images of the Perry expedition and his memoir of it remain his greatest service to America and his supreme achievement. On the expedition he drew, painted, and sketched a handsome portfolio of genre pictures as well as landscapes, portraits, and studies of plants, animals, fish, and birds, thus making the expedition the most widely illustrated American event before the Civil War. A glance at the *oeuvre* verifies plenty of art good enough to certify a first-rate artist and confirm a master illustrator. Heine was also Perry's collector and curator of natural history, a member of the team of surveyors and mapmakers, and the assistant daguerreotypist.

Heine wrote more in his memoir than I have included here. He told the story of Perry's worldwide expedition and added documents translated from English, two volumes in all. The section on the opening of Japan, most of the narrative, appears in this book: his introduction (Chapter 1 here) and Chapters 12 through 27 and part of 29 (Chapters 2 through 18 here). The rest of the voyage, getting to Japan and back, and Heine's discussion of it, are of marginal significance and would detract from the heart of the matter here as they do in the original work. They say nothing my introduction does not say more effectively and with more emphasis. Needless and distracting extras therefore do not appear here.

Of the chapters included, their original sequence has been kept and not a word cut except a few snippets meaningless to today's reader of English. The locations of the cuts have been noted at the point of excision. Within chapters, however, paragraphing has sometimes been changed, and the sequence of paragraphs and sentences altered once in a while. A few sentences and an occasional phrase have been moved a distance. The word or phrase now and then imported beyond translator's license has been put in brackets.

The shifts and the interpolations have not been made to improve Heine's composition. He wrote well; his German wants no alteration. My intent has been to serve clarity, coherence, and emphasis by redesigning where necessary, especially by reshaping Germanic rhythms along English lines.

Likewise, in translating, I have departed from *verbatim et literatim* only when necessity has dictated the *sine qua non* of affable diction and congenial cadence. As the immigrant changes in the melting pot, so the immigrant message changes in the translator's caldron. But meaning has been preserved at all costs, and style where the price was right. True, Heine might not be so kind to me as Gabriel García Márquez was to his translator, Gregory Rabassa. According to Márquez, the translation *One Hundred Years of Solitude* improved the original. But if something has been lost by remodeling Germanic periods, something may have been won with added pith of English points.[1]

I rejected the Germanic forms of Asian names and other words. They are problematic enough in English. Edo, or Yedo, Tokyo's, or Tokio's, former name, appears in newspapers of 1853 and 1854 as Yedo, Yeddo, Jedo, Jeddo, and Jesso. We need not look far in the writings of that time to find *seogoon* and *szeogoun* as well as *shogun*. Authors, including Perry, were divided over Loo Choo and Lew Chew, adaptations of the romanized Chinese Liuqiu or Liu-ch'iu. Today, transliterating the Japanese, we call the island group Ryukyu. Its chief city, Naha, has been Napafoo, Napha, Napachan, Napa Keang, and Napa-Kiang. In spelling I have followed either *Japan: The Official Guide* or the Kodansha *Encyclopedia of Japan* wherever possible. Perforce I have kept Heine's spellings when his names of people and places cannot be checked.

Dates often vary from source to source. I interpolated corrections when Heine's dates are grossly off—a month, say—and patently wrong. Minor deviations I let stand unless the sources agree that Heine was wrong.

However faithfully translated and accurately edited, the text could not stand alone. Time has dimmed what an 1856 reader might have seen in the newspaper and heard on the street. Subsequent scholarship has brought to light what nobody could have known then. I have therefore annotated points that need explanation or benefit from discussion. Annotations are sometimes in brackets within the text but are usually in the notes.

References to sources as a rule support them. The sources compose most of the bibliography and a few more citations complete it, rounding out an up-to-date list. Morison's *"Old Bruin"* has the fullest listing of pictorial and documentary sources, Japanese as well as American, up to 1967. For the best list before 1937, especially of events leading to the expedition, see Sakamaki's "Western Concepts of Japan and the Japanese, 1800–1854."

I have told of Heine's life to its end so that the reader may know the author, yet I resisted the temptation to expand the introduction and apparatus into a life of Heine and a history of the expedition. Both should be written but not here. No source says much about Heine, and the longest are in German. Because the scene must be set and the players put in motion, I have contributed exposition for clarity before the curtain goes up, and my notes are the promptbook against faltering action throughout. Still my task has been subsidiary and secondary, my role at most supporting. I have done my best if Heine looks his best. Therefore—this to be noted above all—my introduction and apparatus elaborate Heine's view of the expedition as an act of aggression against Japan.

Introduced and annotated, the memoir suffices as an eyewitness account of the expedition. I remind the reader that, in addition to the introduction and annotations, my chronology at the end of the memoir puts it in a context beginning with Japan and the West in the 1540s, continuing through Heine's life and the Perry expedition, and ending with Heine's death in 1885. Collateral readings will also increase understanding and enhance appreciation. Robert L. Reynolds' *Commodore Perry in Japan,* though for younger readers, is thorough and accurate. It brings the expedition to life with a wealth of color illustrations, many by Heine and by Japanese artists. Walworth adds an important bibliography to a comprehensive account in *Black Ships off Japan.* Perry's personal journal and official narrative, although not without an occasional bright passage, on the whole serve as encyclopedias that resist prolonged reading. Both have numerous illustrations, many by Heine. Two novels, rich in fictional improvisation yet true to historical fact, illuminate what happened at the time of the expedition and offer scenarios of what could have happened: Lynn Guest's *Yedo* and especially Shimazaki Tōson's *Before the Dawn.* They show daily life and interpersonal relations as they are influenced by historic events. Those books helped with the writing of this one. Had I not been helped, this would have been less of a book, perhaps no book at all.

My gratitude to Beth Trautmann, who cares and understands, always; to Cathy Meaney, Betty Denkins, and Liz Romano of Interlibrary Loan, Paley Library, Temple University, who brought scores of books and reams of articles thousands of miles to my hand; to the friendly faces and helpful spirits at the Paley reference desk, who treated my questions with serious concern and usually had the answers; to Elizabeth Delano Whiteman and Maxwell Whiteman, good readers who value books as much as Milton did; to David M. Neigher, kind, wise, generous, always; to Temple University's James N. Myers, Director of Libraries, and Steven J. Phillips, Professor of Anatomy, who didn't know they were helping and may be amazed to learn that they helped a lot. Thanks also to William A. Bayreuther, Curator, Penobscot Marine Museum; Judith Blakely, The Old Print Gallery, Inc.; Mary Carey, Reference Librarian, The New York Historical Society; Bernard F. Cavalcante, Head, Operational Archives Branch, Naval Historical Center; James W. Cheevers, Senior Curator, United States Naval Academy Museum; Michael Jaehle, Assistant Curator, Philadelphia Maritime Museum; Stanley Kalkus, Navy Department Library; Kenneth M. Newman, The Old Print Shop, Inc.; Lois Oglesby, Research Associate, The Mariner's Museum; Rhoda S. Ratner, Chief Librarian, National Museum of American History; Dorothy H. Schneider, Librarian, Philadelphia Maritime Museum; Mary C. Schroeder, Cataloguer, Mystic Seaport Museum; Jo Anne Triplett, National Museum of American Art; Roberta Waddell, Curator of Prints, The New York Public Library; Galen R. Wilson, Manuscript Curator, William L. Clements Library; A. Paul Winfisky, Keeper of Pictures, Peabody Museum of Salem; and to Lady Luck most of all, the best of muses, who smiled again.

Thanks to them I can offer on Heine's behalf, to a different audience and generation in this century and beyond, his memoir of the Japan expedition: the story of the era's most dangerous voyage and of the argonauts who sailed into the unknown. They did what they set out to do, and they were brave. "As long as God grant me health and the strength of youth," Heine said, "I must bear the obligation to be active and do what I can for the common good." Health and strength to the argonauts of today and tomorrow! May you reach the stars Heine and Perry could only steer by. May you bring home a golden fleece they could not have dreamed of. Let it be for the common good.

INTRODUCTION

He asked what business we had out of our own islands,
unless upon the score of trade or treaty, or to defend
the coasts with our fleet.

Swift, *Gulliver's Travels*

IN JULY of 1846 the USS *Columbus* and the USS *Vincennes* anchored in Edo Bay, Japan. Commodore James Biddle had sailed halfway around the world and into the waters of the capital to ask: Would Japan end two hundred years of isolation and become friends and begin trade? Or would Japan keep its promise to spurn foreign devils and smash barbarians? War junks, girded with soldiers in battle dress, circled and hemmed in the men-of-war. The commodore went in full uniform to a junk for the answer. A soldier pushed him off the junk. The authorities apologized for the shove but not for their answer. "Depart as quick as possible, and not come any more in Japan."[1]

Japan had rejected the United States before. Two fur-trading ships had called in 1791, but the Japanese would not do business. In 1837 the *Morrison* tried at Edo to repatriate Japanese sailors wrecked off the Oregon coast and to land missionaries. Gunfire repelled the unarmed *Morrison* there and at Kagoshima. A few years later the whaler *Manhattan* was sent away while bringing castaways home. Japan seemed determined to remain as it had been since 1638: shut.

Meanwhile the United States wanted more and more to reach this "strange, exclusive" Japan, "which we hoped to open to the world":[2] Secretary of State James Monroe considered Commodore David Porter's proposition to dispatch a squadron in search of a treaty in 1815; Thomas Hart Benton preferred sending representatives to the Orient rather than Europe in 1821; President Jackson authorized a treaty in 1835; a congressional resolution sent Biddle to suffer the insult at Edo Bay in 1846. By then trade with China and the Indies, growing since 1784, had increased America's presence in Asian waters. Whaling north of Japan had been expanding

for decades, and American whalers based in the Sandwich Islands
desired stations nearer the North Pacific grounds, in the Bonins or
Japan. While a ship in sail from New England took as long as six
months to reach China, a merchantman in steam from Oregon
could now raise China in two or three weeks. The Pacific Mail
Steamship Company proposed a regular San Francisco and Canton
run. A brisk traffic quickened during the Gold Rush. Steam begot
the need for coal (preferably mined on site), and Japan was thought
to have coal. Americans also wanted exploration, surveys and
charts, protection for castaways, and trade.

Diplomacy was out of the question. Except for limited relations
with the Dutch, Japan had nothing to do with the West. C. W.
King, writing about the failure of his ship, the *Morrison,* proposed
that a squadron serve an ultimatum for open ports, a legation, and
consulates.[3] Aaron Haight Palmer, director of the American and
Foreign Agency for international trade, had been beating the same
drum to blockade a Japan too weak to resist and to force her open.[4]
In 1849 Commander James Glynn and the USS *Preble* met with
resistence when they attempted to collect Americans lately shipwrecked. Glynn obeyed orders to be respectfully firm, but he
implied a counterthreat. The Japanese released the Americans.[5] This
success seemed to confirm the European view that Japan could neither mount much self-defense nor repel a few Western warships.
Glynn, like King and Palmer, and later Commodore John H. Aulick
in 1851, recommended opening Japan with a naval force.

In 1850 Millard Fillmore became president. To Fillmore America's success in the West ought not be stopped at seaboard. Let head-
way continue, let American interests advance, if not to the ends of
the earth, then to the other side of the globe. But Japan refused to
cooperate. Fillmore changed American policy in a "great Presidential decision."[6]

With Secretary of State Daniel Webster, Fillmore worked to take
America across the Pacific. Although steamers could reach China in
two or three weeks from Oregon, trade still plied between the
northeastern United States and the Far East, a trip of months
around the Horn or around the world. Fillmore's New York and
Webster's Massachusetts owned many of the bottoms, and their
ports dispatched the expeditions and received the goods. To break
through the Central American barrier Fillmore and Webster sent a

warship to the Mosquito Coast to end a disagreement with Britain about a canal. They then told France that the Sandwich Islands would be free or they would be American. With a canal possible and the islands as a stepping-stone, America could proceed to Japan.[7]

Japan had been shut for over two hundred years. Foreign devils knew little of it and had not been there long when the Tokugawa shogunate began driving them out in 1616. By 1638 only the Dutch remained. They had helped suppress Japanese Christians in 1637 and now served as intermediaries with the West. They served so well that the Japanese astounded the Perry expedition with their knowledge of American affairs. Still the Dutch were confined to a few supervised enclaves on the main islands and chiefly to the "Dutch factory" at Deshima in the southwestern corner of the country, remote from all cities except Nagasaki, itself isolated and of secondary importance. "That is where the Dutch traders lived cooped up like chickens for two hundred and fifty years," the captain of the HMS *Topaz* said, pointing to Deshima. "Not even allowed a Christian church or priest. That's how badly the Japanese treated 'em."[8] The Japanese exacted tribute from the Dutch and demanded that it be brought to Edo, where the Dutch debtors must further degrade themselves and titillate officials with lewd acts.

Biddle, Glynn, and the others had tried to enter Japan with a few ships. Be peaceable, their orders said. Arouse no hostility; incur no distrust. Under a new administration Perry went with a squadron and an admiral's power to command and an ambassador's to negotiate. His orders not only exceeded Biddle's and Glynn's but overstepped what Secretary of State Webster would have wanted. Webster had written orders for Aulick, who had sailed for Japan under a Milquetoast's code in comparison with Perry, who was told to show his strength. Be firm but peaceful. Change to unequivocal if necessary concerning shipwrecked and stranded Americans. No armed assertion except to defend the squadron and its officers. (In Heine's words, "Meet force with force.") But be peaceable. Only flex enough muscle to get in. Exert pressure until the Japanese give in. If need be, shoot your way out. The ambiguity suited Perry: The orders were assertive and could be taken as pugnacious. The restrictions did not preclude interpretation. He could shape orders to circumstances and justify what he wanted.[9] He had determined "to drive by force."[10]

Perry probably wrote the orders himself. Webster lay near death when Perry submitted a draft for state-department revision and approval in 1852. For years Perry had advocated a naval policy to secure commercial interests and military advantage. The 1852 orders favored such a posture and sounded like him, calling the Japanese weak and semi-barbarous, mistreaters of American sailors, and the enemies of mankind. The orders provided for not one or two ships but the United States East India Squadron: a fleet in those days, a sight to stiffen American resolve, a presence to overawe the Japanese, and a force to put teeth in proposals. In October, Webster died. In November, Acting Secretary Conrad approved the orders, probably Perry's draft unrevised.[11]

Not all the squadron was in Japanese waters on treaty day, but the parties signed in the sphere of eight ships, over two hundred cannon and heavy guns, and more than two thousand men. American strength prompted Japanese compliance. Perry had told the Japanese to remove their men guarding his squadron—or he would remove them. When the Japanese waffled over taking Fillmore's letter to the emperor, Perry said an appropriate Japanese official would deliver it—or he would deliver it himself. He refused to withdraw his armed survey boats and sent the *Mississippi* with more surveys deeper into Edo Bay. He left promising to return with a larger force. "Heretofore [the Japanese] have arrogantly dictated to all others, but with us the game is changed. We have said, so must you do— this is our way."[12] In "an act of aggression and a virtual challenge to war," Perry's expedition "broke into the Japanese Islands" and "forced Japan into the international arena."[13]

What had provoked the United States? Why a mission of national priority, bristling with guns, and a squadron of the best ships and the finest sailors and marines? Why no compromise to American dignity, no infringement on American rights, and no harm but only a boost to American interests? Why risk hostilities with a country that sought to be left alone and bothered nobody unless bothered by somebody?

The Japanese had mistreated Americans and other foreigners. They had refused everything—would give or sell nothing, not even food and water—to ships at their ports in need of them. They had insulted Christianity and persecuted Christians. Gulliver, in Japan, begged to be excused from "the ceremony imposed on my countrymen of *trampling upon the crucifix* [italics in original]." The Japanese distrusted Americans, seeing them as imperialists of the European stripe. The Biddle and *Morrison* incidents increased and bolstered American resentment against a feudal despotism. Japan's tyranny was reactionary enough to limit what little contact the country had to China, Korea, and the Netherlands. Neither keeping up with the times nor communicating with other nations, an aloof, a hostile, an inscrutable, a backward Japan halted the advancement of science and hindered navigation by blocking exploration, preventing surveys, and refusing to exchange information.[14] Americans maintaining the racial prejudice shown in their anti-Indian policy, viewed Japanese attitudes and actions as unjust, as wrongs to be righted prima facie, and their own as rights to be asserted de facto.[15]

In addition a young America, throbbing with expansive forces, wanted more trade with China and wanted it to begin with Japan. Manifest Destiny would not stop at the Pacific or shy from a Japan shut to the world.[16] The Destiny meant not only material advancement but also ideological expansion; the flag as well as the ledger.[17] Where the flag and the ledger go, the Book must go also.[18] Missionaries, long in the Sandwich Islands, prayed to get to Japan. Steamships and science, progress incarnate, would subdue the ocean. A knock, and guns at the ready, would open the Japanese door. Aaron Haight Palmer, "the man most responsible" for the expedition, had been talking in such terms since the 1840s.[19] Others now talked the same way. Even Fillmore, something of a jellyfish, pompous and pallid, acted like a Theodore Roosevelt about getting to Japan. It was up to Perry to open Japan in the name of the United States.

━━━━

Matthew Calbraith Perry, "Commander-in-Chief, U.S. Naval Forces, East India, China, and Japan Seas, and Special Envoy to Japan," took his dual post at the age of fifty-eight. A midshipman in 1809, Perry served in the War of 1812 and was active in the cause against the slave trade. He was an advocate of steam-powered ships, a reformer in artillery and officer training, and a commodore of the Gulf Squadron in the Mexican War. He held other important commands at sea and shoreside, and his service had been so distinguished that people confused him with his brother, Oliver Hazard

Perry, the hero of Lake Erie. The Japan expedition, his last sea command and greatest achievement, capped the career of "the Fremont of our military expansion in the Pacific."[20]

Perry was a man of thought and a man of affairs; scholar, engineer, and officer converged with bluenose, missionary, and patriot. A stern visage glowers from Irving's portrait and Palmer's bust. The no-nonsense Perry of downturned mouth suffered neither fools nor jokes. He understood theory, respected facts, admired learning, wanted action, and despised frivolity—with a zealous rectitude.

In the Mediterranean during the War of 1812 he taught himself Spanish and translated a book on Mediterranean hydrography, piloting, and navigation. Spurning the antique and haphazard for the thorough, modern, and systematic, he began what became the Naval Academy and turned pedagogy into education. He addressed artillery, gunnery, explosives, armor, and related topics and tested his discoveries at the proving grounds he founded on Sandy Hook, creating the firepower that would give his words authority in Japan. There Heine took comfort in "our big-bored blasters." The Japanese, fearing the latest and best in artillery and armament, came aboard and talked. "The sharp-faced [Japanese] commandant" seemed to have something else to do. Before departing he "went aft to look at the big gun, asked if it was a Paixhan, took its range to the shore, and then examined the locks of the guns near the gangway."[21] In subsequent discussions of Perry's proposals in official Japanese councils, nothing counted more than American firepower.

Mounting the expedition, Perry had to use all his talents and apply every side of his character. As commodore how to assemble and equip a fleet for the other side of the globe? As ambassador how to deal with Asians?

Months of outlay in money, cerebration, and toil followed. The head of a diplomatic mission must bring gifts. Perry collected a shipload that would signify America and celebrate America's achievements. A telegraph and a railroad, complete with poles, wires, rails, ties—down to the last nut and bolt—were loaded on board. Perry ransacked for anything on Japan and the Orient: pictures, maps, books. He pored over them. He talked to missionaries, captains, and whalers who had been there. He bought dear from Dutch navigators the only charts of waters around Japan. Always prepared, this time Perry prepared as never before.

He picked officers to serve as sailor-commanders, men of "talents and acquirements" expected to gather information as well as box the compass, call to quarters, and shoot the sun. He named Henry A. Adams flag captain and chief-of-squadron. Franklin Buchanan, next in rank, had backed Perry on officer-training reforms and had been the Academy's first commandant. The two men had served with him in the Mexican War, and now each commanded a ship: Adams the *Mississippi*, Buchanan the *Susquehanna*. Together they aided and advised Perry: Adams his right-hand man, Buchanan his good right arm.

He took as his flagship the frigate *Mississippi*, which had been his during the Mexican War and built at his order in Philadelphia in 1840, in his days as a steam advocate. The navy's most useful and economical sidewheeler had carried Hungarian revolutionary Kossuth from Turkey into exile in England in 1850 and had logged more miles "than any war-steamer now afloat" by 1852.[22] That year the era's most famous ship hoisted the pennant of its most famous commander on its most famous voyage. Perry moved the pennant from time to time. The flagship *Susquehanna*, another steam frigate completed in Philadelphia, had been fitted out in Norfolk in 1851 and had gone ahead to the China station. The rest of the fleet, if not already there, would meet in China. The *Princeton*, made out to sail with Perry, stayed in Norfolk and never joined him. A screw-driven clipper of the latest technology, able in theory to spank along in sail and steam, the *Princeton* could not overcome a faulty mechanism. Perry, promised enough ships to augur diplomatic success, set out with only one. He would not show the Japanese a fleet until his return for a treaty: the East India Squadron nearly entire, with crews ready to fire guns enough to batter Japanese defenses and pound the Japanese into agreement.

Perry also saw his mission as one of gathering information. Commanders and leaders had been filing reports at least since the military expeditions and diplomatic embassies of ancient Rome. Perry and others like him believed a commander should do more than say "Veni, vidi, vici." He ought to behave in the spirit of the age and according to Science; to observe, study, measure, count, estimate, sample, describe, and record in the service of Knowledge and for the entertainment and instruction of all. Accordingly, though on an errand of "a naval and diplomatic character," Perry expected officers to contribute "to the general mass of information which it is desirable to collect."[23] After the voyage Perry toiled to consummate the mission with the *Narrative of the Expedition of an American Squadron to the China Seas and Japan,* three volumes, heavy to read and hard to lug but big with information. The treaty, printed in facsimile, pales amid hundreds of pages of text, engravings, colored plates of original art, hydrographic and meteorologic data, and maps and charts of land, sea, and sky representing political and natural science, astronomy, geography, navigation, commerce, ethnology, history, theology, and belles lettres.

Captain James Cook had "set the style" for reporting scientific and military expeditions.[24] Napoleon, also a believer in taking a full account, laid down the notable precedent of making science collateral on a military campaign. In Egypt the French army's scientific contingent amassed volumes on antiquities, geography, and natural history; and an officer of engineers found the Rosetta Stone. Egyptology began when Napoleon authorized publication of the findings years later.[25] Charles Darwin, official naturalist on the *Beagle* (1831–1836), accumulated enough data to elaborate the theory of evolution. Perry's friend Commander Charles Wilkes added artists and scientists to the Pacific Exploring Expedition of 1838.

Perry's general orders were concerned first with gathering information, then with inquiry and research. The first was subject to the rigors of censorship. No unauthorized communications, no leaks to the press were permitted. All diaries, notes, journals, memos, etc., had to be surrendered. Security seems part of the reason for such precautions, as well as the need to insure that worthwhile information did not escape rightful notice and useful application. Yet Perry, wanting no "scientific men," rejected the "literary and scientific" from "all quarters of the world." These men, dedicated to disciplines other than military, would (he said) disrespect authority, clutter the ships, cause trouble ashore, and blur the lines of military enterprise. Besides, officers could collect information: George Jones tripled as geologist, astronomer, and navy chaplain. Perry himself knew botany and conchology. Others could sound, measure, survey, and map. Officers would perhaps be better at collecting such information because of their practical experience. Let scientists back home interpret what was found.[26]

Still some civilians had to be included. Perry had no choice but to take agriculturist James Morrow because Secretary of State Edward Everett had appointed him.[27] Perry himself chose sinologist Samuel Wells Williams and Anton Portman, a Dutchman, as interpreters. More Japanese knew Dutch than any other foreign language, and "full communication could be carried on" in it.[28] Perry accepted Bayard Taylor, who dispatched as "letters" the authorized communiqués to the press and wrote the report of the exploration of Peel Island. Taylor had to join the navy, however, and surrender his journal like the others.[29]

But mere words, Taylor's or even those of a modern-day Homer, would not be enough of a record; there must be pictures too. The age of the pamphleteer was over, and the age of the illustrator had arrived. The painter John White had accompanied surveyor and historian Thomas Hariot to the New World and illustrated *A briefe and true Report of the new found land of Virginia* (1590). On his third voyage Captain Cook not only kept a journal that "communicated keenly in words" but he also enlisted the artist John Webber, a professional "Draughtsman and Landskip Painter," for what he could show.[30] Cook had "set the pattern for scientific expeditions to come."[31] As early as 1819 "some of the nation's foremost artists participated in government-sponsored surveys of the West" and "contributed significantly to subsequent reports."[32] By 1852 custom dictated, the government wanted, and the public expected from Perry a graphic as well as a literary document of the expedition.

So Perry added Eliphalet M. Brown, Jr., and William Heine, established professionals with first-rate portfolios for credentials. They were also young and venturesome and not only willing to interrupt commercial success but also eager to take most of their pay in adventure. The adventure itself, if high enough, would be pay enough for these artistic soldiers of fortune. Heine had been and would continue to be one of America's best illustrators. Brown, draftsman and painter, knew better the emerging art of photography. On the expedition he painted and drew but mainly took photographs. Heine collected zoological specimens, especially birds, and painted and drew them for the record. He and Brown assisted the surveyors and mappers and each other, but Heine, the better painter and draftsman, was the chief artist. They shared the adventure of a world cruise and the perils of the opening of Japan and became boon companions. Brown signed Heine's application for citizenship in 1855.

Charged with making as many pictures as possible, Heine set down anything worth remembering and everything worth recording. He had discerned that the expedition, because of its significance, had the power to bestow fame. If he was ever to be noticed, if he was ever to go down in history, this would be the time. He would be recognized and honored today and remembered and revered tomorrow because he would give posterity eyes; he would let the future recall the past. So "Mr. Heine made a drawing of it" as the official narrative says time and again. Heine would go anywhere for a view or an angle. He created hundreds of images: oils, watercolors, pen and pencil sketches, which were later reproduced and published as lithographs, engravings, and woodcuts. He was also a memoirist, sub rosa. He dodged Perry's censorship and disclosed more in his writing than Perry bargained for when he signed a master artist on at a master's mate's pittance. Never before and not until the Civil War did an event of such magnitude get the representation it deserved in print and pictures.

Heine had been trained in his native Dresden at the Royal Academy of Art and in the studio of Professor Julius Hübner. He studied another three years in Paris. What he learned there about art was useful to him on Perry's expedition. The knowledge he gained of French language and culture served him later when he became a consular clerk in Paris. He worked as a set painter at the royal theater in Dresden. He may have fought with the rebels of 1848, for he arrived with the Forty-Eighters in New York in 1849, among the revolution's exiles if not one of them. He lived, kept a studio, taught art, illustrated books, and painted at 515 Broadway. Landscapes were his specialty, and he and his partner Julius H. Kummer represented the landscape-and-genre movement. In search of subjects and adventure Heine traveled to Niagara Falls, the Great Lakes, and Lake Winnipeg in Hudson Bay Company territory, where he sampled the trapper's life.

Probably in 1851 he met Ephraim George Squier, the archeologist and diplomat. Squier, appointed consul to Central America, intended to study the remains of ancient peoples there and asked Heine to illustrate the books he would write. Delayed in the United

States, Squier sent Heine ahead. Heine collected plants, birds, and reptiles; visited the route of the proposed canal across Nicaragua; took notes for his *Wanderbilden aus Central-Amerika;* stood in for Squier as consul; and delivered to Washington a commercial agreement between Central American countries and the United States.

Heine went to Washington mainly because he wanted to join the Japan expedition, sail around the world, and see the Orient. He made the request as he laid the Central American documents before President Fillmore. The president referred him to the expedition's commander.

In September 1852 Heine left New York with Perry in the *Mississippi* for Annapolis and Norfolk, then sailed across the Atlantic, around Africa, over the Indian Ocean, and through the Malacca Straits to China. He painted and drew and described life aboard and on excursions ashore at Funchal in the Madeiras, in the Canaries, at St. Helena, Capetown, Mauritius, Ceylon, Singapore, and in April 1853 Hong Kong. It was an exciting voyage, as colorful in Heine's words as in his pictures. Off China the skeleton squadron formed for Japan. There was a treaty to win. It would turn a page in the annals of America and bring Japan into the modern world. Heine was the comprehensive historian, watching, drawing, painting, and describing from start to finish an event of the century.

━━━━━━

Perry, though promised thirteen ships, met only three in Hong Kong: the storeship *Supply* and the sloops-of-war *Saratoga* and *Plymouth,* three-masted, square-rigged, and handsome enough but growing obsolete in the age of steam. They were not the flaming, smoking, roaring behemoths to overawe a Japanese nation that had never seen a ship in steam. American merchants had caused the *Susquehanna* to be called elsewhere off China to protect their enterprises from the Taiping Rebellion. Perry waited for her. He had no ships to spare, least of all a frigate of the *Mississippi*'s class and a steamer to add fire to a flotilla of mostly sail. At last they rendezvoused at Okinawa, then called Loo Choo, a monarchy subject vaguely to China and Japan. Perry established a base, sent parties into the countryside to gather information and look for coal, and prepared for Japan by testing in this miniature Japan what he had learned from books and talk. Until the mission was accomplished he conducted himself in such a way as to cope with his need to do the work of two. He retired at 8:00 P.M. and rose at 1:00 A.M. Ambassadorial tasks, such as dictating reports, occupied most of his time in the wee hours before he began his day as commander of the expedition.[33]

Perry took his ships to the Bonin Islands, where he had earlier tried to establish a station for American merchantmen and whalers of the North Pacific. Here they would be able to shelter, refuel, and reprovision under navy protection. Perry charted coasts, gathered information, and bought land for the station. Returning to Loo Choo, he left the *Supply* as a stake in the claim to American harbor-and-landing rights and headed for Japan with the *Mississippi* and the *Susquehanna* towing the two sloops-of-war, the *Saratoga* and the *Plymouth*. They were on urgent business for the United States.

The ships anchored off Uraga in clouds of smoke that betrayed their presence beyond the horizon. This fortified town and port of entry asserted Japan's strongest defenses to protect the capital city up the bay, Edo. The steamships excited so much curiosity that a nation turned out to see them. To the Japanese the ships were novel and extraordinary, nonesuch and nonpareil. Leviathans. Sockdolagers. Phoenixes that burned but did not burn up. "Moving without sails against wind and tide [they] have struck, if not terror, at least wonder and wisdom into [Japanese] souls."[34] Black Ships, they called them, after the hulls and the smoke. Bottles, discarded from them, washed ashore to excite wonder, provoke stories, and prompt official action.[35]

The ships represented darkness before dawn. Signifying a new era, they were awakening Japan from "the long sleep that had begun with the closing of the country."[36] What was taking place, what the ships emblazoned, would touch every individual and affect every nation in the world.[37]

The Japanese saw not historic significance but superships crawling with a horde and bristling with ordnance: two frigates, two sloops-of-war, 977 men, 66 guns, and the emissary of a foreign power asking to be let in. Some Japanese snatched up a few possessions and headed for the hills. Others estimated the firepower, counted on the savagery of barbarians, and factored Japanese interests into the equation. The calculation multiplied the confusion and divided the indecisive. Should they ignore their own weakness and the American overtures and put up a fight? Admit their own frailty and allow the Americans as brutish trespassers but inevitable intruders into an empire hitherto sequestered? Was isolation worth defending? Was it even wanted anymore? Officialdom discussed and debated while the military put together a ramshackle defense and diplomats prepared to meet the foreign devils and negotiate.

The Americans meanwhile saw muskets, swords, pistols, spears, and pikes in a harbor ruffled in alarm and swarming with junks. Thousands of Japanese struck an attitude half inquisitive, half hostile. The Americans loaded guns and sharpened sabers while they polished shoes and pressed pants, getting ready for either outcome but wanting to talk, not shoot, hoping for a treaty, not bloodshed.

Feints, skirmishes without violence, confrontations without incident: There were a few of each. Americans went ashore, shoes shined and pants pressed but with "a thousand charges of ball in the escort besides the contents of the cartridge boxes. Any treachery on [the Japanese's] part would have met a serious revenge."[38] Neither side fired a shot except to demonstrate in good humor the marvel of a Colt. They talked. Perry handed over Fillmore's letter addressed to the emperor. Give us friendship, commerce, coal, provisions, and protection for shipwrecked Americans by treaty, Fillmore said, and Perry repeated. The Japanese stalled. This request to open their country was grave; they wanted to think it over and discuss it. The Americans understood the desire to discuss and debate and returned to China. They would come back next year for the decision.

The Japanese talked and argued but did not decide for a while. Accede or fight? Confused, they considered the terms while continuing to ready their defenses. In the countryside rumors abounded. People rushed back and forth. "There had never been any moving of cannon from provincial domains to Edo residences before that day" after the Black Ships left. "Something must be happening in Edo," what with "the constant movement of the daimyo [local lords] over the Kiso road." At times the confusion was wild.[39]

What caused it? Perry had asked for a treaty and, after a show of strength, promised to return stronger. He expected an answer then. His demand on those terms constituted a sufficient cause, a direct and immediate reason for the perplexity and turmoil. Yet the demand itself might not have produced the response. Material, formal, and final causes also obtained: conditions within Japan, of society and government, and of history, motives, and goals.

The Japanese were unsure of themselves as a people, doubtful about national goals, and vague about who governed. Hereditary shoguns had run Japan since the twelfth century, the Tokugawa shoguns since 1615. Shogun rule had made national leaders of these nobility who also represented the samurai or military class. But however firm their control of politics and the economy, the regime was not absolute. The mikado, though reduced in power as emperor, had not been weakened to a figurehead. Authority still attached to him because he had always been in charge in name if not in fact. While a centuries-old bloodline kept him politically influential, he also enjoyed ecclesiastical sovereignty by birthright. Descended from the sun goddess and therefore a deity, he headed what amounted to the national religion. "The actual government of Japan was like an ellipse with two foci."[40]

The shoguns, sensing modern times obtruding alien ideas upon Japan, wanted nothing of notions that might endanger their position. They had had trouble enough with expressions of unrest too modern in tone, too Western in temper. The peasants, once quiescent, at least tractable, now seemed to riot whenever the rice crop failed. Yet, the shoguns had to concede, new ideas might confer benefits, particularly in science and technology. The Dutch had shown them as much. But science and technology could not be laundered and muted. They glowed with undertones as unassuming yet revolutionary as those found in the paintings of the Dutch masters. The Dutch had also been encouraging relations with the West. The hazy lines between imperial and shogunate rule clouded further. Sides formed over who should run the country and how it should behave toward other countries. By the time of the Black Ships some Japanese wanted imperial power restored and contact with the West renewed. The foreign devils' ideas could be let in and the devils kept out, some said. Bewilderment over leadership had so thickened that when the shogun died ten days after Perry's first visit, Perry thought the emperor had died. When Perry concluded a treaty with the shogun, he thought he had concluded it with the emperor. Heine made the same mistake.[41]

Perry's armed insistence and the state of things in Japan produced the perplexity and turmoil. In official circles they also prompted questions never raised before. Should these powerful intruders be evicted like the earlier, weaker ones? If so, when? How?

Early in 1854, to assembled leaders seeking unity and order, Mito Saki no Chiunagon, "the old Prince of Mito," waved the bloody shirt once more. *Fight* else the barbarians abuse, plunder "and end by swallowing up Japan." The British barbarians had lately ravaged India and China. Abe Ise no Kami and other nobles among the assembly knew about the Opium Wars and what the British had done but disagreed with the prince's interpretation. Yes, Japan must fight. But not yet. If we resist now, the American barbarians will conquer us. Japanese artists had studied the squadron and had made picture scrolls. These had been sent to Edo as information on the Americans' strength. It was enormous. Let us not fight and lose. Let us "grant the requests of these people," trade and communicate with them, "learn their drill and tactics," and "go abroad" to prepare ourselves. "It will not be too late then to declare war."[42]

Perry had pledged to return in July. He returned in February anxious to talk. Other powers desired treaties. The British had become pugnacious, and he feared French and especially Russian designs on Japan. He wanted a settlement now and terms equal to what the competition might get. The president's letter had asked for one port and an assurance of good treatment; Perry now demanded five ports and a treaty, promising "in no obscure terms, 'a larger force and more stringent terms and instructions,' if they don't comply."[43] The Japanese had decided to comply temporarily. Perry would get his treaty; his show of strength and his brazen tenacity had prevailed in Japanese councils. Japan would be peaceable, at least for the time being. Meanwhile Perry's surprise return and magnified urgency, with Japan's lingering confusion, encouraged uncertainty and suspicion on both sides.

So each provided against surprise. The Japanese extended a hand while raising a fist. Officials met Perry amid row upon row of their soldiers in armor, horses at the ready, swords sharpened, pikes gleaming. Perry in turn came ashore to sign with an escort of hundreds off the *Southampton,* the *Mississippi,* the *Saratoga,* the *Powhatan,* the *Macedonian,* the *Susquehanna,* the *Vandalia,* and the *Lexington.* All were behind him and positioned should the need have arisen to let the Japanese have it broadside. Perhaps Perry remembered the *Morrison.* He landed with armed pomp and military ceremony: five hundred men on dress parade, each armed, most with loaded firearms.[44] Major Zeilen headed the marines with sword drawn. Two days after the signing, the Articles of War were read on the ships, and the marines drilled and exercised at the guns.[45]

Amid this cordial suspicion Japan and the United States signed the Treaty of Kanegawa at the cannon's mouth. The treaty opened ports to Americans for provisions, stipulated hospitality for Americans in need of shelter, and allowed a consulate at Shimoda. The treaty also made official the entry of Japan into the modern world. This, the first such agreement by Japan, accomplished "the meeting of the East and West, the circling of the world's intercourse, the beginning of American interference in Asia, the putting of the key in the door of Japanese seclusion, the violation of the sanctity of Japanese soil, and . . . a full revenge for the unprovoked firing on the defenseless *Morrison.* . . ."[46]

Perry had come with a fleet, guns loaded. A Japanese had said, "Let us sign now. There will be time then to declare war." The Japanese asked Perry for three cannons. He requested they be sent from the United States. "The gift will be returned a hundredfold," he said.[47] When the time came, Japan sent a fleet to return Perry's call and the gift of cannon a hundred times a hundredfold.

Perry, tired and arthritic, left the expedition at Hong Kong. Taking the easiest way home, he went back part of the way the *Mississippi* had come, then to Suez and across Europe and the Atlantic to New York. Heine, in the *Mississippi,* completed his first circumnavigation in the first warship to cross the Pacific west to east.

Hong Kong. The Sandwich Islands. San Francisco.

At the Golden Gate the *Mississippi* met the American welcome of the expedition and Heine the praise and sale of his pictures, a preview of the enthusiasm awaiting them in New York.

Panama. Valparaiso. Port Famine. Rio de Janeiro.

The *Mississippi* arrived in New York in April 1855. Perry, there since January, joined the welcoming crowds, for the *Mississippi* was bringing him material for his report: memorabilia, logs and other records with members' notes, journals and diaries impounded under General Order No. 1. Seeking more material, he approached

Williams, praising the sinologist's "valuable notes" already filed by Perry, and asked for additional "valuable aid in the way of notes, etc."[48] Under Perry's direction the Reverend Francis L. Hawks, D. D., L. L. D., rector of Calvary Church, compiled the official narrative with the aid of Dr. Robert Tomes, a physician beginning a career as an author. Heine may have helped.[49]

A compendium as diffuse as it is indispensable for myriad facts, the *Narrative* neither reads easily nor kindles attentiveness. Inherent interest begins and ends with Heine's pictures. It does offer, however, an interpretation that might be attractive and compelling: the expedition as an expression of westward expansion in the spirit of scientific and technical advancement and American progress. But another butts in. The cause of the *Narrative*'s diffusiveness poses a puzzle of inconsistency: a Protestant-moralist stand on ethics, chastity, and rectitude, together with a horror of lewdness and intemperance, added to statements against Catholicism mingled with protests of economic misery and monetary injustice in near-Marxist terms and with all of Marx's secular righteousness.[50] The first interpretation can be understood as the dominant tone of the times. The individual persuasions of too many authors probably produced the second. The moral, ethical, Protestant tenor can be attributed to Hawks and Perry. Severe and a profoundly religious Episcopal communicant, Perry conducted services on board ships without chaplains. Hawks was a man of the cloth as if born to it. Tomes must have contributed the Marxism.

The *Narrative* and Heine's memoir, written and published at the same time, treat the same subject. The similarity ends there. Language, English versus German, is the least of the differences. Indifferent to the morality that bound Perry and Hawks, Heine included in words and pictures a scene they avoided: a public bath and men and women in it together. Heine's work, unlike the sprawling *Narrative,* is compact and informative and pleases the reader with its choice of topics and its grace of expression. Neither committed to tell everything nor compelled to tell anything, he dispatched with one phrase the negotiations that fill page after dull page of the *Narrative:* "many long, boring discussions." The artist as writer broached the subject for his words as he might initiate the scene for his brush: by limning it, setting it to scale, and stressing the essentials. A single phrase or stroke may encompass the whole, having the concentrated intensity of a magnifying glass. Yet he observes people, animals, language, history, customs, architecture, landscape, wildlife, vegetation, weather—anything a vigorous, adventuresome young man with omnivorous, insatiable curiosity and a keen eye might notice as remarkable. Recording what he saw, heard, smelled, tasted, and felt, he describes the intimate, the tête-à-tête of the grand expedition. The *Narrative* stresses overall results while Heine's memoir celebrates individual impressions. The former emphasizes the public, official, and professional; the latter the personal. Heine recalls what any member of the expedition might have felt and what many did feel. He walks, buys, observes, eats, works, dreams, wonders, hunts, and shoots. He chases thieves and catches them. He peeks at local people smoking, eating, and sleeping. He encounters salt pork, saltwater, jungle, hurricane winds, typhoon rains, feral goats, sand, coral, and ship's biscuit. He registers exhilaration and evinces fatigue. He confesses the conflict between the call to adventure and the tug of homesickness. He realizes people more clearly, of course. He includes more on Macao and the Bonin Islands, they being of greater personal than official interest. He contributes detail to the *Narrative*'s generalities and speaks where it remains silent, as on the spies that tailed the first excursion to Loo Choo. Left to the *Narrative* we would not know that the "exploring parties" (1:311) were surveyors under Lieutenant William B. Whiting of the *Vandalia*. Nor would we know why the gate to the palace on Loo Choo was closed (1:189–190). We would miss the drama of imminent *harakiri* when Perry advances upon Edo despite objections by Japanese aboard his ship. A little nearer and they must slice their bellies and spill their guts. True, Heine omits what the *Narrative* and every other memoirist mentions: the wrestlers who fling like pillows 125-pound sacks of rice. But he did what other memoirists could not do. He made drawings of them.

While en route from Asia, Heine put his ornithological and zoological specimens in order. (Later these specimens, some never before seen in the West, would enrich the collections at the Smithsonian Institution.) He also finished expedition drawings and paintings begun earlier and did more, about five hundred altogether. These were soon sold and dispersed to museums and private collections. Reproductions of Heine's work, which illustrated the official narrative as well as his own memoir and books and the books and articles of others, continue to illustrate, decorate, and educate. Sarony & Major, the Currier & Ives of the early 1850s, printed lithographs of Heine's oils and watercolors. Various firms—notably Orr, Roberts, and Richardson & Cox—turned drawings into woodcuts and engravings. The lithographs suffered when they were reprinted in the *Narrative* and the memoir. Heine's later publishers, however, did them justice. The woodcuts and engravings, retaining some of the quality of the original artwork, grace the *Narrative,* notably as capitals and tailpieces. Today the watercolors and oils, originals and reproductions, fetch higher and higher prices. Some have returned east with the current migration of Western art, back to the Orient that called them forth. Thanks to Heine's work, no event has been more artistically documented in color.

People crowded to see pictures of the expedition and hear lectures on it. Curiosity about Japan prompted Heine's book *Graphic Scenes of the Japan Expedition* (1856), which was well received: No pictures "superior to them have been executed in the United States, and they have no cause to shun comparison with some of the best productions of Europe."[51] By showing what Japan looked like, by portraying it at the time the expedition excited curiosity in Japan and all the Orient, Heine's pictures probably more than anything else quickened the West's interest in Oriental art and inspired its fancy for *chinoiserie,* coromandel screens, Orientalism, japanware, *japonisme,* and Japanese prints. Things Oriental interested and influenced Degas, Whistler, and Van Gogh, Zola and Goncourt, and the lesser artists who followed them.[52]

Congress voted Heine five thousand dollars for his part in Perry's success. Pupils and commissions appeared at 806 Broadway, where he taught art, painted landscapes, and illustrated books. He exhibited at shows of the Washington Art Association in 1857, 1858, and 1859. He also edited and translated into German the report of the North Pacific Surveying Expedition, which had interested him because it was to have joined Perry's and to have cooperated in exploring and charting. He wanted its report to receive international notice and, having published in German his memoir of Perry's expedition, he felt readers would welcome a companion. *Die Expedition in die Seen von China, Japan und Ochotsk* (1858–1859) improved the original, for Heine, not limiting himself to a rendition of the text, enlarged and enhanced it by drawing on the papers of the participants and adding his own experience.[53]

In search of verisimilitude for new works of art he visited North Africa. He headed back via Germany and prepared a book of North African drawings, *Eine Sommerreise nach Tripolis* (1860), and another important collection with text, *Japan und seine Bewohner* (1860). He had been urging the Germans to follow the example of other Western powers and his lecture before the Geographical Society of Berlin had been effective: The German Economic Union, led by Prussia, decided to pursue diplomatic and commercial interests in the Far East. If other powers had sent Black Ships, Prussia would send Black Ships. Heine joined the Prussian East Asia Squadron as artist, photographer, and correspondent to make a second voyage around the world, hundreds more pictures of Japan, and dispatches to German newspapers. He piloted into Edo Bay the corvette *Arcona,* the first German ship to the Japanese capital. He visited China from Japan, went to Peking twice, and planned to go back to Germany via Mongolia and Siberia. But hearing of war in the United States, he chose to go there instead. Not only an American citizen since 1856, Heine had a wife and daughter, both American by birth, and they were in New York.[54] They had been a new mother and babe at breast when he last saw them. He paused for twelve hours after having been away for several years, then left for the Army of the Potomac.

Though assigned to the First Maryland Infantry, Heine spent most of 1862 as a roving captain of topographical engineers. On the Japan expeditions he had used and been praised for his skill in surveying, mapping, and landscape drawing. When the 26 April 1862 issue of *Harper's Weekly* was suppressed, he was arrested and accused of drawings that revealed too much about Union defenses at Yorktown.[55] He wrote in his excellent English several letters in his own behalf, one of them to the president.[56] Charles Worret and *Harper's* editor John Bonner came forward and said Worret, not Heine, had made and submitted the drawings.

In June 1862, Heine was ridden down and captured by cavalry, briefly imprisoned, and harshly treated. In December he resigned his commission and was given an honorable discharge: unfit for service; injured shoulder, worsened by neglect. Bypassing overcrowded Union hospitals, he returned to Germany for treatment. He prepared his memoir of the Prussian East Asia Expedition, *Eine Weltreise um die nördliche Hemisphäre* (1864). He rejoined the army as a colonel and held three commands: 103d New York; First Brigade, Defenses of the Bermuda Hundred, Army of the James; and U.S. Forces, Folly Island, South Carolina (post commandant). Another flurry of his letters, including one to President Lincoln, helped clear him of charges of disobeying orders in 1864. In 1865 he was breveted to brigadier general for faithful and meritorious service and mustered out as "one of the best-known German officers of the American Civil War."[57]

Later, using his several languages, his excellent written English, and his artist's penmanship, he worked as a clerk in the Paris legation and the Liverpool consulate. The corruption of the Grant administration, and the need for civil service reform, may have arrived in Liverpool ahead of him. According to his letters to Secretary of State Hamilton Fish and the President, dishonesty and mismanagement stained and crippled the consulate. He left amid accusations and recriminations, and in a huff.

Return to America? His wife, who had been of old American stock, was dead. His daughter was making her own way in the world. He had been naturalized for twenty years, but Germany was the land of his birth. His mother still lived there, and her health was failing. His trouble in the diplomatic service further weakened his American connections. He returned to stay whence he had departed thirty years before, to Lossnitz near Dresden. He eked out an author and lecturer's modest, erratic income with an American military pension of twenty dollars a month.

A West still inquisitive about Japan continued to welcome his books, especially when illustrated with his pictures. He had submitted eight hundred to one thousand daguerreotypes for the Prussian East Asia Expedition's report, but none had been used. So he saved fifty for posterity, giving readers a book to satisfy the mind, delight the eye, and challenge the muscles: *Japan: Beiträge zur Kenntniss des Landes und seiner Bewohner* (1873), a sumptuous folio, four inches thick, of halftone engravings on heavy stock and text, one of the finest studies of Japan ever done in the West—a triumph of authorship, a palm to the printer's craft, and a celebration of pictorial art. In

1876, after an earthquake called international attention to the capital, Heine published *Yeddo: Nach Original-Skizzen*. Memories of two expeditions informed its forty pages of text. Daguerreotypes from the Prussian East Asia Expedition composed a foldout, five pictures into one panorama, his largest view of Japan, and his last.

When the book appeared, Heine had not seen Japan for fifteen years. Changes begun by the Black Ships had been transforming the country. By 1885 the war in America overshadowed everything. People had said, "Tell us about Japan." Now they said, "Tell us about the war in America, the big one to free the slaves. You were there. You fought." Heine's words about Japan retained but a tincture of currency, his pictures of Japan only a touch of immediacy, and the events of years ago in Japan merely a modicum of interest.

He had gone around the world twice and had taken part in many of the century's events. His name or initials, on most of the best pictures of the Perry expedition, would be remembered as long as Perry's. Who would know what Perry looked like, what anything looked like, were it not "Drawn from Life, by W. Heine"? With pictures, articles, books, and lectures, he had done more than any other Westerner to commemorate the Black Ships and the opening of Japan.

In those days he had put experience to paper, fresh and vivid. Now he relied on memories, dull and faded. He drew and painted and wrote in retrospect—when he could lift a pencil, hold a brush, or dip a pen. Doctors, on Heine's applications for an increase of pension, spoke of *dementia paralytica progressiva* brought on by injury in war and a "fat heart." The man who had climbed trees, scaled cliffs, and dressed the ranks of a regiment was now "enormously fat," weighing three hundred pounds. Dropsy was causing "constant watering" of the thighs. Doctors certified he could not stoop and could barely walk, a helpless wreck, they said. The pension increase was denied. Heine could no longer write letters or complete applications for an increase. He could scarcely sign them. The signature quaked. *Wilhelm Heine, Brigadier General, United States Army, retired.* The old hand of the artist was barely legible. Soon he was dead.

*The infant settlement has become a giant nation,
and this then rich and flourishing Empire reduced
to feebleness, by its contracted ideas, is forced
to treat with the infant and conform to its more
expanded views.*

George Henry Preble, *The Opening of Japan*

CHAPTER ONE

I GET A BERTH

Purpose and Goal of the Expedition.—Commodore Perry.—Difficulty of Getting a Berth on the Expedition.—A Master's Mate.—I Take a Berth on the Frigate *Mississippi*.—Departure from New York.—Side-Trip to Chesapeake Bay.—Annapolis. President Fillmore Comes Aboard for a Final Call.—Norfolk.—The Navy Yards.—Life and Discipline on an American Ship.

FOR A WHILE in my *Wanderbilder aus Central-Amerika* I (the peripatetic artist) led you (the congenial and patient reader) to all sorts of places. Then I trotted along the Nicaraguan road from León to Granada, swam down the St. Johns River, and at last headed north again. Belatedly let me tell you that before I turned my back on Central America the newspapers spoke often and variously of the expedition the United States planned to send to Japan. I hoped to join it.

I wanted to verify for myself, if possible with my own eyes, diverse reports and claims by travelers to the fog-shrouded, remote shores of the Far East. My attention had been drawn there when I studied the ancient history of the Americas; many allusions suggested that ancient tribes departed the fabulous Orient's island empires and populated the Western Hemisphere.[1] Thus, already attracted to the mysterious Pacific, I could not resist the urge to accompany the American expedition. "Cypango," after all, had been the destination of Columbus himself.[2]

But how was I to attach myself to a squadron scheduled to sail at the beginning of May, when the middle of May found me still in León [Nicaragua], three thousand miles from where I must arrange to become a member of the expedition? Besides, having been gone a long time, I may have lost any number of old friends in Washington. They, in turn, might no longer enjoy the influence I needed there now. (Such lapses occur because national administrations change often in the United States.) In a word my hopes may have been best called chimerical. Still I hoped for a grand adventure.

Mr. [Samuel] Karr, the American chargé d'affaires in León, had concluded trade agreements with Guatemala and San Salvador [El Salvador]. I was to deliver the documents to Washington. What a happy relief when my ship entered the harbor at New York and I saw at anchor in the East River the steam frigate *Mississippi,* the expedition's flagship.[3] Moreover, when I laid my request before President Fillmore a few days later, I realized to my delight that I might yet get what I wanted. Pro forma he sent me to the secretary of the navy [John P. Kennedy], who turned me over to Commodore Perry, the expedition's leader.[4] Perry had taken over a while before and they no longer wanted to meddle in his command.

The glorious annals of the United States Navy would be poorer without the name of the Brothers Perry. The national hero of these pages [Matthew Calbraith Perry] began his career in the Battle of Lake Erie during the War of 1812.[5] That old sea dog tried to dampen my sanguine enthusiasm when I applied to him on 29 July 1852. His expedition was to be purely military, an obstacle to my joining it. Indeed, many important scientists had applied and been rejected.[6]

I had one more chance. Back in the days when the young republic must suddenly make itself a maritime power, officers had to be created even before the ships existed. Many sailors thus entered the navy from the merchant marine—at the rank of master's mate. From there they advanced to lieutenant and up. Though practically forgotten after the founding of the naval academy, the rank remained on the books. Perry, as commander of a unique and special mission, was empowered to appoint six at his discretion. Enterprising young men could thus be got to do artistic and scientific work, albeit military in nature.[7] Presto! The peaceful painter assumed military worth, exchanged his deerskin jacket for a blue one with anchor buttons,[8] and gained the right to put the initials USN after his name.

The reader should not think too well of my new position. The typical master's mate knows neither wealth nor status. He takes orders from the master, who not only navigates but also manages comestibles, drinking water, etc. According to the prevailing scheme of things, I might have done the boatswain's more menial tasks, stood watch, kept the log, issued food and water, tended liquor storage or the "spirit room" (to insure proper dispensation of grog), and in battle either directed the distribution of munitions or led the master's platoon (marines), as circumstances demanded. Such would have been my lot, but Perry quickly excused all master's mates from normal duties for the time being. So I remained a peripatetic artist despite my military blouse.

The many officers aboard included not only the commodore's staff but also those bound for China: passengers on the *Mississippi* and headed for duty in ships on station. Add Mr. [Eliphalet] B[rown, Jr.], daguerreotypist, and Mr. [William B.] D[raper], later to take charge of the telegraph in Japan. What with space therefore measured strictly and issued charily, a little tent on the quarterdeck served as my studio for nearly five months.[9] I slept in a hammock between two iron hooks. For storage, besides my chest in the hold, I had only a drawer (none too large) for linen, clothing, drawings, and artist's supplies. But I knew times when saddlebags on a horse's back must suffice, so why worry over a lack of comfort now? At any rate the inconvenience would end when we reached China. There, in the *Susquehanna,* a ship of some three thousand tons, I should get a permanent studio; the commodore promised to build one and of lumber—and he kept his word. Moreover, we master's mates [later] enjoyed our private mess and took our orders from the commodore himself.[10] Thus we avoided the tedium of everyday naval life and eluded its frequent petty annoyances.

Everything now shipshape below, we longed with painful impatience for departure.

The day hung fire while America and Britain quarreled over fishing rights. Needing a steam frigate off Nova Scotia forthwith, the authorities in Washington detached Perry and the *Mississippi* temporarily from the Japan expedition.[11] I used the time to advantage in New York, preparing for the voyage and the pictures I hoped to paint.

At last the day arrived, 22 October. In the morning the signal fluttered from the *Mississippi*'s forward mast: All officers and boats aboard! The anchor chain rattled as sailors in high spirits at the capstan kept time to the roll of the drum and the squeal of the fife. The clock struck twelve. The gun announcing departure boomed across the bay at the mouth of the Hudson River. A horde of onlookers, some in boats, others on piers, waved handkerchiefs and hats in a last farewell. The bells of Trinity Church sounded their famous notes.[12] Our band played "Hail, Columbia." Joyously we steamed through the narrows and away.

This "departure" amounted only to going as far as Annapolis, there to await the *Princeton,* still being fitted-out at Baltimore.[13]

Although cheerful and in the highest spirits, I felt sad, too, and heavy of heart. Back but briefly in civilization, without time to renew friendships, without even testing peace and quiet, I was leaving for distant shores and hungry for new adventures. But I grieved neither long nor much; the high seas brought good feelings and renewed happiness. A broad and beautiful future beckoned. Entertaining legitimate hopes for fairer circumstances on this voyage than on the last, I expected to benefit accordingly.

We sailed to Cape Henry, Virginia, then into Chesapeake Bay, and anchored five miles from shore, off the little town of Annapolis.

Four weeks proved disagreeable enough, at anchor on dirty yellow water, in cold and gloom, not to mention the *Mississippi*'s cramped quarters, and the general impatience to embark on the voyage proper. This wait in the bay tested everyone's perseverance. To me, indeed, the compulsory pause seemed to drag to twice its actual length.

What a poverty of entertainments! Chesapeake Bay's excellent waterfowling occurs later than the time in question—and the ducks were skittish besides. Annapolis, the little town and its renowned academy, offered scant relief from the monotony of life at anchor. Lacking the commerce of other young American cities and towns, the place also lacks their hustle and bustle. The streets and buildings, many predating the revolution, seem so timebound that you expect for sure to meet at every door an old bewigged colonist out of the year 1775.

Sailors notoriously cannot be kept aboard ship. They will have the forbidden whiskey and, worse, they may take (in the phrase we used there) "French leave." So our boats landed them at the waterfront.

High walls separate academy from town. The buildings themselves, classrooms and quarters for three hundred cadets and their teachers, enclose on three sides a spacious area for drilling and physical training. On the fourth, which opens toward the bay, a circular, covered battery and heavy guns serve to instruct as well as to provide a place for fencing. In the center of the drill field a simple monument memorializes two midshipmen killed in the Mexican War.[14] Indoors a collection of diverse curiosities includes something to be found in nearly every American collection: relics of General Washington. Among the many flags decorating the main hall the big blue one asserts: "Don't give up the ship," motto of Commodore O. H. Perry, brother to our commandant. Flying the flag and in the spirit of its motto, O. H. carried the day at the Battle of Lake Erie.

On 12 November the president and his party visited the *Mississippi:* Mr. Fillmore, his navy secretary [Mr. Kennedy], other ranking officials from Washington, and many ladies. Typically in honor of visitors flags flew in abundance, officers reported in full dress to the quarterdeck, and the crew took to the yardarms. Seventeen guns roared a salute.[15] The band played "Hail, Columbia." After preliminary ceremonies the guests toured every nook and cranny, then lunched, and did not return ashore until late afternoon.

On 18 November the long-awaited *Princeton* arrived at last. Soon she accompanied us to the east end of the bay and the Virginia city of Norfolk. Unfortunately the screw-driven steamer's new boilers proved faulty; she must be left behind and be replaced by the *Powhatan,* a steam-powered sidewheeler of three thousand tons. The switch also effected changes in the *Mississippi*'s personnel. Captain [William J.] McCluney, who had commanded us, departed for the *Powhatan.* Captain S[idney] S[mith] Lee joined the *Mississippi* [as commander] from the *Princeton.*

More days passed with the taking-on of provisions and water. Meanwhile I toured Norfolk, a city of some thirty thousand people. The canal through the Dismal Swamp joins the ocean here; a railroad plys between the city and the capital of Virginia, Richmond, and Norfolk bustles. On the right side of the river, in the suburb of Gosport, a giant navy yard includes huge machine shops and other works, as well as sheds of great length to hold lumber for construction and to store naval cordage. Large ponds contain the kinds of wood best preserved under water. Elsewhere a troop of anchors leans rank and file against a framework for support. The extensive stock offers examples of various weights up to 10,500 pounds. Two frigates, under construction, occupied big covered drydocks. A granite dock, which cost a million dollars and took ten years to build, in its enormity admits the largest ships.[16] There was the *Princeton,* a marvelous sight in that dock, out of the water and propped up by countless wooden beams.

On the river two men-of-war of the largest class, the *Columbus* and the *Delaware,* lay stripped, along with two frigates, two sloops, and two brigs. A frigate and a brig had just been laid to. The new ironclad steamer *Water Witch* was being refitted for a voyage up the Amazon. The gunboat *Pennsylvania* served as receiving ship, a floating barracks for recruits. In active service she requires an immense crew, what with her 140 guns. Hence she will perhaps remain permanently berthed here.

Much has been written of life at sea.[17] Yet I trust it not superfluous to conduct my dear reader about the ship [the *Mississippi*] that would be my home for years. The personnel consisted of the captain, five lieutenants, the captain of marines, six midshipmen of two grades [midshipman and passed midshipman], the purser, three surgeons, the chaplain, the chief engineer and eight assistants, the boatswain, the gunner, the carpenter, the sailmaker, and the captain's and the purser's clerks. The commodore had nothing to do with running the ship; the captain retained command.[18] So Perry himself was only a passenger, along with his flag officers, secretary and clerk, and three brand-new master's mates. (Count my humble self in the incongruous trio.) The enlisted sailors, plus 35 marines and 48 engine-men, brought the total to 380, a large number for a ship of little more than two thousand tons and with much space given over to engines, guns, and essential stores.

The captain's executive, the first lieutenant [or lieutenant commanding, William L. Maury], decides who boards and who departs, and holds each man to every regulation. In battle he takes charge of the deck, the master oversees the sails, and the captain directs tactics. The other lieutenants and the midshipmen work among the guns in their respective divisions. The gunner and the sailmaker hold sway fore and aft, each in his own bailiwick. Musicians, cooks, and officers' orderlies pass the ammunition. On the lowest level, near the stern, surgeons treat the wounded in the cockpit. Commodore and staff take post on the poop, the deck with the big cabins aft. The marines, divided into three units, serve at various points.

The crew eats in messes, or "table groups," usually of ten men each.[19] One of them, designated "mess cook," draws provisions on appointed days, delivers them to the ship's cook, then serves the prepared dishes to his mates. He also washes their tableware, sees to its safekeeping, and secures it along with provisions in a mess locker. Officers must provide, on a monthly cash allowance, their own rations in messes formed by rank. A captain, therefore, usually eats alone. Here, however, lack of space forced him to sit down with the commodore and the captains of the commodore's staff. The wardroom mess consisted of the commodore's clerk, the purser, the chief engineer, surgeons, master, and lieutenants. Midshipmen and clerks composed the starboard-steerage mess; engine-room personnel, the port-steerage mess; and the gunner, the boatswain, the carpenter, and the sailmaker, the forward-officer's mess. Later, aboard the *Susquehanna,* we master's mates separated into our own.

In port the morning gun roars at daybreak. Drums and fifes declare reveille. Piping and shouting, the boatswain orders decks washed.[20] (At sea: no morning gun; deck washing every other day.) Hammocks are drawn up, tied, and put away in lockers. Pumps are manned; buckets and swabs issued. Nothing is heard until 7:00 A.M. but the rasp of brushes and the scratch of scrapers, the moan and groan of pumps, and the rumble of the holystone. Ropes pull the last, a boulder of perhaps two hundred pounds, across decks strewn with sand. Meanwhile the crew sloshes about barefoot and the pumps shoot salt water in every direction. After 7:00 little cleaning remains, only to dry the decks, polish the brass, and do a last touch-up with brooms. Mornings in port the flag is run up at 8:00.

Then the drum sounds for grog.[21] The master's mate of the spirit room issues it on the quarterdeck. (Usually the oldest midshipman gets this disagreeable post.) Breakfast is piped; squares of oilcloth suddenly fill the forward deck. Bowls, knives, forks, and spoons—all of tin—clatter onto them. Coffee or tea follows, served in the bowls, out of large tin kettles. The boatswain's pipe shrills, breakfast utensils disappear; a half hour must do for the needs of the stomach.

At 9:00, after the deck is swept, drums beat the call to station or quarters. The crew rearranges itself accordingly, and officers inspect their divisions, reporting to the first lieutenant whether everything conforms to prescribed order. Tuesday's call is to general quarters— shipwide drill by the entire crew.[22] On the other days, divisions drill independently.

A few minutes before 12:00 the ship's cook delivers to the officer on watch a sample of the crew's noon meal for approval. The master shoots the sun and announces "meridian" to the first lieutenant. The bells proclaim noon, the pipe signals the meal, and it lasts a full hour.

The marines drill in the afternoon, conditions permitting. Or perhaps the ship gets necessary repairs. At 2:00 the purser's steward issues the next day's provisions to the cooks of the messes: salt beef, salt pork, beans, peas, flour, tea, coffee, sugar, syrup, pickles, and dried apples. Each man draws a gallon of water a day, which to suffice must be used with care. Between 4:00 and 4:30 another meal is eaten. Free time follows until sundown, when the crew draws hammocks. The dousing of forward lamps at 8:00 precedes the blackout at 9:00 of all the usual watch and signal lights; others burn only by permission of the officer of the deck. The master-at-arms, making the rounds, orders in every part of the ship, "Lights out!"

During the day at sea in calm weather a quarter of the crew (during the night half) usually stand deck watch. All hands remain topside, however, when conditions demand their presence. Officers and men on watch customarily rotate in four-hour shifts: 4:00 and 8:00 A.M., noon, 4:00 and 8:00 P.M., and midnight. The ship's bells divide each watch into eight half hours. After the first half hour they strike once; after the second, twice; and so forth. Hence the expressions "two bells," "three bells," or "four bells" of the "first watch" (8:00 P.M. to midnight), "middle watch" (midnight to 4:00 A.M.), or "morning watch" (4:00 to 8:00 A.M.). To vary daily the four lieutenants' shifts the oncoming lieutenant halves the 4:00 to 8:00 P.M. shift by starting this so-called dog watch at 6:00 [thus dividing the twenty-four hours into seven watches instead of six].

A midshipman, stationed forward, joins the lieutenant on duty and every half hour throws out the "log" to determine speed. The result goes into the logbook, together with wind, current, barometer, temperatures of air and water, and various other readings and observations.

The first lieutenant receives reports of lapses in discipline. Should he feel incompetent to administer punishment in a given case, he refers it to the captain. Flogging has been stopped in the American navy.[23] Punishment now consists of irons and the brig at the responsible officer's discretion; or confinement and bread and water; or extra duty and restricted movement; or lugging a 68-pound ball for a specified time; or, for officers, suspension from duty and arrest, as well as forfeit of grog for a stated period. In instances of gross misconduct by an officer a court martial always passes sentence.

Sundays, in the general inspection at 9:00, the captain and the first lieutenant scrutinize every part of the ship; at muster at 10:00, every man of the crew. The men present themselves individually to those officers, in the presence of the others, assembled on the quarterdeck. Reprimands—for violations of discipline the week past—occur then and there.

Anglican religious services follow on the *Mississippi* at 11:00: hymn with musical accompaniment, the usual prayer, a psalm, and a short sermon to conclude.[24] Thus a small group of brave men congregate for an utterly simple service amid a wide ocean. They commend themselves to the protection of their Creator; the scene—gripping, stirring, profound in effect—must move the heart to reverence.

Sunday worship in the American navy is as strictly observed as swearing and cursing are expressly forbidden. Rarely did I hear profanity.

Naval discipline *must* be more severe than even the army's, for here every man shall exert himself—much, often, and in close quarters—if duty be done and work finished. Officers accordingly have to excel at the indispensable condition of self-control. It must be total; they shall not be impulsive, lest they lower themselves in the eyes of the crew. Without respect of crew for officers, naval discipline cannot exist.

When a storm tested to the limit the seaworthiness of our frigates [we would have been lost without discipline].[25] At 7:00 A.M. [7 October 1854] the storm's violence had already reached Force 10. (That is, the tenth point [a whole gale] on our twelve-point [Beaufort] scale used when logging wind.) Force 11 [storm], reached later, endured a long while, rising to 12 [hurricane] during most of the afternoon. I shall never forget the hideous tempest of the elements I witnessed then. We lay to, bow windward. Topmast and yards had already been taken down early in the morning, and except for a storm topsail on the spanker to aid steering we showed not a scrap. You had to cling to ropes to get along the deck. The four men at the wheel had to cling to its spokes with all their might or be blown away. The seas swelled so they often stood fifteen to twenty feet over the wheelhouse. A sea broke every minute and flooded the forecastle. Spray and salt water half blinded us. A large number of spars, extra yards, and chicken coops had broken loose; now they danced with one another in a wild cotillion on the slippery deck. An especially heavy sea broke over us once, slanted the deck to an angle of almost thirty-five degrees, ripped away a third of the forward bulwarks on the starboard side, lifted one of the 120-pounders (a cannon weighing some seven tons) out of its emplacement, and rolled it off the larboard side, to drop with a crash to the lower level and smash everything in its ruinous path. By 4:00 P.M. we had lost another section of the bulwarks, two boats on the larboard side broke to bits and swam away, and we expected two others to follows at any moment. The larboard wheelhouse—its captain's mess, barber shop, and gangways in ruins—presented a terrible sight.

Our ship [the *Mississippi*] nonetheless proved itself worth its reputation as one of the American navy's best.[26] The paddle boxes swam beneath every new sea, yet the machinery hummed without pause, working now at the peak of a mountain of water, and now in a lightning plunge to a valley of seething foam.

At such moments a man knows not only his personal helplessness but also recognizes the power of the human mind to master the raging elements. Throw the poor worm alone into the maelstrom: His every effort proves vain. A play of waves drags even the boldest swimmer to a watery grave. Not a trace remains where he lost his fight for life; even his death cry goes unheard beneath the savage howl of the storm. But in a good ship the experienced sailor looks calmly at the surrounding destruction. From time to time a sharp, clear command sounds on the megaphone and a handful of brave topmen or foremastmen rushes wherever danger looms and works to prevent damage or secure things torn loose.

Near sundown the storm abated somewhat. In the morning a warm and pleasant sun beamed on wreckage everywhere. The ship, a sorry sight, resembled one of our belles of the ball after a night of wild dancing, hair tousled, toilette disheveled. Neatness and order usually prevailed. Now chaos: things in an amazing jumble. [But discipline has brought us through, we have weathered the storm. Soon we set things right again.]

And so, dear reader, I'm happy to say that, though often vexed, I look back with joy on the days I served the flag of the United States. Inconveniences and difficulties dim now, my memory teems with the romance of that maritime adventure. I want to tell you about it. Therefore I wrote this little book.

CHAPTER TWO

FIRST LANDING

AT LOO CHOO

First Contact with the Populace.—Ashore!—An English Missionary.—The Harbor at Naha.—Fortifications.—The City.—The Regent Comes Aboard to Pay Official Call.—Expedition to the Interior of the Island.—Nature and Character of the Countryside. — Agriculture. — Official Escorts. — Shuri, the Capital. — Lodging for Travelers. — Affability of the Populace. — The Island's Geology [and Other Features].

T WO BOATS out of Naha approached the *Susquehanna* on the morning of the twenty-seventh [May 1853].[1] They brought gifts from the mayor or *hadji-madji:* two oxen, several hundred eggs, vegetables, sweet potatoes, etc. But we must live up to the principle of taking nothing from the people without giving something of equal value in return. So we did not accept the gifts until later in the day, after Mr. [John] C[ontee], the flag lieutenant, and Mr. [Samuel Wells] W[illiams], the interpreter, saw the hadji-madji himself and presented him with Commodore Perry's compensatory gift.[2] And so nobody but C. and W. went ashore on the twenty-seventh.

Meanwhile several of us left the *Susquehanna* for a boat ride on the bay and viewed the coral reefs that enclose it. We noticed in the depths a school of small fish, beautifully colored.[3] With effort we caught a few, but their azure faded when they died. Local fishing boats cautiously avoided us.

On Sunday the twenty-eighth the commodore gave permission to go ashore. Many went of course, and I among them.

Captain [Murray] Maxwell and other officers had been here before us.[4] Having returned to England, they funded a subscription to send a missionary to this remote island. (Indeed, they began what is still known as the [Loo Choo] Naval Mission.) In 1847 their missionary arrived, the Englishman Dr. [Bernard Jean] Bettelheim.[5] With his family he lives, nearly seven years later, in a small [native] temple beside an imposing crag.[6] Named for what it resembles, the massive rock is called the Capstan.

A tiny schooner [the British *Starling,* Captain McCheyne] landed the party and their modest baggage, then sailed away, leaving husband, wife, and two children on the beach, alone. Practically marooned, they knew neither where to go nor what to do. At wits' end they headed toward a temple nearby and got a night's lodging and a little food. Meanwhile the tide rose and soaked their belongings, left behind on the beach. (The local people, frightened at the appearance of the foreigners, would have no truck with them.) Père [Mathieu] Adnet hospitably offered his help. This French priest had come to Naha not many years before. He lived about three miles away, on the other side of town. Unfortunately he had little to give. So the family spent its first days in sorrow. Later the small temple fell vacant, they moved in, and live there still. A ship or two, calling accidentally, left them a few necessities. In 1849 [or 1850] the English steamer *Reynard* brought the bishop of Hong Kong [George Smith]. As a consequence of this visit the regent of Loo Choo was assigned to look after the family, and they have suffered far fewer of the nuisances and irritations of the days before.[7] Dr. B. has converted no one, however. He starts preaching in the marketplace or elsewhere in a public street, and the people scatter as they have always scattered. The religious intolerance of Loo Choo equals that of Japan. In fact, spies keep watch on the people; nobody dares listen to the foreign preacher.[8]

The city of Naha, the most important center of trade in the greater Loo Choo island group [the Ryukyus], lies on the southwesternmost point of the main island [Okinawa], also called Loo Choo. A river forms Naha's inner harbor at depths to admit Chinese junks. Extensive stonelike fortifications guard the harbor. These walls, great blocks of coral worked into polygonic shapes and laid without mortar, are like the cyclopean walls in Greece. Their good condition belies their obvious age. Indeed, the fortifications seem innocent of bombardment, unless by guns of small caliber. The breastworks measure about four feet high and three thick. The few turrets that project from the walls, though embrasured, are too small to admit a regular mounting of the guard; they must have been intended for observation only.

Our ships anchored in the outer harbor, a basin enclosed on the landward side by a half-moon bend in the coastline and on the seaward by a series of coral reefs. Of the three passages through the reefs, waterborne traffic mostly uses the southernmost, the largest. The city extends beside the coast and the small river of the inner harbor. Perhaps twenty thousand people occupy about four thousand houses along streets quite broad and paved with large blocks of coral. Walls line the streets in the prosperous quarter. Portals lead to the houses behind the walls.

A reserve toward foreigners prevailed. Thus, from behind walls and trees and out of side streets, crowds watched us. At but a hint that we would approach or even address them [from a distance], they fled.

The interpreter mediated several discussions [between us and the local authorities] on why we were here.[9] Then the regent of the Loo Choo islands paid us an official visit.[10] He boarded, and we feted him with military pomp and ceremony; when we fired the salute, several of his entourage nearly collapsed in fright. We wined and dined him and showed him every part of the ship. The venerable man (we were told) ruled during the minority of a twelve-year-old prince.

The entourage consisted largely of long-bearded old men like the regent himself. They wore their hair combed upward all around, worked carefully into a knot on the crown, and pierced and decorated by two metal pins. Their chief garment resembled a long caftan of high-grade material with wide sleeves. Into the silk belt around the waist each man stuck fans, a small tobacco pouch, and a short pipe, its metal bowl scarcely bigger than a thimble. Men of higher rank added a shirt under the caftan, trousers that reached the knee, and stockings of knitted cotton. The stockings provided the big toe its own compartment, isolating it from the rest. Our callers walked about the ship in their stockings, for they had left their footwear behind in the boat, perhaps out of politeness. The gesture resembled behavior in their homes, where (I noticed later) they went shoeless.

Preliminary formalities done, Commodore Perry decided on an expedition into the interior to estimate the resources. The exploring party consisted of the chaplain, [Reverend] Mr. [George] J[ones], the third physician, Dr. [Arthur] L[ynah], Mr. B[ayard] T[aylor], and me, all off the *Susquehanna*. In addition, each ship sent two seamen and two Chinese as bearers.[11] We carried a tent and eight days' provisions. Plenty of carbines, hunting rifles, and other weapons equipped us to repel—to beat back with force—any attempt to molest us. On 30 May our little company landed in Naha and set off at once.

Arable land extends from the city's northeastern edge. Through the fields, on an embankment, runs the road to Shuri, the island's capital. After about a mile we crossed a stream at the little town of Tumai (three thousand to four thousand people). The stream empties into the Bay of Naha nearby. Close to the bridge, thick walls surround a templelike edifice that seemed either a temple or the seat of a person of rank. In any case, it is little used; the three doors through its walls remain shut.

Sometimes the road passes through rice paddies in valleys between hills. Sometimes it crosses the hills. People were working in the paddies, planting. Some paddies are entirely terraced. Continual and copious irrigation keeps paddies soaked like swamps. Ditches bring water, often long distances, to the highest, whence it descends to the lowest. Rice, sown in a corner of a paddy earlier in the spring, sprouts into seedlings to be transplanted, when mature enough, over the rest of the paddy. We saw rice being transplanted in some places. In others it had matured to kernel.

Trees line much of the route, pleasantly shading our march along a roadway eighteen to twenty feet wide and paved with more of the polygonal blocks. Scarcely had we left Naha when an old man and two younger men attached themselves to us. One of the younger was tall and well built. All three, though "natives," were more than ordinary citizens. They did not leave us for a moment thereafter.[12] They were generally passive. But should one of us separate from the rest, one of them would follow.[13] We soon observed that they not only took notes on everything but also compared them every evening. A trio of spies obviously and intent on learning what the peculiar foreigners were up to.

When loads proved too heavy for our Chinese, the mysterious escort would set some of their countrymen to the task. When *they* wearied, others were called up, often from work in the paddies.

They stopped their work at once and followed the order to do ours. The escort repeatedly supplied us with food: chickens, for example, and sweet potatoes and vegetables of every other kind. Yet the escort refused our offer to pay. (We did settle when we returned to Naha six days later. They had kept full and faithful accounts. Dr. Bettelheim served admirably as interpreter, and we paid the modest sum.)

After a hike of something over three miles we reached Shuri. This, the island's capital, resembles Naha, though in style a little more grandiose. A fortress, a castle of sorts, commands the city on the top and the slopes of a hill. Near the city's gates our escort invited us to stop for refreshment.

Inns, places of refreshment of this kind (called *kunk-kwa* in the local tongue), provide lodging for respectable travelers in every town of any importance.[14] The guest goes through a courtyard—trees edge it, beds of flowers border it—and enters a lobby that occupies but a corner of the whole. The inn here is of wood, like its counterparts. An arcade, three to four feet wide and supported by columns, encloses the building, and a wall of thin wooden panels encloses the arcade. Except for a small part at each corner the wall can be removed [by removing the panels] to open the arcade on the inn's every side. In bad weather, when panels are removed, windows of oiled paper may be inserted. Beautiful mats cover the floor of the arcade. Six to seven feet long, three wide, two inches thick, and soft, they can be slept on in splendid comfort. We found this inn and its ceremony of reception identical to those of all others everywhere on the island.

From the huge wooden barrel at the door the guest dips water and washes his face, hands, and feet. He leaves his shoes in the lobby and walks in his stockings indoors. The man who acted as our host was probably a sort of magistrate. He began by bowing, then clapped his hands. Servants appeared. To each of us they brought a small wooden tray, a porcelain bowl, and a segment of bamboo. Embers glowed in the bowl, and the bamboo would take the ashes knocked from a pipe. The host clapped again. The servants handed us tea in small cups. Of course this tea, like tea in China, contained neither sugar nor milk. To me it tasted excellent nonetheless. An effective stimulant, too, it excites the blood.

After a short rest we left the inn. We crossed the town in a column with an advance guard and a rear guard, baggage at the center, and flags flying. The streets were empty and the houses shut, but curious eyes peered at us everywhere. I have already mentioned the castle. We passed it now; its imposing walls, sixty to seventy feet high, and their several entrances, all shut like the doors all over town. Obeying the orders that brought us here, we did not stop to observe anything. We marched through the town and kept going toward the island's northeastern coast.

From one substantial elevation we could see for miles.[15] If a little plot of that terrain can be cultivated, it is cultivated. And more intensively and more carefully than in China. Rice paddies rise on their terraces and stretch away between hills. Water descends from higher terraces to lower, quickening heavy soil to an abundant yield. The distant chains of mountains may be a thousand feet tall.

We continued our march until evening over a ground of slippery clay, then pitched the tent, ran up the flag, and posted sentries. Soon a dinner bubbled and simmered on a blazing fire: rice, pork, tea, and other things we had brought from the ship, rounded out with wild doves shot along the way, and chicken, garlic, and onions furnished by local people en route. Our escort, the mysterious trio, quickly erected a shelter of reeds and camped about thirty steps from us. A crowd of local people clustered around them now.

The excursion lasted another six days: three on the island's eastern shore and three in crossing the island and returning to the ships. (Our official report, submitted to the commodore, contains the particulars. He will publish it in due course.[16]) We cut straight across, about twenty-four miles south of the northeastern tip. We regained the ships via the terrain most willing to accept our line of march: the west coast some of the time but mostly through the interior. Settlements hug the coast on the island's northern end. Thickly wooded hills and mountains fill the interior. Yet wood fetches high prices to the south, so scarce is it there. Hospitality and cordiality, the warmest of both, met us everywhere. Local people supplied us with their foods: chicken, eggs, fresh and salted fish, cucumbers, squash, pickled onions, rice, and something like a sweet potato. Our trio paid for them and (as I have said) accepted our payment, a modest total, when we arrived back at the harbor, our destination.

We spent our nights, all except the first, in kunk-kwas.[17] Many of these khans, delightfully situated, provide superb lodging. Each was immaculate. Even the courtyard and gardens were swept and spread with white, riverbed gravel. Every entrance boasted its barrel of water. The newly arrived could wash his hands, face, and feet, a practice strictly observed not only on arrival but also before and after meals. And how agreeable that not an insect except mosquitoes bothered us!

About in the middle of the island we found a burial site: a considerable area enclosed by a wall. Along the wall across from the entrance was a place to sit, fashioned of stone, and clusters of graves dug into hillsides and rocks, like the graves of ancient Egyptians at Thebes, but open and empty—rifled—now. I compared this site to latter-day ones elsewhere on the island. They resembled those of the Chinese and differed from this one in all essentials. How striking, I thought, that these people should respect modern burial sites and treat older ones with contempt. People here laughed at this opinion of mine. Those old holes, they said (or so the interpreter translated), were graves of men of the Devil.[18]

Next we came upon the imposing ruins of a castle or fortress.[19] Some of the incredibly thick walls still soared to seventy feet. Primary contours proclaimed differences between this and the typical castle: concave walls where typically convex and convex where typically concave, and portals of massive, hewn stone but with little arch.[20] The people responsible had vanished long ago. What sort were they, the builders and their race? Let me withhold my opinion until I learn more about this land and its people, when I possess information instead of guesses and hunches.[21]

As to geology [and other aspects] we met sandstone first; farther north, argillite; then granite, gneiss, and quartz. At this point unfortunately we turned back [short of the northernmost limits], according to instructions. Coral reefs encircle the island. Coral and seashells in various shapes and colors lie in profusion along the shores. The saw-toothed coastline offers more than one excellent anchorage. The most valuable commercial tree, the yellow pine, grows to a considerable height. We saw it in numbers especially in the north. Cattle, few; swine, superabundant; goats and poultry somewhat less abundant than swine. Only a few days deviated from superb weather with temperatures between 75 and a rare 90 degrees Fahrenheit. We could drink the water everywhere.

Finally on 4 June at 3:00 P.M. we regained the coast. We saw our ships, hoisted the flag, and fired the signal. Soon a boat brought us to the *Susquehanna*. Our comrades welcomed us aboard and shook our hands.

Our report, as well as the specimens we brought back, seemed to satisfy the commodore. We had covered 108 miles in six days—as the crow flies. Calculate and add the distance of many small detours right and left, however, and the mileage will double. We had explored and taken a good look at over half the island.[22] To hurrahs and volleys of firearms we had raised the American flag on the island's highest point. Moreover, we had outdone each and every seafaring nation here before us: We had seen more of the island and met more of its people.

CHAPTER THREE

COMMODORE PERRY'S

FESTIVE CALL ON THE

REGENT OF LOO CHOO

The Order of March.—Entry into the Palace.—Ceremony of Welcome.—The Feast
in the Banquet Hall.—Dog Soup.—Some Curiosities of Gastronomy.

O N 6 J U N E our squadron, putting boats on the water, had
covered the harbor with them by 8:00 A.M. The boats took
ashore the officers and their detachments who would march in the
procession. Shortly before 9:00 Mr. Taylor and I, as ordered, got
the commodore's sedan chair and its bearers into the first cutter,
with the commodore himself close behind.[1] Ashore, two companies
of marines with two artillery crews and their brace of light field
pieces drew up for review and awaited him. Arrived ashore, he
reviewed them.

The procession started. At the head were two Loo Choo officials
followed by two boys carrying the officials' sun umbrellas. Then the
artillery, commanded by Lieutenant B[ent], assisted by Mr. [John
W.] B[ennet]t, each piece under the immediate supervision of a
midshipman and all behind a quartermaster bearing a flag. Next the
Susquehanna's band, attached to a company of marines, under a
major. Then the commodore in his chair, conveyed by Chinese and
trailed by Chinese toting the gifts for the regent. Next a staff,
twenty-six officers of various ranks, representing the ships of the
squadron. Then the *Mississippi*'s band. And last another company of
marines, commanded by a captain. Music filled the air, all the way

to the capital city of Shuri itself, either the patriotic airs of the bands or the brisk marching tune of the drums and the fifes.[2]

The venerable regent received the commodore at the city's gate. The regent's nobility and gravity befitted an oldtime Venetian doge. He walked toward us under a large sun umbrella; it seemed to be an insignia of his honorable office. Four officials accompanied him. He and the other dignitaries wore purple silk on their heads. For their plentiful entourage, however, the color was not purple but red or yellow: red crepe signifying lower rank, yellow silk the higher.

An unexpected obstacle stopped us at the entrance to the palace. (I have mentioned the palace on an earlier page [in the prior chapter].) The regent would have received the commodore in his private residence. But when the English ship *Reynard* called, her officers had been received in the palace and our commodore insisted on equal treatment. Our procession—every last element—drew up before the palace. The gates opened at last. The commodore entered, accompanied by his staff of officers, to the tune of "Hail Columbia."[3]

The first or outer courtyard contained another fortification of higher walls to the right of the gates. A small stream flowed down from that area: limpid water that originated at about half the height of the walls and disappeared among the fresh, green plants that encircled them. Straight ahead of the gates a grand staircase ascended through a wide entrance to a spacious courtyard about sixty feet above the first. A few more steps led in turn from the second and up a little to a third. Walkways of large flat stones edged each side of the courtyards and crisscrossed them, while sizeable buildings extended around the courtyards and enclosed them. The upper end of the third courtyard opened into a roomy templelike hall, and spacious gardens seemed to occupy areas beyond the buildings. Yet all this enormous palace seemed [practically] deserted: except for the regent's entourage only a few servants and neither a hint of weapons nor a sign of soldiers or guards.

The reception took place in a spacious hall, off and to the left of the second courtyard. The commodore told the regent why he had come to Loo Choo and assured the regent that the United States felt peaceable and friendly toward this distant island nation. Amid much bowing the commodore gave him several gifts. Tea and pastries were served. Then everyone left the palace, went back to the city, and, in the regent's residence, sat down to a banquet for the foreign guests [of rank]. That is, while officers banqueted, the men stacked arms, wheeled the cannon up beside them, and enjoyed an extra or "bonus" glass of grog.

This hall was of three sections: a main one in the center and one to each side. The four tables of the main [were arranged into two classes and designated as higher and lower in status]. Of the higher two, the commodore took the one on the right, the regent the one on the left. The commodore sat down with his ranking officers, the regent with his ranking officials. The rest of the participants took places at the other two tables and at tables in the other sections.

The tables had been laid with a profusion of small plates, each about four inches in diameter. I cannot describe the array of food on the plates. Attractively arranged, good tasting but of so refined a delicacy that our palates, being those of barbaric sailors, could neither understand nor evaluate them. A corps of waiters brought tea in tiny cups and stood ever ready to pour refills. It was served without milk or sugar but, in deference to us foreigners, there were small bowls of sugar on the table.[4] Yet all of this [food, tea, and pomp and ceremony] amounted merely to the overture to a gastronomical production.

I mean that the true meal consisted of twelve soups, each served as a course. Twelve courses, we were told, compose a banquet fit for a king. (The number corresponds to the status of the guest. There are affairs of three, six, or nine courses. But twelve confer the supreme honor.) The soups came in bowls about as big as a medium-sized saucer. The twelve rang the changes on meat, fish, vegetables, and egg dumplings. All tasted delicious and particularly the one (so I was told) of the flesh of a dog. Now none of our stray curs would do here. It must be a blue-ribbon specimen, young and specially fed. Accordingly I never savored meat of such tenderness and flavor. The most fastidious of gourmands would not—could not—have rejected this morsel.

Was it really dog? Comrades expressed doubt later. True, during my several stays in Loo Choo, I never saw a dog slaughtered. True, one man's testimony is my only proof; the man could have misunderstood my question or misconstrued my drawing; and perhaps he played a trick on me. Was the soup really of dog, then? Yes! Let me tell you how I arrived at this belief. After failing to learn the soup's primary ingredient I drew in my sketchbook a dog and a calf. Pointing to the soup and to my pictures, I pantomimed my question. Which animal was in the soup? My interlocutor, a man of Loo Choo, indicated the dog. So I leave it to you, dear reader. Am I right or wrong?

Tea and saki followed the twelve soups. Saki, distilled of sugared rice, resembles arrack and tastes superb. It came to the table in teapots. We drank it out of miniature porcelain cups, scarcely the size of a thimble. Hence we Occidentals, accustomed to larger portions, needed refill after refill. Yet saki is so mild that I drank fifteen, felt nothing, and noticed not the slightest difference in how I thought or the way I walked. Saki, like every other food here, comes in minute portions, steadily, persistently, and fully renewed, until even the inveterate voluptuary must wail at last, "Enough! Stop!"

Place settings included the so-called chopsticks. The little wooden rods, which resemble their Chinese counterparts, were to be used for the hors d'oeuvres. The eater holds the sticks between thumb and third finger and directs them with the index. I managed the procedure well enough—for a tyro's first effort. With the soup we got small porcelain spoons, an aid to our barbaric lack of grace, and with each subsequent soup, fresh willow sticks, pointed, to spear dumplings and bits of meat.

In the first toast—and there were but two—the commodore saluted "the regent of Loo Choo" and hailed the "continued harmony between his subjects and the American people!" The regent answered with the second toast. "To the United States, its emissary Commodore Perry, and his officers!"[5]

After about an hour we headed back to the ships. We had been cordially and honorably received; we had enjoyed saki, whiskey, punch, and other things, and the combination left us in high spirits. Away we went, flags flying, on the road to the anchorage, past hills, across verdant fields, in the shade of beautiful pines, while the bands played jolly tunes. Many of our comrades—the officers, marines, and sailors left behind—came halfway [from the ships] to meet us. They awaited us on the hills and under the trees to the right and left of the road. They cheered and waved their hats in greeting.[6] They were overjoyed to learn that we had come to good terms and established friendly relations with the locals; initial contact means much for what follows. Moreover, we had been warmly received in a country that pays tribute to Japan. We therefore concluded, justifiably, that a cordial reception boded well for success [in Japan].[7]

I had set to paper many interesting scenes during the reception, as well as on the excursion into the interior. How gratifying, my portfolio, so thick with those drawings! The route to Shuri, through fresh and thriving countryside, offered several beautiful motifs. And then our party on return, and the groups of sailors and marines who welcomed us, composed vivid collective studies.[8]

On 9 June we took the sloop *Saratoga* in tow, steamed back out of the harbor and suddenly found ourselves on the high seas. I presumed (on a military vessel one can only presume) we were bound for the Bonin Islands and would be there in a few days. The story continues in the next chapter.

CHAPTER FOUR

THE BONIN ISLANDS

Location of the Islands.—The First Settlers.—The Islands' Fertility and Beauty.—A Desire to Imitate Robinson Crusoe.—Foreign Ships Call at Port Lloyd.—We Go Hunting on Stapleton Island.—Return to the Ship.

At sea, 16 June [1853]

A T DAWN of the fourteenth—that soon!—we raised the Bonins.[1] The group lies just south of 27° and nearly on the same longitude [142°] as Edo, the capital of Japan. Until recent times only North Pacific whalers called at the islands and only now and then. They would anchor in the superb harbors and go ashore to replenish their fresh water.[2] In 1831 an English sailor named [Nathaniel] Savory deserted one of the ships.[3] He and a few companions hid in the forest until the ship sailed. They came out of hiding and began a life like that of Robinson Crusoe. The soil was fertile, water abundant, and sugarcane, [sweet] potatoes, beans, lemons, tobacco, and other produce plentiful. The many small bays teemed with fish. Turtles frequently came ashore to lay their eggs by the light of the moon in shoreside sands. The colonists not only enjoyed food in profusion; soon they could also deal in vegetables, and they bartered with whalers for tools, seeds, chickens, pigs, and various other things. The pigs ran wild in the forest and multiplied without end. Goats had been released on another island some time before, had gone wild, and reproduced in numbers. The colonists salted and stored an ample supply of meat.

Gradually the original colonists left except Savory. Others replaced them. Some of these left, others stayed.[4] Then a few men and women arrived from the Sandwich Islands. Today the greater Bonins may count a population of forty or fifty.

An English ship had stopped at Port Lloyd as early as 1827 and a

Russian in 1828.[5] In 1838 the English brig *Sulphur*, captained by Sir Edward Belcher, called at the Bonins. They surveyed the area, and, on [Belcher's] excellent chart, the harbor of the biggest island became Port Lloyd. The names Peel, Buckland, and Stapleton went to the three principal islands.[6] Peel lies to the extreme south, Stapleton the north. Between and around them bristle many smaller islands, as well as outcroppings, reefs, and rocks.

The mere outlines of the Bonins promised me artistic treasures.[7] Shortly before noon we anchored in the bay to the west of Port Lloyd. To me it seemed I had suddenly entered upon one of the beautiful inland lakes of upper Bavaria [Germany] or around Salzburg [Austria]. Tall, steep, rocky upthrusts ring the deep, broad, beautiful bay; only one moderately generous inlet pierces the circle. No sight could be more picturesque. A powerful cone of rock, jutting from the center of the bay, looks like a scaled-down Gibraltar. Fortified with a few heavy guns, it would be equally impregnable.[8] Several broad bands of rich farmland extend from the bay toward tall, thickly wooded hills. Rising to enclose everything, they form the backdrop. Settlers have built cottages low on the hills. Trees obscure the cottages while fields surround them with sugarcane, [sweet] potatoes, tobacco, melons, and other crops of this climate.

Wooded hills, verdant fields, grayish-red granite circling the bay in attractive shapes, strips of white sand along the shore—and then the water in a gorgeous blue so different from the rest! The water has washed several passages through the rocks. These grottolike, domed arches, illuminated by reflections of a noonday sun, remind me of majestic Gothic cathedrals in my native land. Seashells in glorious colors decorate every inch of the shore. Down in the cool depths billions of infusoria have planted gardens of stone: many-hued formations of coral that seem to want to hide their mysterious loveliness in the cerulean depths.

You can lean for hours over the gunwale of a boat, gaze into the astonishing waters, exclaim at the work of the Lord, and—be moved to prayer! Tired of the depths? Lift your eyes to the tropical vegetation, see it turn gold in the setting sun, and stare in awe at the miracle. If the sun has disappeared into the ocean's expanses, and should night begin to cast the magic veil of darkness over water, rock, and hill—look to the horizon. Far away, at the edge of the world, a red wafer of a moon rises from the water. Jupiter sends from the heavens to Earth his clear and charming light. Behold these wonders of creation, be amazed, and stare in speechless reverence!

I did not understand Alexander Selkirk until now. That original Robinson Crusoe's experiences suggested the story that became the instructive book for young people around the world. Selkirk grew so attached to the charms of Juan Fernández, his island off Peru, that he could not tear himself away, and there he stayed.[9] During our call at the Bonins I walked about the island, discovered many a lovely spot, and thought, Here I must stay! One valley, nestled among beautifully forested hills, in particular attracted me. Two joyous brooks converged from different directions and formed [in the valley] a small river deep enough to float a boat. Two Kanakas—one from Otaheiti, the other from the Marquesas—lived in the peace of isolation. I felt drawn to this glimpse of Paradise as if pulled by a magic power. *I must request my discharge and settle here, where Peace rules, in calm, quiet, placid asylum.* I freed myself of these thoughts with difficulty and only with the counter-thought that, as long as God grant me health and the strength of youth, I must bear the obligation to be active and do what I can for the common good.[10]

16 June

We landed early, even before daybreak, on the bay's southeastern shore. This time Mr. Bayard Taylor commanded.[11] The party consisted of volunteers, younger officers only, except one sailor and one marine. We failed to engage a guide at a hut near the landing. A path led us into a thicket and disappeared, so from the end of the bay we followed a mountain brook southeasterly and climbed into the hills. Dense vegetation wet with dew slowed us; soft and slippery soil impeded us; and networks of vines blocked us. Crowns of luxuriant palms joined into a roof that the rising sun could not pierce. Slowly, advancing in an atmosphere crepuscular and mysterious, we penetrated a jungle so dense we could barely see twenty or thirty steps in any direction. A second creek brought us down into a valley enclosed by tall peaks. The closer we got to the valley's floor, the more the vegetation thickened—until the sharp and thorny leaves of the pandanus or wild pineapple stopped us dead.[12] To proceed we must get into the creek and wade. Soon and suddenly we debouched into cultivated fields planted to sweet potatoes, squash, and sugarcane. Ahead we saw two palm leaf huts. To raise the inhabitants we fired our guns and shouted and screamed. An answer came at last and then a native appeared, copper-skinned except for a face half blue with tattoos. He and his companion were migrants from Nukahiva in the Marquesas. At a lower elevation, where the creek expanded and deepened enough to float a canoe, we found his companion cutting up a turtle. Half a dozen skinny dogs shared the refuse. One of the natives finally agreed [that the two would] guide us. His name was Judge.

Going east we soon reached the highest ridge of mountains. In this part of the island we discovered the abundant spoor of wild pigs —that is, domestic pigs gone wild—and the deep holes they had grubbed in the mud.[13] Presently our guides' dogs flushed a young boar. It fled—with every one of us in hot pursuit—and dogs out front. We ran as fast as we could for about a mile before the dogs brought the quarry to bay at last. One of our youngest midshipmen, about a hundred paces in the lead, overran the boar as it tussled with the dogs at the base of a hill. The boar broke free and headed back toward us. The midshipman turned and fired. The bullet missed the boar and hit the ground beside my foot. The boar rushed for me. I shot him between the eyes.

A bite of bread from the lunch bag, a swig from the flask, and away we went again, up hill and down dale.

Weary beyond description, we reached a rocky-coasted bay on the southeastern end of the island.[14] The time was exactly noon, so we built a fire and prepared the boar's liver, heart, and kidneys and some things we had brought from the ship: a true and hearty hunter's meal. The morning's exertions, and a dip in the bay, honed appetites razor sharp. Wild garlic and tomatoes imparted a delicious flavor. Did we eat!

We ate so much that for the first two hours of the return our overstuffed bellies made the climb miserable. It took us until 9:00 P.M. to gain a hill on the south end of the island. We fired the signal for a boat, the boat brought us to the ship, and we boarded at 10:00 P.M., worn out and dead tired.[15]

The next day two officers off the *Saratoga* invited another officer and me to go hunting on Stapleton Island. Two of the oldest residents brought us there in a canoe. Immediately out of Port Lloyd, we set a northerly course and passed several rock formations west of Peel and Buckland. These, and the gorgeously rugged shapes of Stapleton, composed views that changed from moment to moment, like a kaleidoscope. Each splendid view gave way to another magnificent view, the next more beautiful than the last. Thus a grand panorama, one superb prospect after the other, unrolled from the start to the end of the eight miles between Port Lloyd and Stapleton.

We landed at a small bay and began at once to climb the rocky heights. For, approaching the island, we had spied what covered its crags and peaks: wild goats. And I mean they *covered* them.

Up and up we climbed, vigorously, spread right and left in a line, each man for himself, I on the far left. No sooner had I reached the top than I spotted, lower and about a hundred paces off, a flock of twenty-five or thirty, including two handsome billies. I took aim in a flash. I hesitated. Which of the two capital beasts should I shoot? Then the so-called buck fever gripped me. The swift, hard climb, and my greed for a trophy, had ignited it. I must sit down for a moment. The fever would not subside, a decision had to be made *now*, so I aimed, fired, and hit the rocks six inches above my billy's head. I sat back down, annoyed. I thought I must look like a schoolboy who forgot his lesson. The goats bleated scorn at me and calmly went their way.

A native on the right had better luck. He shot a fat nanny that became a tasty dinner. Roasting with onions over the fire, she made our mouths water. We took a refreshing dip, then lay on the flat stones of the beach, drank an aromatic cup of tea, and ate the juicy roast.

The remains of a junk, wrecked and broken-up here, provided the firewood. Kiri wood and copper nails—the Chinese use neither—so I concluded that the junk had been Japanese. Moreover, Edo lay a scant three hundred miles from this spot, a fact that lent credence to my conclusion.

Sea turtles often ride the rising tides to shore to lay their eggs in the sand. We took advantage of bright moonlight and quickly caught three, turning them onto their backs [to immobilize them]. The heaviest, at perhaps three hundred pounds, tested our limits. Like the others, it had to be seized and subdued in shallow water. Success demanded the combined strength of all six men to drag the giant to land and turn it over.[16]

After that day's labors we slept, each wrapped in his blanket: deep and dreamless sleep until the end of night. A cup of tea warmed us before dawn. We set off to explore the rocky heights in a new direction. I had determined for the tallest point. Quietly and carefully I began. At last, after much effort, I got above the lush vegetation and beyond the humus-rich soil that covered the slopes nearly to the peak. I reached granite, naked and weathered and seamed here and there with iron. The climb both dangerous and difficult now, I crawled on my hands and knees, gun slung across my back. Finally, just before sunrise, I gained the topmost peak and the abundant reward of a long and grand view. Below, many islands dotted a dark blue ocean and caught the golden glow of the sun. Stapleton's picturesque hills and their tropical vegetation composed a beautiful foreground. The wild goats number easily in the thousands, and the hills teemed with flock after flock.

Twilight still cloaked the valleys at my feet; only the peaks had begun to gleam in the morning's light. A year earlier I had been in the steeple of the venerable cathedral of Léon [Nicaragua] and beheld for the last time the American side of the Pacific. One question, a single thought, possessed my mind then. Would I reach Perry's expedition? I had scarcely dreamed that a year later I would be looking at the same ocean on its opposite side, after sailing nearly three-quarters of the globe. Reflecting on the past, I called up scenes that put me in good spirits.[17] I pondered the future, weighed the possible success of the expedition, and the prospect cheered me. I belted out a pure and lusty Tyrolean yodel that echoed from the rocks roundabout.

The yodel did more than relieve my pent-up emotions. The bushes below began to quiver and shake. A pair of long, yellow horns appeared, followed by an uplifted beard. An old billy, a noble patriarch, thrust his head into the morning air, looking for the hooligan who so disturbed the peace. He may have been 150 paces off, but my gun was loaded, and I fired. The old boy took one leap, then rolled downhill.

As if my gun signalled a battle, shots rang out—Bang!—on nearby heights. Bing! Bang! White cloud after white cloud puffed out of the bushes. Comrades had surrounded a flock and in a flash picked off four. So we had one apiece and began to think about returning to the ships. Shots crackled elsewhere; soon we had five males and four females.

We sang on our way down. A refreshing swim, a hearty hunter's breakfast, into the canoe, and back to the ships by noon. A boat returned for our game.[18] In the evening nine goats and four giant turtles joined us on board.

We sailed the next day and returned to Loo Choo on 21 June. Meanwhile the [American barque] *Caprice* [a collier chartered by Perry], one of our aviso ships, brought mail from Shanghai—a bag of it, carried to the Chinese port by the British overland postal service.

CHAPTER FIVE

SECOND CALL

AT LOO CHOO

A Visit to Naha on the QT.—Design of the Houses.—An Indiscretion.—At the
Market.—We Meet Our First Japanese.—The Character of the People of Loo
Choo.—A Good Time Aboard Ship.—A Visit to an Ancient Ruin.—A Brief Out-
line of Loo Choo's History.—To Nippon!

WE SPENT eight days in port at Naha, taking on coal, food
and water, and repairing storm-damaged ships. Meanwhile I
worked earnestly at my art. For, though nowhere sublime, the
southern part of the island offered in its picturesque places an abundance of studies: bridges and other structures in scenic settings and
usually lovely in form and color, and beautiful groves, especially the
noble pines, as majestic as the cedars of Lebanon. Groups of local
people, their faces and their dress, provided fascinating stuff for the
artist.

Mr. B[rown], the daguerreotypist, had brought his equipment
along. He soon mastered difficulties of situation and climate, and
the daguerreotype proved of exceptional value in depicting the
inhabitants. Locals delighted to sit as models and furnished hilarious
entertainment when they gaped in astonishment at themselves in
portraits a few minutes later. Unfortunately an innate shyness to foreigners could not always or in full measure be overcome in these
good people. Often we no more than glanced into a street whereupon windows and doors were locked. Women in particular would
startle and flee.

At long last, however, I managed to catch a section of the city
unawares and living as usual. I had spent the night in the country
but slept little because of mosquitoes. So, before dawn, Mr. [Wil-

liam B.] D[raper], the telegrapher, and I went after snipe along the river. The hunt took us around Naha and, soon after sunrise, to the opposite quarter, the one on higher ground where it appeared more prosperous people lived. Of course the streets were deserted at that hour, but garden gates, courtyard entrances, and house doors stood open. Thus, in those days, thieves seemed a class of society as yet unknown in that blessed land.

A courtyard typically asserts its boxwood hedges and tidy beds of flowers between a house and the street. Stone walls, eight to ten feet high, enclose the courtyard. One gate lets people in and out. The house, on the other side of the yard, is entirely of wood and simple in design. One or even several vestibules precede the rooms proper. Wooden panels serve as walls. Inserted or removed at will, they are usually removed on the side facing the yard. I have already mentioned windows of oiled paper. Also removable, they are usually installed in bad weather. During heat waves, jalousies are lowered over the verandah. Because of the jalousies' split-reed construction, people inside can see out, but people outside cannot see in.

Not a soul did we see or hear. So we continued to explore—even to the garden behind the house. A miniature of its Chinese counterpart and beautiful in flowers, this garden showed more taste in its arrangement. Goldfish swam in the pond at the garden's center, and seashells and multicolored stones decorated the pond's edges. Quietly we approached the rear of the house and peeked through the open jalousies. Straw mats covered the floor. Three women and two small children in scanty nightwear were sound asleep on the mats. Had we spied on women in these circumstances in Constantinople on earlier travels and been caught, our lives would not have been worth a red cent. Things were different here. The worst consequence of our illicit curiosity would have been terror for the sleeping beauties. But we would have been sorry to cause even that disquiet. So we withdrew as silently as we had approached. Probably nobody has yet suspected that two audacious foreigners dared penetrate what the good people of Loo Choo deem their holy of holies.

Descending again, we crossed other lower-lying quarters and found them gradually coming to life. In the marketplace, business boomed. Several hundred lower-class women sat behind baskets and counters and offered pork and chickens and various vegetables: beans, [sweet] potatoes, onions, cucumbers, and others. Some of the women took one look at us and fled. Some sat motionless. When those who fled saw that we meant no harm, they returned. I bought a nice-looking watermelon, and we savored it for breakfast. An especially popular item seemed to me a mild cheese, done up in blocks about the size of our Limburgers, eaten fresh or toasted over charcoal, and delicious either way.

We continued down to the harbor. During the last eight days sixteen to twenty Japanese junks had put in, and many lay at anchor. Here we met our first Japanese nobleman, identified by two swords in the belt. Part of his head was shaved clean while the hair that remained was oiled, combed neatly, and knotted at the crown; the beard thin but carefully groomed. He wore a long robe of a thin, almost transparent cloth, checkered in gray and white, with wide sleeves; and on top of the robe, another piece of the same fabric, patterned like a Scottish plaid, distinctively folded over the chest and shoulders and looking like armor, though of cloth. He carried in his belt (besides the swords) a fan, a short pipe with a small bowl in a silken case, and a small tobacco pouch also of silk. In his hand a sun umbrella of paper lacquered in black. He passed without paying us the slightest heed. We did likewise of course. The swords of this noble Japanese were the first weapons we had seen anywhere in Loo Choo.

We boarded one of the junks to a welcome of tea and saki. The crew, though a little shy, generally behaved friendly and cordially to us.

On a subsequent day we took the road to the capital city of Shuri, daguerreotyping apparatus in hand. By evening I had sketched numerous studies. Some of them featured groups of local people in one or another of the city's squares and streets as they sat—quiet and rigid, like statues—smoking their tobacco in the shade of beautiful trees: perfect subjects for artistic rendition. If (to serve the needs of the daguerreotype) I wanted this or that person in this or that place, I needed but take him politely by the hand and lead him there. He would strike a pose and remain, as rigid and passive as if hewn in stone, until I waved my thanks that I no longer needed him. He would bow courteously and go his way.

It seems thus that hard work, here as in other countries, must be restricted to the lower classes. For, at most times of day, I saw men of slightly higher status sitting in pleasantly shaded places, smoking their tobacco, or drinking tea or saki, and eating the foods they had brought along. The "lunch boxes" were of lacquered wood, small but pretty, and fitted with several drawers.

Generally speaking, I found the local person gentle, kind, and well behaved. I doubt whether conversion to Christianity could improve his conduct. I never witnessed throughout my stay one instance of punishment, nor so much as an act of rudeness, nor even a quarrel.

On 28 June, aboard ship, the commodore threw a farewell party for the regent. We had heard the early rumors that he had been deposed by imperial decree because he had welcomed and feted us in the castle. Were the rumors true? I do not know. At any rate, he did step down. An intelligent-looking, somewhat younger man now holds the office.[1]

Our guests, helping themselves boldly to our food, dug with hearty appetites into turtle soup, vegetables, fricassees, sliced meats, salad, roasts, fruit preserves, pies and other pastries, and every other delicacy of our table.[2] They cared little for the wine except champagne. In inverse proportion, however, they savored the sweet liqueurs and finer spirits. That is, they drank deep of them, with partiality to the maraschino, and became merry and bright. And so they rose from the table and departed, each a little tipsy.

During this second stay in Loo Choo I was able to study the ancient castle. I confirmed my assumption that the massive ruin belonged to a civilization lost in the mists of time.[3] Several people tried to direct me to it, but the way proved elusive nonetheless. Following the river from its mouth in Naha I went east about three miles. Sometimes rock formations cover the gently undulating hills, sometimes forests. Rice paddies fill the level places in between. The river, meandering across the landscape, embraces two wooded islands. The region would be idyllic, only the paddies and their symmetrical terraces slash through it and crisscross it like a chessboard. The eye rests agreeably on the occasional village half-hidden in a bamboo thicket. As for the rock formations, their bizarre and weathered shapes often led me astray; they resemble the wreckage of man-made walls. At last, after I hunted and hunted, I reached my goal.

The river bends abruptly there. On the peninsula and from a rocky height of about three hundred feet, the castle dominates its

surroundings: a picturesque sight. The ground slopes down on the
landward side. There the evidence of three circular walls remains
plain, though they have mostly collapsed and original shapes must
be deduced from heaps of rubble. Toward the river the upthrust of
perpendicular rock creates naturally a fortress practically impregnable. So there is but one man-made wall on this side. It is the castle's
best preserved wall except for the circumvallations of the innermost
fortifications. I have mentioned on a prior page the peculiarity of
the newer castle at Shuri, and I observed the same here.[4] That is,
every other people built castles with convex bastions. Here the bastions are concave.

To the right and left of the gate the second circle of wall has
largely collapsed. The massive arch of the gate should also have
crumbled. But the roots of a tree growing out of the rubble have
kept the arch partially intact. This part of the ruin, and the glimpse
of the river and city that appears with it, offer a lovely picture.

The last circle of wall encloses an area overgrown with trees and
shrubs. Yet something contradicted the desolation and glared in
wondrous contrast to the ruins besetting it: a wooden gate well preserved and firmly shut. (I had to climb over it.) Inside the enclosure
I discovered a mound of earth about four feet tall, with a slab of
fluted stone, eighteen feet long and four wide, on top of it. A few
characters of Chinese had been engraved on the slab. Remnants of
incense, like the incense used by Chinese at prayer, clung to sticks
protruding from the earth beside the slab. A path, narrow but clear,
led from the gate to this spot. The incense, and a path beaten plain
by feet that followed it, made the place look as if prayers and religious sacrifices were being offered there even now.

Perhaps I should present a little of the local history.

These islands, thirty-six in all—variously called Loo Choo, Lew
Kew, Lieu Kieu, Liu Kiu, and (by the Japanese) even Riu Kiu—sub-
divide into the northern or Sanbok group, the middle or Chusan
group, and the southern or Sannan group. They pay tribute to
China and Japan, being subordinate to both while pledging alle-
giance to neither. The Chinese scholar Su-Poa-Kuong [or Su-Poa-
Koang] sketched best the distant past of these islands. He traveled
here as an ambassador in 1719. Captain Maxwell included the
sketch in his report of his voyage of exploration here in the British
frigate *Alceste* in 1817.[5]

The history of Liu Kiu or Loo Choo starts with the legend that in the beginning the world was chaos. The first man and the first woman, both named Omo-Mey-Kiou, had three sons and two daughters. The eldest son, Tieu-Son (grandson of heaven) was Loo Choo's first king. The second son became the progenitor of the tributary princes. The third gave rise to descendants who multiplied into the populace. It is not recorded whether the brothers shared the sisters or somehow divided them or whether the third obtained a wife elsewhere. The older daughter was called the spirit of heaven, the younger the spirit of the waters. Tieu-Son died. According to the way time was reckoned here, rule passed down the millennia and through some 17,802 years and twenty-five dynasties to our year 1817 and the man said to have reigned then, the regent Chun-Tein. The local people believe this fabulous story—indeed, respect and maintain it with jealous regard.

The true story reads otherwise. The islands seem to to have come to the attention of the outside world in the seventh century A.D. About the year 650 the emperor of China, Yong-Ti, demanded tribute of the people of Loo Choo. When they rejected the demand, he mobilized an army of ten thousand men and fitted out a fleet in Amoy and Fou-Kieu. The force landed in Loo Choo, killed in battle the king and many of his subjects, burned the capital, and carried five thousand people back to China as slaves. In 1291 another Chinese emperor, Chit-Soo, assembled another fleet in Fou-Kieu. Though intended to strike Loo Choo, it got no further than Formosa.

By 1372 civil unrest had divided the islands into three smaller kingdoms. In 1372 the emperor of China, Hong-Ou, dispatched a mandarin [as emissary] to Prince Tray-Tou, who ruled [the part of Loo Choo called] Tschou-Chaw. The mandarin succeeded so well in his diplomatic mission that he persuaded this segment of the islanders to become tributary to China. In China their mission met a warm welcome and received a shower of gifts before departure. The example moved the kings or princes of Chan-Pe and Chan-Nau (the other parts of Loo Choo) to accept tributary status. When thirty Chinese families emigrated to Cha-Ou-Li, the present Naha, they introduced books, the Chinese way of writing, and the teachings of Confucius. Loo Choo's noble sons were brought up and educated in Nanking, at the emperor's expense. At long last, in the reign of

Chau-Pa-Chi, Loo Choo reunited. Relations with China and Japan continued, and Loo Choo enjoyed advantageous trade with them. Loo Choo has remained one kingdom.

In time, however, the famous Japanese emperor Tay-Cosoma demanded control of Loo Choo. Chang-Ning, Loo Choo's regent, rejected the demand. Japan dispatched a fleet. When it returned, it brought the king of Loo Choo to Japan. He proved so royally firm that the Japanese, though victorious, sent him (with admiration and awe) back to his kingdom.

Later when the Tartar dynasty acceded to the Chinese throne, changes occurred in the tributes paid to China, and ambassadors from Loo Choo had to travel to Peking only every other year. The name of Chang-Hi, the regent who effected this change, still enjoys reverence in Loo Choo.

I had little opportunity to observe religious ceremonies. It is said that about a thousand years ago the foreign big shots introduced to Loo Choo the Fo religion, which endures. Yet the local people seem rather to follow a simple paganism. Temples tumble down in disrepair. Some of the old idols suffer neglect, and others have been mutilated. I saw evidence of fresh mutilation.

Polygamy, though permitted, seldom occurs. The king must marry one daughter of one of three princely families. There is another such family, but the king is not to choose his queen there, for it has not been determined whether the bloodlines will mingle. Royalty and nobility are hereditary but deserving men can rise. Those who misbehave can be stripped of rank. The king derives income partly from estates, partly from taxes on salt, copper, tin, sulphur, and other commodities. He uses the monies to pay officials and maintain his household.

My source for this history [M'Leod's *Narrative*] also has a long discussion of the ceremony to be conducted when one ruler dies and another is crowned. Necessarily I omit it here.

The name of these islands appears in a different form on every map. Controversy still rages as to the proper spelling. The Japanese have *Riu-Kiu,* the English *Loo Choo* or *Liu-Kiu.* Captain [Basil] Hall wrote *Lew Chew.* French maps have *Lieu-Kieu.* We decided at last on *Loo Choo* for our maps. . . .[6]

The next day we put to sea again, this time on our most important passage, the crucial one—to Nippon!

CHAPTER SIX

EDO BAY: FIRST CALL

A View of the Coast of Nippon.—Its Beauty.—Entry into the Bay.—Uraga Harbor.
—First Contact with the Japanese.—How They Looked and What They Wore.—
Precautions. — Taking Measure of the Bay. — Coastal Fortifications. — Hostile
Demonstrations.—The Effect of a Whistle.

ON 2 JULY we left Naha: the *Susquehanna* first, towing the
Saratoga, with the *Mississippi* and the *Plymouth* a quarter-mile
astern.[1] As we expected to raise the coast of Nippon at dawn on the
eighth, I took post on the *Susquehanna's* deck before dawn.

The sun made slow progress against thick fog. We would occasionally see a Japanese junk, which would beat out of sight the
moment it spied us. Though of eighty to a hundred tons and built
solidly enough, junks run and maneuver rather well, usually under
one enormous cotton sail.[2] (Sometimes two smaller ones may be
hoisted on special masts, one fore, one aft.) In contrast to the
brightly painted junks of China and Loo Choo these show merely
the color of wood, and salt water has turned their few copper acces-
sories green.

At about 6:00 A.M. we went through a scatter of small islands
southwest of Edo Bay. At 9:00 we watched the peaks of Nippon's
mountains rise above the fog. Now as a rule, a warship can begin
action at a moment's notice; at most the guns must be recharged
and the crew issued live ammunition. We saw the peaks and the
order rang out, "General quarters!"[3] We were ready in a flash.

We saw beautifully picturesque mountains and rocky slopes
plunging to the water's edge. Forests cover some of the heights.
Attractive fields and meadows also occur up there if the incline
moderates or a plateau opens to them.

The nearby mountains might rise a good six thousand to seven
thousand feet. Yet at about 10:00 A.M. a volcanic peak could be

seen above and beyond them. The grand Fujiyama seemed about
thirty to forty miles off. (Later I learned the truth: It was over a
hundred miles off.) We observed the truncated cone, the shape of all
volcanoes, its rim some forty to fifty feet above the core. The light-
colored stripes and patches—were they snow or bright sand? We
could not tell the difference, what with vapor and haze.

We reached the entrance to Edo's outer bay at about 2:00 P.M.
Moderate elevations frame the bay in a hilly landscape; mountains
rise higher at a distance. The hills sometimes end in bluffs [at the
water's edge]: picturesque, lush with vegetation, and crowned by
sublime and lovely pines. Elsewhere the hills expire into meadowed
valleys and small flats. Towns and villages often occur there, as well
as green, handsome rice paddies wherever tillage is possible. Paddies, rocky knolls scattered among them, and a dotting of groves
add up to a fetching aspect. To heighten the charm, a haze cloaks
the land in a delicate gray, softening and calming the impression.
And, as foreground, the deep blue sea harmonizes beautifully.

The number of junks increased the closer we approached the
coast. When we entered the bay, junks and a conflux of small fishing
boats covered the water. At first they avoided us. Then a little fisher
craft could not dodge fast enough and passed hard by us. The rest
observed that we not only left it alone but also ignored it.
Emboldened, they paraded by, gaping in curious wonder at the fabulous sea monsters that moved without sails and against the wind
besides.[4]

At 4:00 P.M. we reached the place where the breadth of thirty to
forty miles narrows to ten or twelve: the entrance to the inner bay
or true [harbor]. *This* Bay of Edo extends another thirty to thirty-
five miles to Edo at the far end. Here at the entrance a fair-sized city
occupies the western out-thrust of the narrows. At several locations
on the hills artillery bristles. When we had got to about three miles
from that point of land, a battery puffed a cloud of white smoke.
We expected a missile to hit the water. Instead, above the battery, a
bomb or a rocket burst in the air. It proved to be only a signal, three
times repeated, and answered from hills farther off.

Our ships did not hesitate but proceeded. Soon, a mile and a half
from shore, we anchored in battle formation, each ship facing a land
battery broadside. Presently many boats of appreciable size put out
from land toward us. Two rowers worked each of a boat's six or

eight oars. They rowed Chinese style: not from front to back [in horizontal strokes] but in a circular motion at the side of the boat, like a fish propelling itself with tail and fins.[5] The boats carried officials who wanted to board us. After a parley the ranking one gained permission and boarded with his Dutch interpreter. Since he was not the top official hereabouts, only our flag lieutenant [John Contee] met and talked with him.[6] In a few words the official heard our purpose and in a few more an invitation to the local head of government to visit us. Meanwhile the number of boats had multiplied. They threatened, as on earlier occasions, to surround and confine us with boats upon myriad boats.[7] The commodore soon had it made clear to the officials that the boats must leave us alone; he would not suffer such a violation of maritime law. They looked nonplused. His statement was repeated—in a threatening tone.[8] They sent the boats home, then requested plainly and frankly that none of us go ashore for the time being, as they would have to answer for it. We gave our word. They returned to land in a calmer frame of mind.

Very early the next morning the commander-in-chief of local military forces came aboard with a kind of lord mayor or prefect.[9] They being of higher rank, the flag captain met them and informed them of the American government's charge to the commodore.[10] The captain stressed that the squadron intended to go up the bay to Edo to deliver to the proper authority the communication from his government. Both officials would have remonstrated but nobody paid attention, so they requested four days to report to Edo. They got almost what they wanted, insomuch as the squadron would stay put until noon of 12 July. The officials behaved with decency and politeness to the most agreeable surprise of us all.

Only a hint of the Asiatic countenance touched the features of these upper-class people. Nor did it assert itself disagreeably even in the faces of lower-class people, the fishermen and the boat crews. Indeed, only one characteristic struck us as peculiar: a body either too short in the lower half or too long in the upper, and all the more noticeable because of belts and sashes worn low.

Dress differed little from what I had seen worn on Japanese junks at Loo Choo. The roomy garment resembled a caftan, with short, wide sleeves, culotted at the bottom and gathered by a belt at the hips. In the belt: a pair of swords, one long and two-handed, the other short. (What a bother it must be, carrying swords that shift and swing with every step.) Undergarments consisted of a short tunic and ankle-length trousers, both light-colored and in a thin, diaphanous fabric. Stockings, of a dark knit, provided the big toe its own compartment. The sandal's two straps, neatly woven of rice straw, passed thereby between the big and second toes and to the right and left across the foot and [toward the back of] the sandal, also of straw. Again [as with Japanese at Loo Choo] what remained of largely shorn hair had been braided into a tuft on the crown and put flat toward the front to touch the upper forehead. Care and concern went into this hairdo, combed to a nicety and oiled. I saw no beards. Nor anything for the officials' heads except the fan held to protect them from the sun.[11] Soldiers wore hats, broad and flat, and lacquered to a luster. Ranking officials wore black overcoats ornamented with embroidery like coats of arms, in colored silk, on the shoulders, the back and the chest, and at the hems. I noticed a kind of coat of arms on military officers' hats, too, in mixed colors or in gold. Of the strapping fellows who manned the boats, nearly all wore nothing but a piece of cotton around the loins. Nearing our ships, however, these boatmen donned short, bright smocks in colors distributed according to boats. (The crew of a boat wore only the colors of the owner of the boat.) The helmsman stood in the stern, a flag to his right, a flag to his left. One flag displayed the owner's coat of arms; the other, a black stripe between two white stripes. Black and white, we learned later, are the imperial colors.[12]

All our while in the bay we never let down our guard. Our every precaution against mishap included measures to forestall a Japanese surprise attack.[13] Three times the usual number stood watch. Officers—assigned [as extras] four in each of two-hour shifts—joined them, between sundown and sunup, in various parts of the ship. Orders stated: Allow no boat during the night to approach within rifle range. At any unusual movement ashore or on the water, sound the alarm.

Nothing of the sort occurred. Earlier incidents on the Japanese coast justified precautions nevertheless. Note especially the surprise attack on Captain [Vasilii M.] Golovnin, which landed that brave officer and his companions in jail for years.[14]

After dark the shore presented a marvelous view. Large signal fires burned everywhere on the hills. Sentry fires strung lights along the several lines of batteries and forts. Many hamlets and villages dotted the length of the coast and speckled the hilly seaside. Illuminated by fires and torches, which often moved from place to place, they looked like swarms of fireflies.[15]

At 9:00 P.M. [the first evening], the flagship's gun as usual sounded retreat, the other ships answered, and we saw strange movement ashore.[16] Many people ran about with torches, and some sentry fires were put out, as the Japanese probably feared attack. Calm returned after a while. Quiet reigned until, ashore, a great clock struck. Now and again during the night it would send its full but gentle notes to us across the water.

We lay opposite the city of Uraga, home (it seemed) to some eight thousand to ten thousand people. It apparently serves Edo as a port of entry [and exit]. Traffic, to and from Edo, stops here. Easily more than a hundred large junks arrive each day, understandably, as every Japanese high-muck-a-muck spends part of the year in Edo. During his stay provisions of all sorts, for him and entourage, follow from his province.[17]

We had given the officials three days [to communicate with Edo].[18] We used the days to survey the bay, headed by the *Mississippi*'s Lieutenant Bent. He also commanded the first cutter, where I was assigned. We sounded for depths, then traced the coast, counting batteries, establishing their positions, and determining their range. Japanese patrol boats, stationed along the coast, tried a few times to stop us. Our orders: In such instances meet force with force.[19] A crew of sixteen manned each of our boats, armed with handguns, muskets, and bayonets. Officers carried the excellent six-shot pistol that, under the name Colt Revolver [or Colt's "revolving pistol"], won universal applause at the London fair.[20] When Japanese boats tried to intercept us, half our crew would drop oars and pick up muskets from under seats. Without fail this demonstration cleared the way for us.

We saw many forts of nothing but earth. Half-circular or elliptical, a shape typical of [fortifications in the] seventeenth and eighteenth centuries [in the West], they of course could not deliver crossfire. Their flanks, as well as the hills behind them, lacked any protection whatsoever. Along three miles of coast, 120 to 130 guns could have been placed in the embrasures of the several forts. But scarcely a quarter of the embrasures held guns, and none bigger than nine- and twelve-pounders. At the worst [if armed clash occurred] we could anchor beyond their range and at leisure bombard them with our sixty-eights. The forts thus amounted to unsatisfactory defenses, easy to overpower.

The boats of the Japanese—fast, well built, skillfully maneuvered —therefore remained the greatest threat. And in battle the sturdy Japanese soldiers would have proved to be champions of the cold steel.[21]

Our survey boats [working until now in the lower or outer bay] shifted to the upper or inner. On the eleventh [of July] the *Mississippi* moved there to protect them. When we lay at anchor before Uraga, an extended point [later Point Rubicon] blocked sight of the upper. This point was fortified and, in coast artillery, well gunned. Ordered aboard the *Mississippi* for the day, I would be able to get a good look at that upper bay.[22]

The *Mississippi* and the boats rounded the point. From assorted places along the [western] shore, some 120 sizeable Japanese boats, each with a crew of twenty to twenty-five, moved as if to intercept us. Meanwhile we saw shove off across the bay about an equal number of boats similarly manned. This flotilla seemed about to unite with that from the west. Our four—themselves of good size—halted perhaps a quarter-mile in front of the *Mississippi* and thus under the protection of a frigate's cannon.

Our four boats moved, in line, slowly forward. In each, one man cast the lead. On the *Mississippi,* where I was, four each cast a lead. These soundings produced the best possible results: The sand bars and coral reefs, widely rumored to make the bay dangerous, did not exist.

In this way we went up the bay approximately another twelve miles without significant resistance. The Japanese did attempt, once, a kind of battle formation. The *Mississippi* steamed calmly on. So near that their boats might be run down, the *Mississippi* blew her whistle—with the desired result. The blast, an ear-splitter, shrilled and shrieked over the water, and boats beat to safety right and left as fast as possible. I could not help but laugh, in that comic moment, at the amazing effect produced by a whistle.[23]

When we reached our limits, we saw a city, way off, spreading far and wide at the bay's upper end. Located there, the city must be Edo. But under strict orders from the commodore, we could not approach near enough to confirm our assumption.

Meanwhile several embassies called on the commodore.[24] Word had arrived at last, authenticated by an imperial certificate shown to him, that two imperial officials from Edo would see him on the twelfth. The president of the United States had sent [with the commodore] a message to the emperor of Japan; the imperial officials would receive it. [Perry had refused to give it to anyone low in rank.] The meeting would take place in the little town of Kurihama, about two miles before Uraga. According to the embassies, preparations to receive Perry had already been made there.

CHAPTER SEVEN

THE MEETING WITH THE

IMPERIAL DELEGATION¹

Tricked Out and Ready.—The Japanese Dress for the Occasion.—The Commodore Goes Ashore.—Japanese Soldiers.—The Imperial Representatives.—Negotiations Begin.—The Commodore Stands Firm.—The Governor of Uraga Comes Aboard to Visit.—The Japanese Show Us That They Have Been Educated and What They Know.—Return to Loo Choo.

THIS MORNING, the twelfth [14 July 1853], we saw a medley of flags decorating the batteries and forts. Long sheets of black-and-white cloth had been stretched inside the walls. Earlier travelers, discussing these sheets installed above the guns, assumed that they served to conceal the armed interior below. Our interpreter, Mr. Wells Williams, did not agree. (He and Dr. [Peter] Parker passed along these coasts sixteen years earlier [as missionaries] in the *Morrison* from Canton.²) He thought that the sheets, erected close together, were to protect the cannoneers from rifle bullets. To me, this interpretation seemed the better one. For, however ineffective against bombardment, they would be of some value as a screen against small arms.³

At about 8:00 A.M. the governor of Uraga and several officials came aboard with an announcement. Everything was ready for the reception ashore, they said. This time each Japanese wore full dress: something like baggy trousers of heavy black silk, ankle-length, held up by strips of silk like our suspenders, and hemmed generously, top and bottom, in dark blue silk; a close-fitting sleeved vest or jacket, of silk, tucked into the top of the trousers; around the waist the usual belt and the pair of swords; and over the whole a kind of cloak like the Spanish poncho or our Catholic priest's surplice except for the slit down the front and the clasp to hold the halves together. Cloaks differed according to wearer's rank: for higher ranks, a heavy silk, woven like brocade, in gold, silver, and [other] colors; for the lower, a nondescript fabric, usually red but occasionally yellow. All cloaks, regardless of wearer's rank, were edged and hemmed with gold and silver and coats of arms embroidered on the shoulders and across the chest.

At 9:00 A.M. the call to boats sounded—after some ships had anchored opposite the meeting place. From there, should worst come to worst for us [ashore], they could protect us with their cannon. Fifteen boats took four hundred men from the several ships. Shortly before 10:00 A.M. the *Susquehanna*'s gun announced the commodore's departure. The flotilla of boats set off for the rendezvous about two miles west of Uraga, in a small inlet. The village of Kurihama lay on the inlet.

About 150 [Japanese] boats ringed the inlet. We saw a group of richly dressed officials in front of two spacious pavilions that had been erected ashore. To the right and left, sheets of black cloth had been stretched at a height of six to eight feet for about two miles. Units of soldiers ranged along them. The number of soldiers could not be readily estimated, their formation being ragged and ill-defined. The Japanese announced six thousand; it had to be at least five thousand. Most carried spear or musket, others bow and arrow; but all the ubiquitous pair of swords. Why *two?* I see no reason except pomp: mere show.

About 150 soldiers, armed with muskets and bayoneted rifles, had been arrayed near the pavilions, in two ranks, military style, weapons at the order. The rest of the soldiers formed irregular groups here and there. Two cannon on the left flank, three- or four-pounders, in bronze and on carriages of ancient vintage, looked like old Spanish or Portuguese. They probably dated from the Japanese war of extermination against Portuguese Christians. Officers of the various units sat on low seats, each under his unit's insignia. Orderlies, behind the ranks, held a number of horses of small breed but strong and well built: their saddles, harness, and trappings showy and inlaid abundantly with silver and gold; manes cut short; and tails brightly decorated, sometimes enclosed in a container of vivid fabric, sometimes entwined with pieces of colored cloth. When our band played, the horses pricked up their ears, cut hoof-stomping caprioles, and caused disturbances among the soldiers. Other soldiers, carrying pikes of various shapes and fifteen to sixteen feet long, did nothing but keep close, a few to each horse.

Four companies of ours, two of marines and two of sailors, had formed where the commodore would land, marines right, sailors left. Two bands—one of marines, one of sailors—provided music in addition to the usual complement of red-jacketed drummers and fifers. A major [Jacob Zeilin] and a captain [William B. Slack] commanded the marines; four lieutenants and two midshipmen, the sailors. The remaining officers, about forty (the commodore's staff), awaited the commodore himself at the spot where he would debark.[4]

The moment the commodore set foot on land, the governor of Uraga and his entourage appeared. (The governor had arrived a little earlier.) He welcomed everybody, and then the grand procession started for the pavilions, not far off.

Long sheets of black and white formed a kind of outer courtyard. Japanese and Americans stayed outside it except the governor and a small retinue and the commodore and a small staff. Each leader thus left most of his followers behind.

The governor escorted the commodore into the courtyard, across mats that had been laid there, and up several steps to the open adjoining pavilion. The imperial councilors—Toda, prince of Idsu, and Ido, prince of Iwami—waited in the pavilion. Toda sat a bit higher than Ido. To Ido's right another official kneeled [until we drew near], Yezaimon, whose rank I was unable to learn.[5] He, the governor of Uraga, and the interpreter Tatsonoske bowed deeply before Prince Toda, kneeled there, and remained kneeling throughout [the day's] negotiations. The commodore and the senior captains were asked to take the three seats of equal height opposite Toda's. The other American officers gathered behind the commodore. The rest of the governor's retinue stayed in the courtyard, kneeling.

We had been told that these were imperial representatives of the highest rank. In the lives of their people ceremony and formality took precedence over everything else. The councilors' underlings always removed their shoes upon entry and, when speaking to the councilors, kneeled and touched their foreheads continually to the ground. Dutch and Russian emissaries in Japan before us had been compelled to disgraceful humiliation.[6] And now we entered with such little ado, and we remained erect.

What an outlandish and insolent spectacle we therefore presented to the Japanese. How different our behavior from that of the Russians and the Dutch, what a lurid contrast our manner against that of the councilors' underlings, and how egregious we alien barbarians must have seemed to the councilors.[7] Perhaps the Dutch and Russian emissaries had been instructed to respond with obeisance to every impudent Japanese policeman and to kneel and crawl, backward and forward, time after time. Not so with us, thank God! The commodore had made up his mind; no disgraceful humiliation would be inflicted on *him*.[8]

Accordingly he issued the strictest of orders, and we paid each Japanese the courtesy that would have been paid a man of his position in the United States. This policy produced obviously excellent results.[9] Yes, the Japanese sycophants at first looked askance. But they took comfort at last when they saw aboard ship that our officers enjoyed respect and that each subordinate obeyed every command with prompt assent—all without shameful subservience and servile formalities. The Japanese also observed that we received their representatives aboard and, without degrading ourselves, treated them with cordiality and warmth.

True, the Japanese had objected to our survey of the bay and to our anchoring wherever it suited us. They had tried to justify their gestures of resistance: "You have contradicted the wishes of our government, and we must do as we are told." But we retorted: "We are honoring the wishes of *our* government, and *we* must do as *we* are told. Besides, we are accustomed to behave this way all over the world. So we shall behave this way here, too!" We also declared, however, and at the same time, that the United States felt nothing but friendship for Japan. At any rate, the Japanese could do nothing but comply, though our actions be new to them. For, in the end, small boats and twelve-pound cannon would have been a squeak against the roar of our mighty steamships and heavy artillery.[10]

The Japanese again showed the commodore the document that vested imperial authority in them.[11] The commodore responded with his diplomatic credentials and the letter for the emperor from the president. Each of these document bore the Great Seal of the United States in a dangling gold skippet. The two handsomest cabin

boys brought them forward, each in its container: a case with a
golden clasp and a golden lock. After the cases were opened, a short
speech set forth the purpose of the commodore's mission. Then the
documents—and translations of them into Dutch, Chinese, and
French—were presented to the imperial councilors, and they accepted them. The documents were then placed with much ceremony in a roomy chest, and the chest shut, locked, wrapped many
times with a stout cord of silk, and tied with an array of astounding
knots.

"No doubt," the commodore added at the end of the meeting,
"mature deliberation will have to take place on my mission and my
message. Therefore I shall leave now and return in the spring."[12]
Again the Japanese were seeing and hearing what they had never
seen or heard before. The commodore behaved nothing like the
emissaries of other nations who had preceded him. Those unfortu-
nates had waited long months in ignominious semi-imprisonment
until it pleased the Japanese to answer them equivocally and let
them go at last.

"I shall leave, I shall return," the commodore had announced.
The Japanese made no bones about it; the announcement astounded them.[13] Then Perry explained that the awesome military
power [of our ships], so close to the imperial capital, could give rise
to incorrect assumptions. "I do not want in the least to influence
discussions." As an act of politeness, therefore, we will go away, he
said, and the Japanese calmed down.

Everyone exchanged courtesies in farewell and left the pavilion.
We embarked in good order.[14] For Major [Jacob] Z[eilin] had gone
to the marines and assembled the drums and fifes, and we got into
the boats to a famous old tune. It had never been heard on the
shores of Nippon, but now, with drums obbligato, "Yankee Doo-
dle" rang out—to the delight of all.

The governor and his officials accompanied us to the ships and
came aboard.[15] They behaved with the reserve of people who think
it indecorous to let one's curiosity show. Yet they studied everything below; it had been out of their sight until now. The ship's
machinery, the heavy cannons and their percussion locks, the rifles,
the revolvers—that sort of thing provoked the greatest astonishment.[16] On the other hand, familiar with maps of the earth and
charts of the heavens, they pointed out—on the globe and with pre-

cision—not only Japan, Russia, England, Holland, and the United States but their capitals and other features. And they asked a variety of questions, indicating considerable knowledge of international affairs.[17]

"Does Mexico still exist? Or has the United States conquered it by now?"

"Has the giant railroad been built from New York to San Francisco, really?"

On and on, question after question. With each, a finger went—correctly—to the place meant.

We received numerous gifts before we departed: fabrics (including gold brocade), over a hundred fowls, over a thousand eggs, all sorts of lacquerware, saki, fans, and other things. The commodore responded with gifts. Politely the Japanese declined the several valuable arms and weapons. But wines, jams, preserves, and candied fruits seemed all the more welcome; the Japanese enjoyed them aboard whenever possible.[18] Especially on the last day, when champagne flowed and Uraga's lord governor and suite left in uncommonly good humor.

We remained in the bay for two more days, completing the survey and choosing a good anchorage for next spring. During this interval relations grew better each day: terms friendlier, harmony more general.[19] The governor paid us still another visit. Time and again our survey boats laid alongside boats of the Japanese. Crews smoked pipes together and gave and received little gifts.[20] Delicious fresh fruit [from the Japanese] included magnificent ripe peaches.

On the fifteenth we steamed out of the bay the way we had come in. South we went the entire day, among the various islands.[21] When we reached open ocean again, we steered straight for our former anchorage at Naha on Loo Choo.

A savage storm struck.[22] Cruelly battered, we [the *Susquehanna*] lost some masts, spars, and rigging. Worse, the *Mississippi* surrendered two of her boats. At least we suffered no further deprivation, no other casualties, and, happily, no deaths. Around noon on the twenty-fifth we lay at anchor again in the old place. We had left comrades behind in the *Supply* (storeship), and now they met us with a warm welcome. Happy to be welcomed, we were equally happy to be able to replenish our fresh meat and vegetables, recently depleted.

A few days later the regent invited us to Shuri for a reception and banquet. Our second here, this one lacked the formality of the first but resembled it closely otherwise. This time we also dispensed with the escort of sailors and marines. The commodore used the occasion [to gain the regent's ear]. The people of Loo Choo now believed enough in our peaceable intentions, the commodore said, and he politely declined the official escorts of the earlier visit. They had been at the heels of each of us, ostensible aides, in fact watchdogs. He said he wanted to select and pay for food and other things at the market. "In short, let your people and mine mingle freely." The regent hesitated, unwilling to agree. As an excuse he pleaded that nothing of the sort could be allowed without approval by the prince, no less. "I'll go to Shuri," the commodore said, "and take care of everything myself." The regent agreed at once.[23]

Difficulties also arose when we proposed a shed to store our extra coal during our absence next year. What amazing objections! "A storm might blow the shed down as it would be of merely the same construction as the indigenous houses." Or "Local people might steal the coal." And more of the same. Suffice it to say that all objections bit the dust while relations remained amicable.[24] And the shed was built.[25]

At last, on the morning of 31 July in Naha, a kind of bazaar opened to sell us fans, fabrics in wool and silk, lacquerware, and all sorts of other items. Money was the precious commodity, however. Accordingly I bought one of those handsome [lunch] boxes in lacquerware, with four drawers, [one each] for rice, meat, fish, and vegetables. I bought shoes, a tin container for saki, some small lacquered cups, a caftan with a silk belt, a pipe and tobacco pouch, fans, and other things. And all for the pittance of $3.00. We paid prices equally low at the food market but with Chinese money called *cash*.

And so we gradually overcame the shyness of the inhabitants of Loo Choo. Let us hope that the friendly relations thus established with those good-natured people will get better and better in the years to come.[26]

CHAPTER EIGHT

AN INTERVAL OF REST

IN MACAO

Cum Sing Moon.—Daily Life in Macao.—A Friendly Tone and Cordial Relations. —Pleasant and Entertaining Cruises on the River.—A Granary for Rice.—South Sea Islanders Rescued.—News from Japan and Reflections on It.—A Painful Loss.— Hunting Parties.—The Murder of Governor Amaral.—[Macao and Environs].

W E LEFT Loo Choo on the first of August [1853].[1] Winds against us, we proceeded inchmeal. The sloop *Vandalia* meanwhile had been headed straight here from the United States; we met her at the end of the day on the third. On the seventh we anchored once again in the famous harbor at Hong Kong. Typhoon season at hand, we stayed but three days before the *Mississippi* moved to Whampoa and the *Susquehanna* to the somewhat more sheltered anchorage of Cum Sing Moon.[2]

The name of this place—whoever bestowed it—must answer for it. Cum Sing Moon means the Golden Gate of the Rising Sun.[3] But Cum Sing Moon is a big basin surrounded by bald, stunted hills. A few miserable fishermen's shacks huddle among the hills, and ships of the international opium trade anchor in the basin.[4] In heat intense unto suffocation, starched collars had been heard of but never seen around somebody's neck. For entertainment we could either visit opium ships or go fishing. The fishing did not amount to much, and I find little entertainment in fishing. Bored, I threw a line over the side anyway. After a long wait I pulled out a denizen of the yellow depths. Its huge goggle-eye reproached me with a glare. Shame on you, I said to myself, for the heroic act that tricked this poor creature with such a scrap of bait. I set my captive free.

After four days the word arrived. The entire artistic section [or artists' mess] would move their quarters to the newly established hospital at Macao.[5] The Portuguese *lorcha* arrived for us, we boarded with a song in our hearts, and we were in Macao the same evening.[6]

I believe I have already said that Macao's beautiful situation has made it a favorite summer and fall resort of rich foreign merchants from Canton and Hong Kong.[7] This year they stayed longer than usual, especially because of the political unrest. And they filled with colorful life this place that would otherwise have been quiet.

During my first five or six weeks here—my winter, or rather my autumn, in Macao—I tried to avoid the many temptations of its social whirl. My drawings of Japan had to be organized and completed, my duties in the hydrographic department demanded time and attention, my hands were therefore full and my mind had to be on my work.[8] I took evening walks, however, to refresh myself after the day's enervating toil. Out walking, I met people and formed agreeable acquaintanceships and entered pleasant social affiliations. These grew until in the end I could not rightly decline the numerous invitations to dinners, suppers, balls, promenades, and hunting parties—lest I seem a rude misanthrope. Meanwhile, as my work progressed, so I gained time for leisure. I could yield with a clear conscience to the pleasure of sociable gatherings.[9]

Call Macao Portuguese, call it Anglo-Indian, call it Oriental; in short, anything before Chinese. I had never experienced such a place. In general a Latin informality and ease of association combine with genuine English decency in a unique blend that produces the tone.[10] What a contrast it poses to the indigenous strictures, especially here amid a nation where the reverence for ancient ceremony regulates modern life. The rules of so-called good manners can thus be followed with ease, and they cause the newcomer no trouble. True, a few strange ways constitute exceptions, but everyone adjusts to them readily and quickly.

The newcomer (for example) customarily pays a visit as soon as possible to everyone he wants to meet. If he has a good friend or an acquaintance who will take him around, so much the better. No matter, however, if he lack such a guide. Even the courtesy of a letter of introduction can be dispensed with. One's card, sent only to the lady of the house, will suffice, and the request to visit will usually be granted at once. That is, in response, in most instances, the man of the house will return the call or his wife even extend an invitation in writing. The newcomer can then consider himself a friend of the family.

It even happened several times that I wanted an evening visit with a lady of my recent acquaintance. Then I heard she was planning to call on someone else or had been invited elsewhere. According to custom in my northern part of the world, she would have politely declined my request. But in the friendliest way she said: "I've been invited elsewhere. You come, too."

In the hot months the men here usually wear a short, white tunic of a light fabric. This practice considerably eases the problems of etiquette: It eliminates the necessity to dress for an occasion. Moreover, you can forget what must be observed in London, Paris, Vienna, and New York: You need not choose an outfit for the time of day, as the tunic suffices at all times everywhere.

I spent many agreeable hours in the home of the French minister to China, Mr. [Alphonse] de B[ourboulon]. Macao's French officials repaired there regularly. Madame de B.—a delightful conversationalist fluent in several languages and a better-than-average musician—attracted the intelligentsia to her house, and they always regretted to leave.[11] I had grown up, become a traveler, and no longer heard the good music—indeed, the best in music—that I heard during my years at home. At Madame de B.'s, however, a few proficient and enthusiastic amateur musicians often gathered, and I heard much fine music, to my supreme delight. Several officers off the French corvette *Constantine,* excellent singers, presented many a lovely quartet for male voices. Frequently I drifted into reverie and dreamed myself back in the city of my birth. I would wake and, astounded, find myself again on the outermost edge of the Celestial Empire.

My intimate friendship with Dr. W. provided another opportunity for relaxation and entertainment of body and mind. This English aficionado of landscape painting was himself a capable amateur in that genre. He owned a superbly beautiful hong boat, its cabin spacious enough to seat four at table, and equipped with every other comfort. We cruised many a time upriver for the day and exploited the numerous views the shores offered our sketchbooks. Mornings, out to shoot snipe for lunch, I would roam the rice paddies a while, gun in hand. When the sun began to take its work too seriously, I would find a shady spot and from there—also from the boat sometimes—draw the interesting scenes along the banks: boats and junks, groups of picturesquely situated fishermen's huts, pagodas half-hidden by trees, and the like. Later in the afternoon we would dine aboard the boat. Madame W., woman's work done and her hours of reading finished, would join us. We would close the day with a stroll in the cool of the evening, sketchbook or gun in hand again. On several of these little excursions we visited nearby examples of the villages that occur along the river. The most important, Casa Branca, counts about ten thousand residents within its walls of stone.

At another point on the river a strange towerlike building contained in its three stories many altars and idols, old but in excellent condition. Incense burned on some altars as if to say, This temple has by no means been abandoned. Yet I found as few worshipers at prayer and as few priests on duty as in temples I had previously observed. Thus it would seem that the Chinese do not practice religion with any excess of zeal.

As far as I could determine, peasants in this part of China divide into a certain number of clans or tribes. Several families rule them, require specified services, and exact an annual tribute of rice. Along with tribute, however, these noble families also accept the obligation—or perhaps they do it out of custom and tradition—to supply their poorer vassals with rice in hard times. Immense buildings serve the purpose [of storing the rice]. These granaries display more or less pomp according to the small or large fortunes of the families who own them. Thus at still another point on the river a grandly spacious structure, rich in gilding and wood carvings, radiates three hundred and four hundred feet in every direction and serves as granary and temple. The second harvest was in progress, and rice was being brought in for storage. Dr. W. has visited here on several occasions, sometimes to find the granary almost empty, sometimes full. I was unable to learn whether the same arrangements exist everywhere in the Chinese empire.

Let me report a curious incident.[12] Our storeship *Southampton* arrived at this time. After a voyage around the Horn she had fished out of the open ocean a fifteen-foot native canoe and its seven passengers. Obviously from one of the South Sea islands, they must have been driven, according to the most conservative estimate, at least 1,200 nautical miles. Questioned, the seven said little except *salibabou*. It could have meant the name of their island as well as their tribe. When a French officer entered the sick bay where they had been sent for treatment, they flew into a dither and addressed him with much gesticulation in a language of many gutterals. That episode, and the rosary among their few possessions, prompted speculation that perhaps French ships had called at their island. But the location could not be determined. Another of their possessions was of Malayan metal: a tin pot. The people's features nearly mirrored those of Malays, but their hair was kinky. Though the canoe was of fairly substantial boards, not nails but thin strips of bamboo bound them together. It remained a riddle to us how these people could sustain such a voyage in such a fragile craft.

We received word via Shanghai of what happened to the Russian expedition in Japan.[13] We heard too that the Japanese would communicate with nobody until further notice. Reasons (such differing reasons!) accompanied this news of a supposed end to communication: (1) the Japanese wanted no discussions with any other nation until those with Commodore Perry had been concluded; (2) the emperor of Japan had died on 26 August—so the Japanese allegedly said to the head of the Russian expedition—and no affairs of state could be conducted during the three-year period of mourning.[14]

The second, depicting the Japanese as the worst of idiots, sounded like nonsense; we had seen that they are not idiots. This reason had to be discounted also because it confounded what we had learned of Japanese statecraft; in other words the death of an emperor would never be announced until his successor had been installed. And all aspects of installing him would be kept secret *(ne-boen)* so that nothing interrupt or frustrate the operations of government. Perhaps this story therefore amounted to subterfuge.

Had such an event occurred, there might have followed a conflict so large and so fateful as to bear upon the American overtures to Japan. For, when a difference of opinion divides the emperor from his ministers, representatives of the nation's ranking nobility convene to adjudicate it in a court of arbitration. The decision is final. If rendered against the ministers, it means public execution for them. Moreover, thus punished, a man can leave nothing to his family; he forfeits all rights of will and inheritance. Nothing [honorable] remains to the condemned but to slash the belly [in ritual suicide].

Should the court decide against the emperor, he would of course not be expected to disembowel himself. But he would be considered politically dead, and steps would be taken to install a successor. This event, had it proved true, would have occurred immediately after the commodore presented himself and his proposal and would have coincided with the official deliberations over it. There would have been little doubt as to who would win that clash. The only question left open would have been, What will they resolve to do? At least the answer would be quickly known. That is, perhaps the Japanese would match their sturdiness with determination and decide against [foreign] penetration. What a task we would face then! But our observations would suggest otherwise. For, being clever as well as sturdy and admirably knowledgeable of world affairs, the Japanese would be more likely to realize that their two-hundred-year isolation must end soon. Accordingly they would choose relations with a power that did not intend grand conquests on foreign soil. Especially since the same power, in exchange for such cooperation, would make trade as advantageous as possible.[15]

Prepared for either alternative, we would bring the negotiations to an honorable and glorious conclusion regardless which was chosen. One of the most interesting moments in modern history was approaching, no doubt about it. How I delighted to be both observer and participant!

Our sloop-of-war *Plymouth* followed us to Macao later. Stationed at Loo Choo, she had left when the *Vandalia* relieved her.[16] The *Plymouth* had suffered tragedy at one of the islands we visited the prior summer. Lieutenant [John] Matthews and thirteen men in the first cutter had left the ship at anchor and gone fishing. A savage typhoon hit, battered her, and drove the cutter into the open ocean. Everybody in the cutter perished by drowning.

The *Plymouth,* on the way here, called at Amoy and Ningpo, cities in the hands of the imperialists again [in the Taiping Rebellion]. In Amoy, after the rebels departed without much of a fight, the nationalists wreaked carnage among the populace. Of particular horror was their alleged murder of many women and children. Of course whenever and wherever the rebels held sway, they too spilled buckets of blood. Still, the rebels supposedly tended to limit their atrocities to mandarins and other officials, whose heads they mercilessly cut off. Such things ought not to incite wonder; similar motives and consequences prevail wherever civil war rages. Let a broader view be taken and such brutalities deplored as outbursts of man's animal nature.

Let us leave such sad events for happier ones. Let me continue the description of my stay in Macao, where several hunting trips offered pleasant diversions. It was autumn, and snipe abounded in the stubble of the rice paddies. A snipe hunt in the paddies of Macao in autumn confers superb exercise, let me tell you. A paddy, after a summer under water, emerges in autumn as soft, soaked soil: a *mire*. Several hours' wading in it—while wearing heavy boots—equals a trek through three feet of snow. How then to reach outlying paddies, the ones more abundant with snipe because farther away, and not be exhausted? The answer is usually the sedan chair.

I set out to hunt with my old shipmate, Dr. [Arthur M.] L[ynah, assistant surgeon of the *Mississippi*], who worked in the [Macao] hospital at that time. Mr. D., an old Frenchman and passionate hunter, put at our disposal his sedan chairs, provision baskets, dogs, dog handlers, gun bearers, and other employees who would serve us on the hunt. (I know no other name for "dog handler," an occupation best called *Hundejunge* in German.) Handlers in Macao reminded me of Saxon nobility and the romance of the hunt in the good old days! Six coolies or bearers accompanied each chair and took turns carrying it. The bearers, plus the others in our employ, added up to an entourage of eighteen.

We had to cover ten miles before dawn, so we left at 3:00 A.M. You should have seen us setting off for the hunt and wending our way through the murky, deserted streets of Macao, the panjandrums in their sedan chairs, followed by gun bearers, dog handlers, provision baskets, and the rest of the lackeys—what a spectacle! We reached open country soon. Dr. L. and I puffed excellent cigars and chatted about experiences of the past year and hopes for the year ahead. The bearers meanwhile trotted through the keen, fresh air of night. Indeed, the air stung with a chill—remarkable amid the warm days of so southern a latitude. I could not but think of the old buffoon in Gozzi-Schiller's *Turandot*.[17] Called by the anxious princess to the harem at 3:00 A.M. and unable to restrain himself even in the imperial presence, he blurts: "My beard shivered, it was so cold!" And "I believe I've said harsh things to you. Ill-humor made me do it—and the savage cold!" As for *me,* not only the beard but also the rest of the man shivered. And the doctor matched me, shiver for shiver.

On we went, and shivering, for about ten miles inland. We passed houses and villages, occupants already awake, preparing for work in the fields or to take produce to market. At dawn, beyond the town of Casa Branca, we stopped for a sip of whiskey and a bite of bread. Then we released the dogs and marched into the paddies. One gun bearer followed the doctor, the other followed me; the one carried the doctor's second gun, the other mine; each bearer would reload for his gunner. We gunners banged away, each trying to outshoot the other. At noon, as the day became as warm as the night had been cold, a grove beckoned with a shady place to rest on the bank of a creek. We opened provision baskets and spread on the grass their abundance of good things. The tasty meal calmed and restored our frayed nerves. The doctor had wearied, however, so I renewed the hunt and beat the paddies for a while alone. Joyfully to our grand bag of snipe and partridge I added two woodcock (called, I believe, *Holzschnepfen* or "wood snipe" in German, though I have never seen one in Germany). At last I gratified my desire to hunt and returned to where I had left the doctor at rest.

My weary fellow hunter and his half of the party had already gone. No choice for me but to head home with mine. On the way here we had bypassed Casa Branca. Moreover, the shortest route home led straight through it. Therefore I decided to visit it. All day long in the paddies I had found its people friendly and agreeable. They watched what we did and frequently would bring me a downed snipe or show me a good paddy [for hunting]. Yet when I, riding in my chair, had but neared the gates, an old, long-pigtailed burgher of the Celestial Empire sprang out and intercepted me. What a flurry of gestures, what a flood of words! Through my gun bearer I asked, "Why all this anger?" Answer: "Since our last troubles with the Portuguese, no foreigner has been let into our town."[18] Well, I felt no special curiosity to see Casa Branca (Chinese towns more or less resemble one another anyway), and it would have been useless further to vex this honorable idolater. Besides, the instant I had appeared, a great gong over the gate boomed three times. A decidedly unfriendly crowd had gathered, and I was [virtually] alone. I submitted, called retreat, and took the short detour around the town.

I did not want to return to Macao in the delightfully mild evening while daylight remained. Thus I halted my coolies and climbed a hill to the ruins of a small Chinese fort on the crown. If I forgot to discuss Macao's situation earlier, I must do it here. The city lies on a hilly peninsula about five or six miles long and a mile and a half or two miles wide. A narrow, level isthmus connects the peninsula to the mainland (or, more accurately, to a second, huge peninsula). Halfway along the isthmus a wall pierced by a towered gate [the Porta do Cerco] divides Portuguese territory from Chinese. Chinese soldiers [once] stood guard at the gate. At the extremities of the isthmus, however, both powers—China at its end, Portugal at the other—have fortified the hills that command the road.

If I am not mistaken, Macao's one-armed governor, [João Ferreira do] Amaral, quarreled with Chinese officials in 1849.[19] The quarrel had so intensified that the Chinese put a price of forty thousand taels on his head. Still, though a mediocre horseman, he rode often in the vicinity, accompanied only by his adjutant [Lieutenant Leite]. One evening he met on Portuguese territory five or six coolies with farm tools on their shoulders.[20] Suddenly a coolie swung a heavy bamboo pole and hit him in the face. He seized the reins with his teeth in order to be able to draw his pistol with his left and only hand. But the horse, nervous by now and not to be checked, pitched him off. Several coolies fell on him while others attacked and wounded the adjutant. He shouted for help and attracted several pedestrians. Him they found on the ground, gravely wounded but alive; the governor, dead—a corpse plundered of its hand and head. A carriage happened to be passing; it brought the wounded man and the mutilated corpse to town.

At the moment of the assault the Chinese guards at the central gate [Porta do Cerco] fled to the [Chinese] fort [Passaleong]. A Portuguese lieutenant and thirty men took over the gate at once. Next morning, from the fort, the Chinese began firing on the Portuguese at the gate. The firing soon grew onerous, and the brave lieutenant did not wait for reinforcements but led his little unit against the fort—in fact, stormed and burned it, supposedly killing some two hundred Chinese.[21] In time the sides came to terms. The governor's hand and head came back to Macao and the dignity of a funeral. To this day the fort and the towered gate remain in ruins.

As I made tortuous progress among the wrack and ruin of the

fort, the setting sun lighted my way and illuminated the devastation hereabouts. The lurid light, together with the bloody associations of this place, doubled its mystery and its dolor. The granite outer walls still enjoy fairly good condition. Unusually large embrasures, and the gun emplacements of stone behind them, show that twenty-six cannon once armed the fort. I doubt their presence when the Portuguese attacked unless ammunition ran short; otherwise the little unit's heroism must verge on the miraculous. The guardhouses, of oyster shell, have quite collapsed, and a chapel along with them. At the center of the fort a huge and ancient block of granite rises to become the fort's highest point. Chinese characters, hewn into the block, endure, perfectly legible. An old tree spreads its branches over the one place agreeable to pause for rest. I sat on a stone bench under the tree. A vespertine landscape extended before me, the beauty refreshing to my eye: picturesque Macao and the surrounding islands, soaring with ease and grace from the calm waters, and in the roads of Macao, slim masts of two of our ships, the *Mississippi* and the *Powhatan,* and of several merchantmen, drawing delicate lines against the evening sky.

Usually I indulge nostalgic reveries on such occasions. The barking of my dogs woke me from those. Slowly I returned to my chair, awaiting me at the foot of the hill. From there my men and I turned homeward.

I have thus described accurately and faithfully one hunting trip during the stay at Macao. Soon another would bring back something better than snipe.

CHAPTER NINE

AN INTERVAL OF REST

IN MACAO

(CONTINUED)

A Dream Comes True.—Words of Solace?—A Manhunt.—Much of Interest but Nothing of What Was Wanted.—Sniffing Out the Rascals.—The Utility of Long Pigtails.—A Lucky Catch.—Getting Ready for the Second Voyage to Nippon.—An Inventory of the Squadron.—A Review of Our Gifts for the Emperor.

D O   Y O U remember, dear reader, the lovely verse about the Chinese boy who slept under the stars, Hyolin, whose name— praise be to history!—has come down the millennia to us? The poet sings of an event said to have happened ages and ages past. Let me tell of an event barely past. The poem shows that rascals lived in China in times out of mind. My story proves that they live there still.[1]

I shared a bed with Mr. W[illiams] at the hospital, our home in Macao. We were going on a hunting trip, my second, in the morn- ing. I was asleep—sleeping like the virtuous Hyolin had slept—and dreaming marvelous dreams. Near the end of them I looked at my watch, found it broken, and grew so angry that I woke. Because we intended to go hunting, I got out of bed at once. It must have been about 4:00 A.M. I opened my writing desk—to dismay! I could not find my watch. Nor could I find Mr. W.'s. Both had disappeared without a trace.

We had, each of us, suffered a grievous loss. No mere watches, these were chronometers. I had bought mine for one hundred dol- lars shortly before leaving New York, expressly for the expedition, and could not easily replace it. The thieves had cottoned to many other things, too, as we discovered while raising hell over the time-pieces.

We soon picked up the trail. Two Chinese employees of the hospital had scrammed, lowering themselves on a rope from the second floor to the street, and left us at a loss. We gave up the hunting trip immediately, as you can imagine.

Instead we went with our story to the American consul as soon as possible; we wanted to proceed properly and according to law. The experience saddened me. If dealing with the police is awkward, unpleasant, and ticklish anywhere in the world, it is especially so here. Yes, a law enforcement agency does exist, but it is the police in name only. They told me merely that as soon as I could nab the thieves, punishment would be meted out. If I desired to conduct house searches, soldiers would be assigned to help. Some news for a law-abiding German who supports the police! Still, I had lived long enough under conditions that demanded I be my own policeman. I decided on the spot to do it again.

First I posted a handsome reward for the capture of the thieves and for the goods. People think that whoever promises such munificence usually has no appetite to take much trouble himself—which is what I wanted them to think now. Meanwhile I hired all the spies I could find. I spent the day from morning to night in all manner of sleuthing, trying on the sly to scout out places where my scoundrels could have squirreled themselves away, wherever such a hideout might be. I acted alone and kept everything from the others. At nightfall I armed myself and two of our sailors, added a squad of four from the watch, and began to comb Macao's Chinese quarter.[2]

The search led me of course into dives of the lowest sort: tea houses, opium dens, casinos, brothels, and similar cosmopolitan establishments. Had I not been on a manhunt, I would probably never have penetrated such depths, though my destinations proved engrossing to the student of human affairs. I must praise my soldiers for their measured dispatch. In a flash they would secure entrances and exists of the den in question and—equally fast—the corporal, my sailors, and I would ransack it.

At those moments, as I have suggested, I got interesting and fabulous glimpses of life as lived by the honorable Chinese. Tea and other refreshments were usually served in the brothels, and much opium smoked. The back rooms offered unusually large places of repose: couches furnished with mats. Customers might be eating a variety of meats and other delicacies and drinking with this dinner either tea or *sam-chou,* an intoxicating beverage prepared from rice. Or they lay on couches and smoked opium. A lamp with a short wick (necessary to opium smoking) burned on a small, simple table beside the smoker. The pipe itself, though eighteen to twenty inches long, has a bowl even smaller than those of Oriental tobacco pipes. Prepared opium resembles a thick syrup, brought to the pipe on a needle and in a quantity the size of a grain of millet. The smoker, reclining, puts the pipe to the lamp, then consumes the bit of opium in three or four pulls drawn into the lungs. Some smokers satisfy themselves with still less; they feel only an effect similar to what we feel from a strong cigar. Others repeat the normal dose until they collapse in a stupor, to lie benumbed for several hours. And others smoke while surrounded by women who sing with amazing nasality to the accompaniment of a long-necked zither. This musical entertainment hit my barbarous ear with a screech rather like the nocturnal caterwauling from the rooftops of May. But perhaps to the ear of an opium smoker in a semistupor it sounded charming, lovely, and sweet.[3]

In another of these houses ten or twelve well-dressed men sat with as many or more women around a table laid with a fine dinner. (If one adulterates the meaning of respectable in order to apply it here, then this house appeared to be the most respectable in this quarter.) Songs were sung and a zither plucked, as in the others. Here, however, an ensemble also produced loud and vigorous music. The ensemble's vocalist accompanied himself on two small kettledrums, joined by a kind of a violin with three metal strings, a flute, and a boy with castanets. I noticed not only that everybody wore exquisite clothes but also that the women were large and well developed, and their faces attractive. Overall, a certain decorum seemed to prevail—the more astounding to me, to find it in a place like this.

Unfortunately all our searches turned up nothing. We ransacked all locations on the waterfront, then spent part of the night rummaging through the Chinese ships in the harbor. At that hour, near midnight, we surprised crews sound asleep. Many woke terrified that pirates had attacked and boarded them.[4] Yet all cooperated, opening everything and exposing each nook and every cranny where somebody could have crammed himself. These probes, like the earlier, proved futile. I went home, exhausted.

Next morning one of my spies brought news of the two individuals. He described them briefly and added a few words on the place where they had been seen. I cogitated a short while and hit upon a workable plan that would bag my quarry. Meanwhile, the better to keep the plan secret, I pretended to ignore the report. I spent the day as I had spent the one before: searching, searching, searching. My soldiers laughed over "wasted effort" and began to grumble. I ignored them.

Macao lies on a peninsula, as I have noted. Portuguese authority stops at the gate, which I have also mentioned. An arm of the ocean reaches between the mainland and the peninsula's inner or mainland side. Several fishing villages and a few isolated pagodas occupy the shore of the mainland, a scant mile from Macao, across the arm. One of the pagodas concealed the quarry: So I had been told. I knew the area—I had hunted snipe in it—ergo I could plan and conduct a manhunt there.

Next morning I woke the two sailors at 3:00. As quickly as I could I filled them in and sketched a scenario. They agreed at once to help. I gave each a shotgun and a six-shooter, armed myself likewise, and collected the dogs as if setting off to hunt snipe. I also brought a true and faithful Chinese servant; he, should it prove necessary, would be interpreter. We boarded one of the ferries that ply at all hours, day and night.

We landed a few hundred paces above our destination—just at the first gray of dawn. Quickly I assigned my party their posts. When all were in place and the pagoda surrounded, I signalled: Secure the exits! No sooner had they been secured when the old building quivered. My two rascals were there with ten or twelve others of the ilk, and now the gang struggled to escape. By accident—or was it intent? —they chose the door guarded by my Chinese. Feebly he tried to resist. The gang knocked him off his pins, left him with his thick-soled shoes in the air, raced clear, and intended to scatter.

I and the rest of my posse had spotted the birds trying to fly the coop. One of my sailors, an Irishman—he who had shouted to bring me to the fine wild boar at Singapore—yelled to me now, "By Jasus, Sir, thare he is!"[5] In a flash the same sailor, being nearest the fugitives, seized a long pigtail. Its owner, a husky fellow as strong as an ox, turned and put up a fight. The future looked black for my Irishman. But Dick Short, in a rage, let fly, "By Jasus, you damned son of a bitch, I will knock you down!" The gun butt struck the shorn head, and the man collapsed, knocked flat.

Meanwhile, I had captured another. But when the second sailor grabbed a long, flowing pigtail, a jerk of its owner's head left it in the sailor's hand, and the sailor smack on the ground, open-mouthed, watching his man depart with a leap. (That Chinese blackguard had paid with his tail for an earlier crime and had replaced it with a false one.) Our skirmish now affirmed the impracticability of sentencing a thief to lose his tail. Should he steal again, as had happened here, how could he be caught and held?

Two were ours yet. I have said that I nabbed one [and the other had been clubbed with the gun]. Mine had been a frequenter of the hospital. We tied their hands behind their backs and their genuine pigtails into a genuine Gordian knot sailor-style and took them to a boat. Both were agitated and unnerved—with good reason. Chinese law, as I learned later, prescribes death for a second offense of theft.

After we had secured them in the boat and the boat had left the shore, a frisk discovered Mr. Williams's watch sewn into my scoundrel's pants. He said he had sold mine to pay a man for food. He pointed out the house, beside a stream near a fishing village not far off. We lost no time getting there and found the man together with shirts, stockings, and other things of ours but not my watch. For the moment we satisfied ourselves by taking this rascal into custody and carrying along the stolen goods. At 8:00 we arrived back at the hospital. How we amazed people there! My search-and-seize operations had been unknown to them until now.

Secret societies of thieves exist among the Chinese. I learned of them after I turned my key on my prisoners. (Members help one another when in trouble.) Our receiver of stolen goods, the last man caught, lived in that village as an otherwise upright citizen. Shortly after my return [from his village, with him in tow] two well-dressed men, cutting a figure as good as his, presented themselves and offered bail. I refused. They promised my watch if I released him. I agreed. We struck the bargain, and I had the watch, undamaged, the same afternoon.

This affair in sum caused quite a stir in Macao, and people gave credit for much more courage than had been needed. True, the Chinese are sly and crafty in exceptional measure, and they consider it meritorious to kill a foreigner when it demands little risk. But they are as cowardly as they are cunning, and they yield readily and in awe to a show of force. Indeed, they respect force. Thus three of us could capture a Chinese in his house and lead him through a mass of Chinese. The affair vexed the Portuguese authorities; their law enforcement had been proved inadequate. I believe I nonetheless rendered an essential service to non-Chinese who live here. For, as I have said, nothing impresses the Chinese more than energetic and fearless *action*.

At the end of December we returned to the *Susquehanna,* every man jack of us. With energy and diligence we prepared for the second visit to Edo. The *Lexington,* arriving at the turn of the year, brought the squadron to full strength.

Steam Frigates (2,000 to 2,500 tons in all, armed with true Paixhans guns: 68-pounders and 120-pounders)

Susquehanna (flagship)	9 cannon
Powhatan	9 cannon
Mississippi	10 cannon
Macedonian (refitted as a ship of the line and now a deck lower)	10 cannon

Sloops of War
Saratoga	22 cannon (32-pounders)
Plymouth	24 cannon (32-pounders)
Vandalia	22 cannon (32-pounders)

Storeships
Supply	6 cannon (32-pounders)
Southhampton	6 cannon (32-pounders)
Lexington	6 cannon (32-pounders)

In sum: 10 ships, 130 cannon, 52 of them Paixhans, and 2,600 men.[6]

We waited daily for Commander [Cadwalader] Ringgold's flotilla of five; they would be our reserve.[7]

Meanwhile, aboard our ships, turmoil: scarcely quiet anywhere. Crate after crate of provisions came aboard. Machinery, farm implements, and fancy goods constituted an incredible conglomeration, gifts to the emperor. (I shall discuss these in detail at the appropriate place.) Printing presses, high-pressure pumps, mowing machines, threshers, looms, mills to spin cotton, even a portable field oven: They filled each ship's every corner. A railroad had been brought, disassembled. Unpacked and inspected now, there were the cutest little locomotive with tender, a fifty-person car tricked out in imperial luxury, and several miles of rails, all of first-rate workmanship and in perfect condition. When the time would come to unload and parade these many splendid things, we would create a nice, full-sized industrial exposition all our own.

CHAPTER TEN

THIRD CALL

AT LOO CHOO

Departure from Hong Kong.—Undersea Volcanoes.—Arrival in Naha.—Taking up
Quarters in Our Station There.—Thoughts of Home.—The Missionary's Family.—
Excursion to Locate Coal Deposits.—An Accident.—New Year's Celebration on
Loo Choo.—Increased Trust by the Local People.—A Change of Ships.

Aboard the steam frigate Powhatan
Sea of Japan, 10 February 1854

O N 1 3 J A N U A R Y we departed Hong Kong bound for Loo
Choo. The first division, our sloops of war, preceded us, having left on the third. What a beautiful sight, our three steam frigates
—stately, imposing, magnificent—weighing anchor one after the
other, each with a storeship in tow, and steaming out of the harbor,
passing men-of-war of other nations, their crews in the rigging as if
on parade, and Admiral Pellew's flagship *Winchester* roaring "Bon
Voyage" with a thunder of guns![1] From boats many of our Hong
Kong friends waved hats and white handkerchiefs to send us off
with a hearty farewell. Even Chinese vessels, bringing provisions to
ships or serving as ferries, staged a grand *yin-yosh* (their word for a
public celebration) to wish us—with drums, gongs, firecrackers, and
the boom of cannon obbligato—a safe and prosperous journey.

On the fifteenth, rounding the southern tip of Formosa, we
observed small volcanoes at two separate locations. The storeship
Southampton, on her last crossing to Loo Choo, had discovered near
Formosa an undersea volcano that billowed smoke from water that
churned and seethed in weather perfectly calm. The *Macedonian*
passed the spot a short while behind the *Southampton;* after several

hours, white ash lay thick on the *Macedonian*'s decks and covered every rope of the rigging.

The crossing [of the South China Sea] was short and pleasant. On the twentieth we arrived at Naha, on Loo Choo. The artistic corps of master's mates went ashore at once to remain from the twentieth to the day the division would put to sea again.

Quarters had already been engaged. During the last stay in Loo Choo, Commodore Perry rented from the regent a former temple with outbuildings and garden adjoining as hospital and billets for the squadron. This small, handsome temple, in acquiring its peculiar historical significance of sorts, played a role in every prior meeting between foreigners and the people of the island. In 1817, Captain Maxwell landed supplies to dry them. Admiral Cecille did likewise later [1846] and so did the small American *Preble* in 1849. Père Adnet, a French missionary, lived here a while and also died here.[2] Last year [1853] we installed a telegraph, set up the daguerreotype, and added other things; the temple had been our hospital since then. On the coast nearby we had erected our coal warehouse. Our cemetery lies a little farther away, in a grove of pines.[3] There, unfortunately, many a brave comrade sleeps the sleep from which no one awakens here below. Three graves have fallen into neglect by now, having been here since Captain Maxwell's time. Admiral Cecille buried three officers and two seamen; the *Preble* left a grave to memorialize her visit; and our squadron had already added fresh mounds and increased the necrology by seven.

I often took a walk in this little graveyard after the day's work. How I love the evening wind in the pines, soughing through the crowns: the only sound in the peaceful isolation except the murmer of the ocean intermingling from far away. Let me confess, I cherish the pine above all trees. True, the soar of slim palms into deep blue sky captivated me at first sight; I marveled at the beautiful forests of Ceylon and their thousands upon thousands of slender trunks supporting a graceful and elegant dome of leaves like the rotunda of a temple of God. But then a fresh morning breeze in the palms and the clatter of stiff fronds broke the spell. My love for our northern pines reawakened, stronger than ever. For me, only the pine plays my soft, mysterious music. In an hour of solitude, when I hear gentle evening breezes in the boughs, my soul responds with sweet harmonies. I have never known a tree that evokes so many feelings in me, no tree that fosters devotion, nostalgia, friendship and love, no tree that stirs *all* feelings esteemed in this earthly life, no tree—except my beloved northern pine!

I came ashore in the afternoon and spent the rest of the day putting my things in order. In the evening I took a walk the scant mile from our station to Naha and the house of the missionary Dr. Bettelheim.[4] Night had fallen, and I entered the outer courtyard in darkness. The dogs, recognizing me, bounded in my direction, tails wagging. Unseen by anyone else, I advanced to the open door of the living room. The family had just gathered at a circular table for evening prayers. A lamp on the table cast a warm, friendly glow. Lucy, the youngest child, recited the prayers in a loud voice. Involuntarily I drew back that my approach not disturb the congenial, pleasant scene. I folded my hands, also involuntarily, and prayed along with them but to myself. I stood there in the dark long after the prayers ended. A flood of thoughts engulfed me, the homeless wanderer, and I felt lonely and alone. Love and affection, of parents, siblings, and friends, bind people together; and these ties are strong. The heart that can feel them feels them in a thousand ways. For the most of us, however, these ties reach us from the past; only people of the greatest good fortune form them with the present. Empty places remain in the heart, and nothing but family and fireside can fill them; for a man has no future except in wife and children. A wonderful thing, the human heart: From its most basic and most powerful impulses spring also the highest virtue! How many more people would be happier did they but know these truths and know them well!

I went into the house.

"Good evening," I said.

"Good evening," they said.

My words were friendly and amiable, theirs hearty and joyful. The children danced and skipped around me, pulled my hand, and tugged at my coattail, so happy were their memories of me. They played daguerreotype for me, their game of taking pictures. An old crate, topped by the round cover of a tea can, represented the apparatus. Bernhard, the oldest, acted the daguerreotypist and directed the procedure. Rosa polished old pieces of tin; they stood for the metal plates. And—that the subject cooperate for a successful photograph—tiny Lucy must sit on the chair and cling to the family dog or the old tom cat. The photograph existed only in the children's imagination of course.

Conversation lasted to a late hour; we had much to ask of one another, and much to tell. The family invited me to stay the night, but I felt the need to walk a while yet and started back the way I had come. If good wishes equal prayer, how fervently I prayed that evening!

Free to do as I pleased for the next eight days, I devoted part of them to a number of careful studies in oil of landscapes and objects. Then I filled gaps [in pictures] left earlier for lack of time. Often, after a day's work, I shouldered my gun and hunted specimens to increase our ornithological collection. Or at dawn I would prowl the rice paddies or follow the river and shoot a string of snipe or a few wild ducks. Snipe and ducks so abounded that an hour's hunt would bring to our table an abundance of the tasty creatures.

During the commodore's absence Lieutenant [William B.] Whiting of the *Vandalia* had commenced a detailed survey of the Loo Choo group. Whiting returned to the station about eight days after we arrived. According to his glowing report, he had found a far better harbor somewhat to our north and signs of coal close to it. At once the commodore assigned officers to proceed overland to check this doubtful assertion.[5] Our tireless chaplain off the *Mississippi,* Dr. [George] J[ones], would go; for he, as I have said on a prior page, was also the expedition's geologist.[6] And the party would include my humble self.

We went some forty miles by sundown the first day, an exhausting trek. Yet that day's destination, Ou-Nu, remained about six miles off. (We had stopped there on our first overland expedition in 1853.) Local people led the way, illuminating it with torches and flaming stalks of bamboo. We arrived spent. (We had done a two-day march in one, to our depletion.) It took us merely a moment to bolt a modest dinner of foods we had brought, but we were scarcely able to last even *that* short time. In a few minutes we lay wrapped in blankets against a sharp chill, sound asleep.

In the afternoon of the second day's hike I sprained my foot in a gravelly terrain and had to go to bed in the next village. Dr. [Charles T.] Fahs of the *Susquehanna,* overtired at that moment anyway, remained to look after me, what with the severe inflammation and swelling that set in at once. The remainder of our party proceeded immediately, reached the destination, and returned to us two days later. Their expedition produced notably gratifying results.[7]

My foot had greatly improved during that time, but I could not demand much of it yet. Exhaustion gripped the rest, every last person. Therefore we took sedan chairs, made of bamboo poles and expressly for us: one of us to a chair, each carried by four local men. On the fifth day we arrived back at Naha.

The commodore had called on the regent in Shuri while we were gone. On a prior page I have described the first visit. This second duplicated the first, without the imposing show of military force.[8] Our officers consumed with gusto the famous twelve soups and other mysterious dishes—and the obligatory saki with them.[9] The visit occurred on the [lunar] New Year, 28 January on the Christian calendar, a day when people in Japan and Loo Choo call on one another and exchange gifts. Indeed, during the first eight days [of the new year] I saw much going in and out of houses by people better dressed than usual. Even work in the fields stopped. Pine boughs decked every house. Small pines, like our Christmas trees, stood at the doors, pushed into the ground there. Sprigs of pine had even been nailed to junks and fishing boats.

I observe with delight that the local people had almost entirely overcome the diffidence shown us during our presence the year before. They no longer run when we approach. Doors and windows remain open when we pass outside. Women, most notably, when we appear, remain quietly at their wares in the market or on their thresholds—and we had barely caught sight of the tip of a woman's nose before![10] Many people take the trouble to learn a few words of our language. Street urchins never vary, whatever the corner of the world, but how droll to hear Loo Choo's little charmers call to us: "American! American!" Or address us with the world-famous "How do you do?"[11] Two handsome young men, Nagador and Yusizato, have from the start been supplying us with fresh food. They applied themselves so diligently to English that they can soon express themselves tolerably. Each time they meet a new word, they transcribe it according to sound in the Loo Choo alphabet. We do the reverse: their words into our alphabet. In this way I have acquired more than three hundred words and phrases, valuable in my getting necessities during our last excursion.

On 4 February our party returned to the ships. Commodore

Perry had received orders from Washington. The secretary of the navy said, "Put a steamship at the disposal of our ambassador in China." Perry sent the *Susquehanna* and made the *Powhatan* his flagship instead.[12] As usual the corps of master's mates followed him. By and large the two ships, both about three thousand tons, were twins. But some of the *Powhatan*'s differences—in this respect, her merits—particularly her sharper-defined features and more powerful machinery, made her the better flagship. In addition I experienced once again the joy of serving under our old and amiable Captain [William J.] Mc[Cluney]. I have already related, when discussing that part of the voyage, how he left the *Mississippi* in Norfolk to take command of the *Powhatan*.

Our sailing vessels had left on the first [of February] and we [in steamships] followed on the seventh. We cleared the harbor and presto! The *Saratoga* greeted us. In our eyes, a good omen, this meeting with the *Saratoga* arriving from Shanghai. For she too had been ordered to Edo.[13]

This time we steered east from the Loo Choo group. On the eighth we enjoyed a rare spectacle of whales. We happened onto a school of at least three hundred; they sported around us and sometimes their spouts erupted within fifty feet of a ship. We were then east of the Van Diemen Straits and passed through them the day before I wrote these words.

CHAPTER ELEVEN

RETURN TO EDO BAY

A Storm.—A Beautiful View of Nippon.—The Commodore Stands Firm.—Arrival in Uraga. — Reception Hall. — Negotiations. — Friendly Intercourse with the Japanese.—Preliminaries.

A T D A W N on 11 February we saw land, the island groups south of the Bay of Edo. There was a volcano on the southern tip of the first island, four thousand to five thousand feet tall, crater covered by sulphur or yellow ash. Meanwhile a fresh nor'easter strengthened hourly. We held course until a little past sunset, when the wind changed to a storm.[1] The commodore signalled, Heave to! Maintain intervals of one mile! I had been topside all day to photograph the coastline with Mr. B[rown]. The temperature had dropped from 65 to 40 degrees Fahrenheit. Nearly frozen stiff, I [went below and] lay down. About 11:00 P.M. the storm got so bad that the pipe called, "All hands about ship!"

Nature raged. The storm drove dense fog before it, reducing visibility to a scant one hundred paces. A downpour of fine sleet, icy needles, cut our faces; we could scarcely open our eyes. A roar and a clamor filled the air, as if gigantic gongs were being struck or steel drums pounded. The terrible fog blacked out the lights of other ships, rendering our situation near critical, at least for the ships of sail, as we faced the danger of collision. But we stood off the lee shore, therefore in seas not extremely high, and a powerful steamship could hold position without hardship. Toward morning the storm diminished somewhat, and the commodore signalled again, Resume normal intervals and follow the flagship. Cape Izu lay to the west now, and the steep and rugged coast ran north.

We were to the north of the Bay of Odowara and west of the Bay of Edo. During last night's storm the *Macedonian* had run aground on one of Odowara's coral reefs. The *Mississippi*, sent at once to help, easily pulled her free; but, having therefore been forced to stop for a while, we could not that day reach the Bay of Edo.

We anchored for the night. A little after sunset the *Lexington* joined us. We saw nothing of Captain [Lieutenant J. J.] Boyle and his *Southampton,* and the absence worried us. On the morning of the thirteenth some took others in tow: the *Powhatan,* the *Vandalia;* the *Mississippi,* the *Macedonian;* and the *Susquehanna,* the very tardy *Lexington.* We steamed straight for the Bay of Edo.

I cannot remember a more beautiful view than the one I beheld that morning. The breeze had freshened again; it was pleasant. Several snow-capped peaks could already be seen during the night. When the sun rose in a clear sky, a chain of snowy mountains, five thousand to seven thousand feet high, described about a third of a circle before us. The volcanic Fujiyama lifted its gigantic head above them. Streaks of lava drew black lines on Fuji's snowfields. The panorama might have been of an array of alpine glaciers—dwarfed by Aetna itself. Morning mist still cloaked the ocean and, in the light of the new day, cast over everything a tone of delicate rose. I had to get my paint box—the bite of the cold could not stop me. I had to put the splendid scene to canvas as well as it could be done on such short notice.

We rounded Sagami Point at noon and passed our old anchorage at Uraga at 2:00 P.M. The moment we reached Point Rubicon (so-named by us on our first visit) we saw to our delight old Captain [Lieutenant] Junius Boyle and his *Southampton:* anchored, as cosily and attractively as could be, in a fine and spacious inlet about fifteen miles up the bay.[2] Boyle's anchorage being excellent, the commodore signalled to the squadron, Anchor here. We formed a half-moon, facing the coast.[3]

On the fourteenth an embassy came aboard and invited the commodore to go back to the anchorage of the year before.[4] "Preparations have been made to receive you there." The old sea dog acted friendly while at once declining with energy and resolve. "I don't know what it means to go back."

During the following days each ship dispatched its first cutter, and up the bay they went to finish the nautical survey unfinished the year before. Lieutenant Whiting of the *Vandalia* and I joined the work together. The Japanese interfered not a bit, but cold and storm encumbered it. A piercing chill, and twelve hours of turbulent rolling in high seas, left my head empty and me confused. Evenings I often could not write a decent sentence—or even think straight—so nasty was the work.

23 February

Many long, boring discussions with Japanese officials ended at last.[5] It was decided that Flag Captain [Henry A.] Adams would confer with the imperial delegation in Uraga over preparations. On the twenty-third Adams boarded the *Vandalia* to be carried to Uraga. His party consisted of Major [Jacob] Zeilen (Marines), Lieutenant [James H.] Jones (Marines), Lieutenant Boncraft (of the *Macedonian*), Captain [Robert] Tansill (Marines), Purser [Joseph C.] Eldridge, Secretary [Oliver H.] Perry [II] (the commodore's son), Mr. [Antón L. C.] Portman (Dutch interpreter), Mr. [N. B.] Adams (Captain Adam's son and secretary), and my humble self.[6]

We did as we had done on this occasion [the year] before. We boarded [the *Vandalia,* the ship that would land us]. A Japanese group, our escort, crossed to us from the coast. We must go about fifteen miles from our anchorage back to Uraga, as I have said. The wind, light and favorable at the start, shifted and roared in a sudden betrayal; we had not so much as rounded the Uraga peninsula (our Point Rubicon) when a bumptious storm, a nor'wester, opposed us. We strained to exhaustion for two hours and must finally anchor in the shelter of the lee shore. Our escort declined our invitation to spend the night on board. They had been ordered to arrive at Uraga by sea, and they held fast to the order. Every last one of them climbed into the two boats that had brought them to us. Lives at risk, they rowed toward shore and through the surf along it and disappeared at last around the point.

The storm persisted in its rage. We had to drop all four anchors. A cold rain, with ice, slammed and poked us—in the apt words of one of our sailors—"like boarding pikes with points downward." Luckily the *Susquehanna*'s band was there; they, together with the hospitality of our hosts of the *Vandalia,* helped pass the long, hostile night as agreeably as possible. The storm subsided toward morning. We weighed anchors and set sail again.

It was the twenty-second of February, birthday of the great

Washington.[7] Could a better day have been chosen for our fateful rendezvous? Large American flags waved from our masts, fore and mizzen. A banner streamed from the main nearly to the deck. The squadron wore the same decorations; we saw the ships poised on the horizon. At 11:00 A.M. we reached approximately the place, opposite Uraga, where, the year before, our ships had ridden happily and auspiciously at anchor. The Japanese delegation returned and boarded. Soon we went ashore in the first cutter and the long boat, arriving punctually at noon. Exactly then, to celebrate the historic day, our cannon thundered. This time we had nothing military about us; even the usual sidearm at the belt had been left behind, to prove to the Japanese our trust in their assurances of friendship.[8] Our officers retained only their dress sabres.

Uraga might as well be called the port of entry for Edo; no vessel can enter the bay without stopping at Uraga and being inspected. Perhaps that is the reason the Japanese wanted to meet us there. Among Uraga's waterfront houses, at the shoreline, several buildings had been erected for the purpose. One black-and-white cloth barrier enclosed them. From the other side an inquisitive crowd surged against the barrier. A number of men, though armed with long truncheons, could scarcely restrain them. Within, first, there was an outer court [or reception area], with a guardhouse hard by the entrance. Eight to ten soldiers occupied the guardhouse, their weapons arrayed behind them in red flannel cases. At the second [inner] door of this area another squad, of six this time, carried only the customary swords at the belt.[9]

We passed from that area into a grand hall about fifty paces long and twenty-five wide and twelve to fourteen feet high. New mats of finely woven straw had been laid. Pillars at the [far] end circled a small section covered by a canopy of violet silk. Seats for each of us had been installed on the left and on the right for the imperial councilors, with tables of corresponding height in front of the seats for us, but none for the councilors. Galleries, with windows of oiled paper, ran along the right and left walls. About 150 to 200 Japanese occupied the galleries in the Japanese way: kneeling or squatting on their heels. In the center of the hall eight stands each held a metal brazier filled with something white. The stands were of wood lacquered black and fitted with gilded metal; the white substance was ground pumice or limestone, and on it a warming fire of coal burned in each brazier. These appliances, like the fitting-out of the entire hall, though simple, looked nonetheless extraordinarily genial.

We took our seats. Presently the three imperial councilors entered and sat opposite. We exchanged courtesies, then got to the point. The Japanese wanted to conduct all negotiations [here] in Uraga, but Perry did not want to return to Uraga's less favorable anchorage. He would move the negotiations to the city opposite his present anchorage. The distance would be too great for the councilors? He countered with the offer of one of our steamships to convey everybody to where he wanted to negotiate. Captain Adams carried this proposal and several other points in writing across to the commissioners and orally added several explanations and comments. The councilors listened with attention and promised an answer the next morning. (In important transactions the Japanese regard haste as a lack of good manners.)

They withdrew. The governor of Uraga, Yezaimon, and his officials now did the honors. Refreshments were served: tea, pastry, fine confections, and oranges. The pastry, confections, and oranges came on lacquered plates; the tea, in blue-and-white porcelain cups on a tray of lacquered wood. The first-rate craftsmanship of the plates included gilt-work of exceptional artistry and handsome in relief. Guests by pairs shared two silver tankards, about a bottle and a half [each] of saki in one and miri in the other. Miri and saki are prepared of rice, but miri tastes savory with the flavor of muscatel. I had never regretted an absence of those thimble-sized cups [from the banquet at Loo Choo], but I missed them now as we drank from tiny and shallow dishes of lacquered wood.

Meanwhile the wind strengthened until we dared not return to the boats. So we tarried long after negotiations ended. Alcohol and tobacco made everyone happy, and international relations approached intimacy. One of the [Japanese] interpreters spoke rather good English, learned from Captain Maxwell. (This American whaler, shipwrecked on the coast of Izu and four years a prisoner in Matsmai, had been surrendered at last to the sloop-of-war *Preble* in 1849.) Mr. Portman and I chatted with the interpreters in Dutch. With others we used sign language and achieved as much understanding as that medium permits. The Japanese examined and studied our uniforms, sabres, watches, and every last trifle we had on us. In turn they eagerly shared Japanese curiosities, even show-ing us their small swords. (We knew that the sword would otherwise be kept punctiliously in the scabbard.) They were of bluish steel, these swords, superb in quality, and so sharp that we could cut thin paper on the razor-like edge. Even our money must stand in-spection, and the scrutiny included questions about the value of each piece. Conversely we saw not one Japanese coin. A map of the United States, in pocket edition, caused intense study and prompted urgent questions about climate, products, and other aspects of individual states. Questions continued with equal ur-gency:

"Is it true that anyone can go to California and find gold?"

"How many ships are in the squadron?"

"How long did it take to get here?"

"In one year, 160 American ships have been sighted, passing through the Straits of Matsmayae [the Tsugaru Straits]. Why are so many coming to the Sea of Japan?" (The ships were American whal-ers. I note, by the way, that their frequency in these waters seems to have done us much good.[10])

As for the Japanese things that I saw, let me mention a quadrant of delicate and graceful workmanship; a book with woodcuts; a musket, superbly crafted, with a beautiful barrel and gold fittings; a small, flintlock pistol, complete at a length of two inches; and a book of various flags, among them the flag of the emperor himself, which was pointed out to me.

Joy so increased and relations grew so friendly that at last several young and stylish Japanese put on our caps and coats, strolled to and fro, and disported themselves with this masquerade.

Toward evening the wind subsided enough that we could return to the *Vandalia*. Four or five of us rode in the boats of the Japanese who accompanied us, and our presence seemed to please them to the utmost. Thinly dressed, they obviously suffered from the biting cold. Therefore I took two with me under my huge cape. One was a cultivated and likeable young man, the interpreter Tokojuru. A comrade of mine took another two with him under his. I thus caused hilarity, and so did he. Japanese and Americans parted with regret when we reached the ship. The generous, the proper, the gra-cious manner of our hosts had impressed and touched my comrades and me, each and every one of us.[11]

On the morning of the twenty-third, the day after Perry proposed to meet somewhere other than Uraga, Governor Yezaimon came aboard with the reply. "The law, hitherto permitting Japanese trade with nobody but the Chinese and the Dutch, has been changed expressly to include the Americans. Nothing remains but for Commodore Perry to appear in Uraga, where the imperial councilors await him, to settle the details of the agreement."[12]

On board the Powhatan
26 February

Captain Adams suggested changes in the communications between the councilors and Commodore Perry, and we had to remain during the twenty-third; that is, until the changes should reach their destination.[13] On the twenty-fourth we set sail on our return. Rounding Point Rubicon, we expected to see the squadron. It was gone. A riddle—soon solved. The commodore that morning had gone about ten miles farther up the bay to where he had found an even better anchorage. By evening, rejoining the squadron, we had put into our old position, two cable-lengths from the *Susquehanna*.

Punctually, the morning of the twenty-fifth, a delegation reappeared at our latest anchorage, off Kanegawa, a city of some importance. In this last try they proposed to the commodore again, "Return to Uraga." He refused; he would not budge. Then, at last, they said that the councilors would come to us. They asked Captain Adams to pick the place.[14] The choice: a piece of open field a half mile east of Kanegawa. At Uraga there was haste to dismantle the buildings erected for negotiations and to reassemble them in the place now so designated instead.

PRINCETON   VERMONT   ALLEGHANY   ST. MARY'S   MACEDONIAN   VANDALIA   PLYMOUTH   SARATOGA   MISSISSIPPI (Flag Ship)   SUSQUEHANNA   POWHATAN

Perry's fleet, from a contemporary magazine. Note ships' names in lower border.
(Library of Congress)

"Return of Commodore Perry, officers & men of the squadron, from a visit to the Prince Regent of Lew Chew, 6 June 1853," by Heine, lithograph prepared by Brown, printed by Lewis. (Library of Congress)

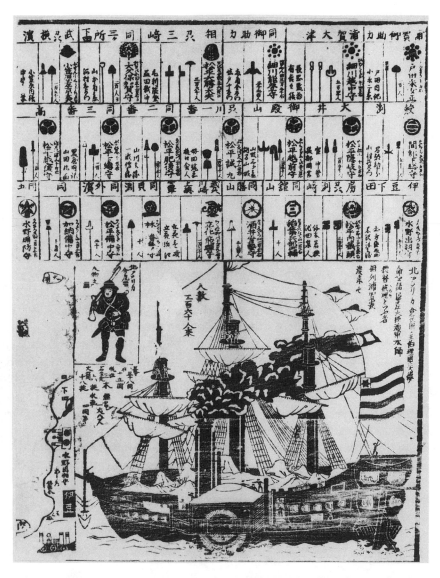

"American boat which visited Japan, 8 July 1853, with coats of arms of various lords" by Japanese artist. (Library of Congress)

"Passing the Rubicon: Lieut. L. Bent in the 'Mississippi's' first cutter forcing his way through a fleet of Japanese boats, 11 July 1853," by Heine, lithograph prepared by Brown, printed by Sarony. (Library of Congress)

"First landing at Gorahama" by Heine, lithograph prepared by Queen, printed by Duval. (Library of Congress)

"Eight American ships in Yokohama," seen from Urashima temple in Kanagawa, and "The Landing of the Americans," by Japanese artist. (Library of Congress)

"Landing of Commodore Perry, officers & men of the squadron, to meet the imperial commissioners at Yoku-hama, Japan, 8 March 1854," by Heine, lithograph prepared by Brown, printed by Sarony. (Library of Congress)

"Landing of Commodore Perry, officers & men of the squadron, to meet the imperial commissioners at Simoda, Japan, 8 June 1854," by Heine, lithograph prepared by Brown, printed by Sarony. (Library of Congress)

"Tensions ease between ship and shore: Perry goes sightseeing" by Japanese artist.
(Library of Congress)

"A Lilliputian locomotive delights Perry's hosts," woodcut by Hiroshige. (Library of Congress)

"Exercise of troops in temple grounds, Simoda, Japan," by Heine, lithograph prepared by Brown, printed by Buell & Sutherland (?). (Library of Congress)

"Dinner given to the Japanese commissioners on board U.S.S.F. Powhatan" by Heine "from nature," lithograph prepared by Queen, printed by Duval. (Library of Congress)

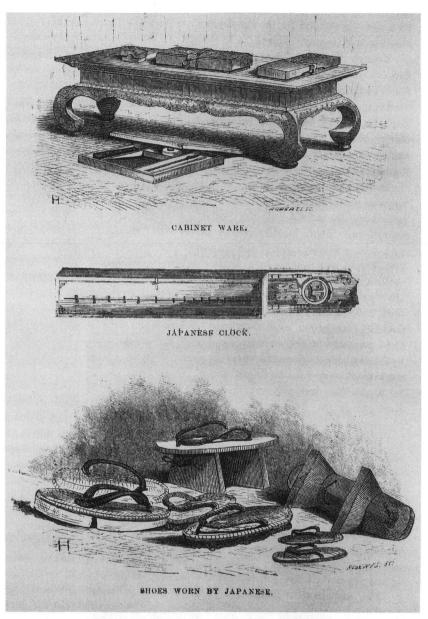

CABINET WARE.

JAPANESE CLOCK.

SHOES WORN BY JAPANESE.

Japanese articles, drawn by Heine, engraved by Roberts. (From the *Narrative of the Expedition*, photograph by Gary Donnelly)

Commodore Perry, "Peruri, a North American," woodcut by Japanese artist. (Library of Congress)

Commodore Perry after the return from Japan, portrait photograph by Brady. (Library of Congress)

HE port of Singapore is a great resort for ships of all nations. Vessels from China, Siam, Malaya, Sumatra, and the various commercial countries of Europe and America, are to be seen anchored together at the same time. The products of these different parts of the world are all to be found in Singapore, brought thither for reciprocal exchange. The policy which has made Singapore a free port has been fully justified by the prosperous result. Its commerce, being entirely unshackled, flourishes even beyond the most sanguine

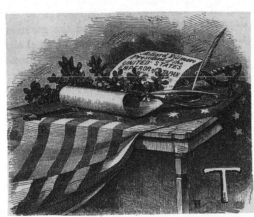

HE Commodore had, previous to setting out on the expedition ashore, placed his two steamers in such a position as to command the little bay, and had given orders that the decks should be cleared and everything got ready for action. Howitzers were placed in boats alongside, in readiness to be despatched at a moment's notice, in case any trouble should occur on land, and the ship's guns were prepared to send their balls and shells in showers upon all the line of Japanese troops which thronged the shore, had they commenced hostilities. There was, however, no serious apprehension felt of any warlike termination to the ceremonies of the day, although every precaution was properly taken to provide against the least untoward occurrence.

Display initials by Heine ornament the text of *Narrative of the Expedition*. (Photograph by Gary Donnelly)

Camida Creek, Bay of Hakodadi.

In the Bay of Yedo.

Tailpieces by Heine in the *Narrative of the Expedition*. (Photograph by Gary Donnelly)

CHAPTER TWELVE

A TREATY AT LAST

Joyous and Festive Preparations.—The Commodore Goes Ashore.—Reception and Entertainment.—A Stroll on Japanese Soil.—Reminders of Home.—Gifts from the American Government.—The Signing of the Treaty.—"Hurrah for Commodore Perry!"

In the Bay of Edo, 11 March 1854

THE EIGHTH of March arrived in spring weather at its finest. Only a few small white clouds dotted a deep blue sky; from that sky—to announce the first, the beautiful season—a warm sun beamed bright. On all ships since early morning, life had throbbed. Action, action everywhere. Boats, lowered into the water, received guns and ammunition. Marines, in parade dress, gave weapons a final polish and checked the white leather. Had any spots appeared overnight? Meanwhile, Jack Tar of the navy cut a handsome and dapper figure: blue jacket and trousers, the thirteen stars on a tricolored band around the cap, dress sabre at the left hip, and pistol at the right.[1] On the quarterdeck, epaulets shone and gold braid gleamed. In short, every man had done all he could to look as becoming and as impressive as possible for the long-awaited, momentous, fateful meeting between Commodore Perry and the imperial councilors.[2]

At 10:00 the flagship signaled, all boats prepare to rendezvous. Whereupon from each ship boats full of men pushed off and assembled into a line of cable-length in front of the ships. Ten longboats composed the line's center. Four of them carried twenty-four pounders off the *Powhatan* and the *Susquehanna*, and the rest carried twelve-pounders. The lighter boats, all twenty-eight, arranged themselves into two wings.[3] Captain Buchanan of the *Susquehanna* [in charge of the day's military proceedings] commanded this small flotilla, from a position [in a gig] out in front.

The choirs off the three frigates had been distributed along the line. At 11:00, slowly and like a battalion on the parade field, the line began to move amid the singers' cheerful tones. What a beautiful sight: the squadron's eight ships in a row over a mile long; the three steamers and the *Macedonian* asserting sprung batteries (that is, turned, with the aid of spring cables, broadside to the coast to cover our landing with their cannon[4]); parallel to them, the line of boats, filled with officers, marines, and sailors, their cannon polished and shining, and their personal weapons gleaming in the sun; and flags fluttering their joyful stars and happy stripes in the mild breeze.

Six hundred men landed without trouble. The marines and sailors, in eight companies, drew up first into review formation, facing the water at the landing site. Then they assembled into three sides of a square.[5] The square's upper end enclosed the hall erected for the reception. In effect the boats, anchored off the beach, completed the square on its fourth side.[6]

The *Powhatan* fired the commodore's salute, thirteen guns. The commodore's boat burst at the same moment out of the white smoke, the commodore's grand flag flying. His escort awaited him, thirty and more officers already at the landing site. He stepped onto Japanese soil and strode through our midst, and we at once followed him to the reception hall [often called Treaty House in days and years to come]. The troops presented arms, flags dipped, and the band played "Hail Columbia," the national anthem. Simultaneously the *Powhatan* hoisted the imperial Japanese flag, and the ships fired to it a salvo of twenty-one guns. Another followed immediately, seventeen (the number for a minister plenipotentiary) in a salute to the flag of the imperial councilors.[7]

The reception hall was the one used at Kanegawa but more festively decorated. The proceedings began as they had begun [there], with everyone taking seats in the big room. A few pleasantries were exchanged. A second special area, a kind of alcove or conference room, had been added to the far end, with eight to ten seats for the commodore, the imperial councilors, the interpreters, and the rest of the chief participants. They went in there now, and curtains of violet-colored silk closed behind them. Refreshments came for those of us remaining outside: four or five kinds of fish and an array of dishes that defied description. I thought it funny to find among them, yes, minced radishes. The seasoning to be used at table, a small cup of soy sauce and another of a dressing similarly piquant, proved by their composition that gastronomy had not trailed the other elements of Japanese culture. A sort of soup of eel, served in small covered bowls, tasted superb to me.[8] Cheese replaced bread (a peculiar substitution), a sort of fresh cheese, sliced thin. Yet with all those dishes nothing to drink but tea until the dessert of cakes and all sorts of sweet things and a first-rate saki in silver containers.[9]

Japanese officials had made several visits to the ships, and I had gotten to know some of them. On such occasions they delighted in the custom of drinking one's health.[10] Having to join them therefore in so many such toasts here, I must at last take recourse in a few cups of tea, just to keep my balance.

This meeting with the imperial councilors was *very* long.[11] Some of us began to smoke with the Japanese. Others, I among them, took a stroll.[12]

The breeze was gentle, the air warm, the oncoming crowds innocuous. At the commodore's explicit request the everlasting black-and-white striped canvas had not been set up as a barrier this time, and nothing kept me from a little excursion into the open fields. Only the highest mountain peaks retained signs of the aftermath of winter. Even the towering Fujiyama had begun to show a few black specks on its snowcap. Several small units of Japanese soldiers—standards bright, weapons gleaming in the sun—added their brightly colored uniforms to the scene. They enlivened a landscape otherwise monotonous. I wandered about in the fields of greening wheat. Suddenly, just ahead, a lark took flight. Up, up it went, singing joyously. I stopped, I stood unaware that I had stopped, and I listened reverently to that little feathered singer's devout hymn. It spoke to my heart like a voice from home, of a friend I had not seen for a long while. Larks had sung the last time I rode through the meadows of home. I had been a wanderer about to depart then, and I cannot remember having heard the song again.

Nothing worth mentioning happened the rest of that day. After 4:00 P.M. we all returned to the ships.

30 March 1854

A few days later [9 March] we had to bury in Japanese soil a marine off the *Mississippi* [Private Robert Williams], the first of our expedition to die here.[13] The *Mississippi*'s chaplain, [George] Jones, several officers, and a corporal's squad composed the funeral party. When we passed the gates of a village on our way to the graveyard, a Buddhist priest joined our procession, and as nobody objected, he assumed the place behind Dr. Jones. The graveyard lay near a small temple. The grave had been dug. Dr. Jones read the customary prayers. When he finished, the Buddhist asked, with much modesty, might he be permitted to conduct *his* ceremony? It would consist only of burning a few pieces of paper inscribed with prayers and offering a few sacrifices: tea, rice, etc. Quite a number of Japanese had assembled meanwhile. When the request was granted, the courtesy seemed to make on them a very good impression. Let us hope that a few more prayers, together with the priest's innocent and inoffensive obsequies, did no harm to the soul of the departed.[14]

Official duties occupied me much thereafter, taking me daily into the countryside. Meanwhile our engineers [Chief Engineer Jesse Gay in charge, aided by his first assistant, Robert Danby, both of the *Mississippi*] and mechanics worked and worked to unpack and assemble our gifts to the emperor.[15] The astonishment of the Japanese increased with the opening of each crate.[16] Indeed, these American gifts to Japan were so beautiful they would have caused amazement and produced applause in any country in the world.[17]

The Japanese marveled most at the railroad. Locomotive, tender, and passenger cars (built by Norris [Brothers, locomotive works] in Philadelphia, all of course at reduced scale), paneling in two varieties of rosewood, metalwork of superior craftsmanship—these features amounted to the most attractive example [of a railroad] that I had ever seen. The rails were laid in a circle about a mile in circumference.[18]

One of our mechanics tested a high-pressure fire-fighting apparatus.[19] What hilarity when the stream hit a crowd of gawking Japanese and knocked them into a heap! All sorts of agricultural machinery took shape. (America had rightly won first prize in this category at the London World's Fair [the Great Exposition of 1851].) The Japanese gaped at the metal [copper-clad] lifeboat by Francis and the famous covered [and copper-clad] surfboat that can be pulled back and forth, between shore and the ship in distress, on a line fired by mortar from shore to the ship. The others included a number of the well-known Colts (six-shooters), as well as beautiful examples of Hall's rifles (twenty-four-shot), manufactured articles of all kinds, cloth, and finally the most lovely editions of books by American authors (among them even a splendid Audubon, *Birds of America,* the renowned monument to natural science).[20] In sum, these things constituted one of the most valuable gifts ever brought and presented by one nation to another. And, what enhanced the value much, the inventors and manufacturers with few exceptions contributed their products voluntarily and free of charge; the government had only to round them out with a few supplements.[21] This can probably be called unique, a pioneer act of generosity never duplicated.

Then, finally, the long-desired commercial treaty was agreed upon and on 24 [31] March solemnly and ceremoniously signed by the ministers plenipotentiary of the contractual powers.[22]

On the twenty-sixth the commodore hosted the imperial councilors aboard our ships with their escort of some sixty other Japanese.[23] These festivities ended in a most agreeable and a most joyful manner. While cannon thundered, we drank the health of the shogun (the present emperor).[24] Our guests in turn, revealing a brilliant talent for our way of toasting, proposed the health of the President of the United States. Then, with equal enthusiasm, they offered and we all of us accepted, "Hurrah for the Stars and Stripes!" "Hurrah for Commodore Perry!"

CHAPTER THIRTEEN

SHIMODA

Officials Frightened Out of Their Wits.—View of Edo.—Izu.—Shimoda: Situation and Harbor. — In a Japanese City. — Houses. — Baths. — Contrasts. — Temples. — Worship.

Shimoda Bay, 7 May 1854

THE COASTAL survey, proceeding in bad weather during and beyond the last days of negotiations, ended on 6 April despite storm and fog. The pace, and the tasks to complete, ran me off my feet. Agreement had been reached by the treaty just signed to open to American traffic the harbor at Shimoda near Cape Izu and forty-five miles west of the entrance to the Bay of Edo.[1] Before the squadron removed there, however, the commodore wanted a look at Edo itself. He was encouraged because the survey ships had approached within four miles and sounded depths of fourteen fathoms. His wish, communicated to the imperial commission, alarmed them. Foreigners who would not humble themselves to Japanese ceremony dare state they intended to see the imperial palace? The notion boggled the officials' minds.[2]

There were suggestions as to how a bad situation might be avoided. Perhaps, for example, Perry could proceed overland to Edo and request an audience in the manner of Dutch envoys earlier. It is readily understandable that this alternative was rejected as unacceptable and as degrading as the numerous others. Finally the commodore spoke with compromise but categorically. He would approach but only near enough to see Edo. They replied, "Please consider that if your flotilla anchor outside Edo's walls, nothing remains for us but to kill ourselves."

On the eighth, the day set for our advance up the bay to Edo, the legation came aboard and expressed every hope that the plan would be abandoned. Our handsome and impressive flotilla weighed anchor and set off. Despair twisted the faces of the wretched Japanese and they plied our officers:

"Are you really headed for Edo?"

"Do you intend to anchor there?"

"You will actually anchor there?"

Our officers replied, "We don't know what the commodore intends. We shall obey his orders, whatever they are."

"No, no"—I quote the Japanese verbatim—"let not the ships anchor at Edo. Perry is a man of good heart and magnanimous; he does not want us to die!"

At 10:00 A.M. we saw Edo at the upper end of the bay: white buildings curving almost to a half circle along a low and level shore. To our left a suburb, Shinagawa, leaned upward against a chain of low hills to a height of, say, 120 to 150 feet. What the Japanese called a lighthouse, a tall towerlike structure bulking near us, consisted solely of wood in the shape of a squat pyramid. Boards enclosed only the upper part; it rested on a naked framework below.

Thousands upon thousands of small fishing boats swarmed along the shore. Between us and the city, about three miles from us and a mile from it, a concourse of junks lay anchored, surely over two hundred, huge ones, probably warships. In the distance, above the buildings of the city, we could see a hill and several grand walls and edifices: the imperial palace, we were told. The commodore signalled a halt and ordered all officers on deck for a last look at Edo; we would approach no nearer.[3] After perhaps a half hour's pause our ships turned and set a reverse course—to the inexpressible relief of our Japanese. Only then did they begin to revive.

For those poor devils' sake I wanted to be happy at the commodore's decision. But (I cannot lie) I felt no joy whatsoever. Rather, at that moment, I and many others knew nothing but disappointment—twice over. First: What we had seen of Edo's size and aspect did not confirm our expectations. Second: I had longed to stay a while in the imperial city—a hope now shattered. Still, all things considered, everyone must concur with the commodore. Our mission having been better accomplished than could have been wished, more could not be achieved at the moment. Indeed, what could be gained but the satisfaction of our curiosity, perhaps at the price of innocent lives? For, as the officials subsequently assured us in all earnestness, the splash of anchors before Edo would compel them to commit *hara-hini* [*hara-kiri*], suicide by slashing the abdomen, to avoid being executed in disgrace.[4] Worse, regardless whether they killed themselves or were killed, our disrespect for their requests and our scorn for their remonstrances would have so humiliated the Japanese that a wall of bitterness would have divided the two nations, perhaps for a long time.

In the afternoon we returned to our anchorage of the year past, the "American anchorage," and undertook exact corrections to the coastal survey done then.[5] After several days we completed the work successfully on 15 May [April]. Captain [Henry A.] Adams, bringing home the treaty, had been at sea in the *Saratoga* since the sixth.[6] On the fourteenth, while he proceeded via the Sandwich Islands and San Francisco, our assembled ships of sail moved to the harbor at Shimoda; the *Powhatan* and the *Mississippi* followed on the sixteenth.[7]

Fog, so common along those shores, on that occasion denied us the beautiful view of grand Fujiyama and the chain of mountains around it. About 10:00 we sighted Oshima Island, four to five miles southwest. The island's highest point encloses a magnificent gorge filled then with clouds of white steam always billowing upward and surging far outward. As we saw this steam whenever we approached, I feel justified to assume volcanic emissions, perhaps similar to Iceland's, occurring in the whole island.

About 12:00 the outlines of Cape Izu appeared in the distance. For about two hours we edged along the coast. The lead, cast continually to either side, contradicted our caution and belied our fears: forty fathoms all the way.

A peninsula of tall majestic mountains extending north–south into the ocean constitutes the province of Izu. At many coastal spots, walls of rock soar from the water, vertical for a thousand feet and more. Plateaus can often be descried, several thousand feet above sea level, with wild-looking rugged ridges towering still higher. Here and there green valleys pose delightful contrasts running inland from the water's edge. Lusty brooks dance through them to the ocean, and cities and towns nestle like strings of pearls on the emerald velvet of meadows and fields. Many fishing boats pursue continually the denizens of the blue depths. Large junks with black masts and ponderous sails—marvelously-shaped craft—

transport the goods of trade between one harbor and another. If we neared a junk, its crew would gape in curiosity at the strange ships of fire. One junk crossed within pistol shot under the stern of the *Powhatan*. The junk's crew waved handkerchiefs, lifted hands in greeting, and laughed. None of us, unfortunately, could understand the badinage they shouted at us except our interpreter, Dr. Williams.

The harbor of Shimoda, near Cape Izu, at the southernmost point of the peninsula, consists of a spacious inlet surrounded (except the entrance) by rolling countryside rising to hills of several hundred feet. Even our large ships could anchor within rifle shot of land, so abruptly does the shore slant to depth. At the northwestern end of this harbor basin a valley widens to something more than a mile. There at the mouth of a small but vigorous river the town of Shimoda numbers about a thousand buildings; beyond, north from the shore, a second town, Korsaki, about five hundred.

The river and a creek descend from the east to furnish the harbor with ample fresh water. The hills protect anchored ships from storms out of every quarter but one. Southern storms ruffle the water to the innermost harbor but too little to endanger security of anchorage, especially as anchors grip the bottom's viscous mud. A rock pointed out of the middle of the bay; from it we measured in all directions. (Americans shall by treaty be subject solely to American law within a ten-mile radius. Henceforth, Shimoda is the American harbor in southern Japan.)

First, with respect to Perry's enduring concern, we undertook a scrupulous coastal survey of the harbor.[8] The shoreline and contiguous areas, and especially the isolated rocks and a series of reefs, must be charted. The rocks and reefs extend crookedly west of the harbor's entrance and some ten miles into the ocean. Partially submerged and hidden, they could easily wreck an ignorant mariner. This aspect of the work demanded much of me because, to ensure safe passage, prominent landmarks [had to be described and represented to guide navigators]. On such excursions we brought food and water for three days, should storms interrupt return.

In rough weather fishing boats seek refuge in an inlet of the spacious outermost cliff. There is even a small meadow to grace the narrow defile. The somewhat ruinous temple on the meadow contains porcelain vases, two small copper gongs, several idols, and a box for offerings. To its few coppers, gifts of fishermen, I added some American small change.

In Shimoda the surveying taught me much, for, until that late date, I had been overly innocent of practical experience in such matters. What a profound difference, I learned, between a topographical survey on solid ground and its marine counterpart! On land the plane table, diopter, compass, and chain operate almost on their own. Afloat, however, you have only mathematics aided by compass and sextant. Consider yourself richly rewarded if, soaked to the skin, you derive a few good and correct angles and establish a true meridian while the boat bobs and you shiver with cold.

Shimoda—small and unimportant when compared with Edo, Osaka, Miako, Nagasaki, and others—nonetheless teems with novelty and abounds in things worth noting. Amid houses usually of one story, streets form squares and end in gates locked at night, blocking nocturnal communication.[9] Smooth and well-paved sidewalks, elevated six inches, run six feet along the center of the streets. Verandahs front all streetside houses. The shop gives onto the entire width of the verandah where a merchant lives. The average nonmercantile home features a kind of antechamber there: an empty room with a bare floor, a little higher than street level. The next, still higher (about two feet up), seems to serve transient visits and inconsequential business. The more-or-less attractive Japanese mats, found in most Japanese interiors, furnish this "intermediate room." (How wealthy is the owner? Look at the quality of his mats.) The parlor, or "best room," the nicest part of the house and boasting the choicest mats, occupies the rear and typically overlooks a yard. People of means usually plant an elegant garden there and often add a pond of goldfish. The kitchen, normally relegated to its own side-annex, remains inside the smallest houses but in the remotest corners.

Fireproof mortar, white in color, or a structure partly of stone, both roofed with tile, distinguish farmers' and merchants' storehouses from the unpainted wood of residences and their roofs of straw. Doors and windows of the Western sort exist in China but not here. Japanese differences extend even to walls. Panels, installed in upper and lower grooves, serve as windows and doors to be slid back and forth, opened and shut, as desired. All partitions can thus be pushed aside and many rooms made into one. Indeed, outer walls themselves can be closed and opened at will. In the thin wood of outer wall panels, paper appears where we would expect glass. A second panel, of sturdy lumber, joins the first in nocturnal security or as protection against the elements. Large lanterns illuminate the rooms at night: a paper wick burning in a shallow, oil-filled dish inside a shade of oiled paper and thin wood.

Obviously the houses' fragile structure poses the clear and present danger of fire. During our stay in the Bay of Edo at least one fire reddened the sky nearly every night.[10] Against this menace the Japanese exercise eternal vigilance and assert defiant countermeasures. Even the smallest village has a fire station. (Unfortunately its buckets, hooks, ladders, and primitive wooden pumps too often cannot do the trick.) Towns and cities have more stations, of course, as well as a corps of firemen always on duty to answer the alarm and rush to help.

In the houses and in the streets immaculateness prevails. The streets are swept once a day at least. The people bathe daily and in warm water. By "the people bathe" I mean not only the well-to-do [at home] but also the poor at public facilities. And I ought to say *hot* water, for it inflames and chaps the skin. What a shock the first time I saw a Japanese in the bath—he had turned as red as a boiled lobster! I wondered, Whatever is he doing? He sat shrouded by steam in a wooden vat of water, while a second man stoked the fire roaring beneath. A man taking a bath looked like an oldtime saint immolating himself. I could not so scald my hand for a minute; yet the man in the bath—I should say the man being cooked—seemed comfortable. Nor did my presence embarrass him. When finished in the water, he climbed out naked and, in the next stage of cleaning himself, proceeded to rub his body dry from top to bottom.

In public facilities, heated water must be rationed; each patron gets but one small jar of it. He squats on the stone floor and washes himself, then pours over himself what remains. A gutter, running the length of the center of the floor, carries the waste outside. Finally he enjoys a last scalding in the common tank, a huge receptacle full and hot.

An array of patrons one after another use the same water in the tank. Moreover, a single bathhouse serves all comers. Old and young, men and women, boys and girls: they scramble about together in a remarkable medley as naked as frogs. Yet they stay calm even when foreigners appear. At most the sight of us would elicit what I took to be an off-color witticism. I assumed it because one or another of the women would then abruptly plunge headlong into the tank or squat and hold her arms as if imitating the Venus of Medici.[11]

In lurid contrast to the love of cleanliness, another practice reeks to high heaven in Japan. Every bit of organic matter must be saved, composted, and used in agriculture. Giant tubs stand, not only at specified intervals on country roads, but also on street corners and even in the houses. The tubs receive all manner of refuse vegetable and animal: trash, rubbish, garbage, offal, and excrement. You'll see clean and tidy streets, therefore, but hold your nose when near a tub, especially as passersby freely relieve themselves there.[12] Yet if these public facilities stink in the nostrils, unsoiled streets and sidewalks spare the eye the sore of the urban contribution to agriculture, which often disfigures the streets and defiles the sidewalks in the supercivilized cities of the West.

At home in Japan, in huts separate from the house, two small private spaces serve this physiological exigency. In Number One a long trough empties into a barrel, like the setup in German saloons. In Number Two a simple twelve-by-eighteen-inch hole in the floor accepts feces. Outside each hut a container of clean water and a washcloth provide for immediate cleanup. When in Rome, do as the Romans do!

At Shimoda's edge, among the farthest houses, eight buildings stand at the foot of the hill. Being fairly large, they contain places of worship, quarters for priests, and (as is common in Japan) lodgings for distinguished travelers. I allocated my studio in one building. The adjoining garden answered the needs of Mr. Brown's daguerreotypic procedures. The priests, as especially attentive observers, joined the many astonished visitors who marveled at the ocher wooden box. How fast, how accurately it produced those diverse images!

In a spacious hall of the temple proper reserved for worship the main altar resembles in every appointment the altars of China and Indochina, with vases of lotus blossoms notable in particular, as well as candelabra and incense burners. To the left of the altar a low table holds two bronze gongs of different sizes, each with its own striker. Both, when struck, emit beautifully rich sounds, the smaller a fifth higher in tone. Beside the table, three prayer books lie on a short lectern. To its right a stout wooden globe looks like a giant sleigh bell: hollow, about a foot and a half in diameter, with a slit. Usually the globe gleams attractively in red lacquer trimmed in gold.

At sunrise and sunset, the principal hours of worship, the priest kneels at the table and strikes the larger gong. While it resounds he begins to recite prayers in a nasal voice, beats time on the globe, and occasionally hits the smaller gong to add its tone. Worshippers kneel at the altar and continually rub a kind of rosary between their folded hands. Before leaving they either throw a small contribution of money into the box or bring to the priest an offering of rice, fish, or other comestibles. I saw not a hint of the superstitious ceremonials of China, a noteworthy fact. The Japanese service seemed to consist of genuine prayer, no less, and nothing else.

CHAPTER FOURTEEN

SHIMODA

(CONTINUED)

Japanese Women.—What Happens When They Are Impetuous.—Manners and Customs.—Priests and Mendicant Nuns.—Our First Hunt on Japanese Soil.—Of Birds.—Frictions.—Departure.—Oshima.

I SAW many women here. They wear the kimono, a calf-length wrap, usually black, with a wide sash and broad sleeves that fall to the wrist. The kimono closes at the front, the ends being brought together, one atop the other, and fastened with the sash, which rides around the lower torso and low on the hips, frequently even below them. The sash, the most important accessory in the Japanese woman's wardrobe, often represents the ultimate in extravagance: a monster band some twelve inches wide, decorated in as costly a manner as the wearer's means permit. The kimono provides a seemly cover to the body—when the wearer is quiet. A quick movement often exposes the breasts, perhaps also part of the legs. For this reason, decorous ladies of the upper classes walk slowly and take small steps.[1] Well-to-do wearers put on several kimonos at once in layers. The obtrusive length of some kimonos forms a train that twists about the legs and hinders movement. I saw modest young ladies pull their layers together from back to front, close their knees on them, and therefore have to walk by describing half-circles with the feet. In addition, women wear sandals that, with wooden soles and heels three to four inches thick, look like short stilts. In long kimono and on stiltlike sandals, the woman totters and wobbles when she walks, her progress a miracle of locomotion. In the dialect of my native Saxony we would call this *lätschbeinig:* the "clumsy-footed gait" or "shuffling like a bear."

The woman's hair is usually black and very soft. (I have seen two red-haired children, but only lately, after much time in Japan.) Women of every class take pains with the coiffure. On the crown of the head they shave smooth a spot the size of a large coin. Then, pulling the hair together from all sides, they gather it above the spot and tie it in a loose, full knot. The knot's shape varies according to the hair's density and length. Whatever its substance, the hair seems fuller and more luxuriant in this style because neither cords nor bands but combs secure the knot and hold the hairdo together; and unlike the style of Chinese women, the hair does not lie tight on the head. The combs are of wood or horn, or of tortoiseshell for those who can afford it. Pins provide ornament in metal, glass, horn, or tortoiseshell. On festive occasions a net decorates the head: a mesh of brilliant color, usually red, on the hair or woven into it.

On one occasion I saw six or eight young women tricked out in their most elegant. At the commodore's request the prefect or governor of Shimoda selected them to be daguerreotyped.[2] All were attractive, and some so prepossessing that they would have been called lovely in different cultures and other lands. (When I expressed this opinion to the interpreter Tatsnoske, he contradicted it. "No exceptional female beauty occurs in such a small town. It can be found, more of it certainly, in Miako, the city of the *dairi,* the chief priest."[3]) Anything but shy, they let us examine their garments. When I chucked one under the chin, or pinched a cheek, or shared some other familiarity, merriment ran the circle round and spread to everybody present: relatives, prefect, and officials. (About a hundred people had gathered to witness this experiment with that miraculous box.) No other member of the expedition reported more evidence of goodwill up to the date of this chapter [7 May 1854].

Japanese society knows good manners and practices social graces. I reproduce here the best proof: examples of Japanese calling cards.[4] [See Figure 1.]

Japanese cards cannot compare with ours for quality and durability of paper and elegance of format. But Japanese cards, long and narrow in contrast to ours [have a charm and a courtliness of their own]. Many that I examined seemed printed on [rice paper or] a thin sheet made of plant pulp.

The notorious Japanese tea houses, mentioned by several travel-

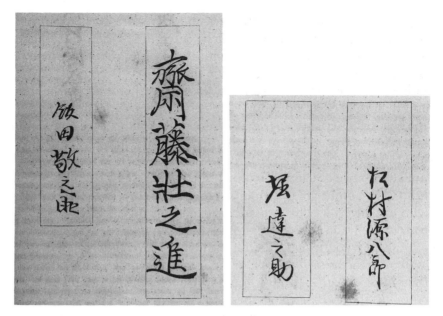

Figure 1. Japanese calling cards. (In Heine's original publication, the calling cards were printed upside down.)

ers, seemed absent from Shimoda, or they escaped our notice. I did observe things about Japanese women that I would call ugly and repulsive: fashions as ugly as the severe corsets of civilized Western beauties and practices as repulsive as the binding of the feet among aristocratic Chinese women. Consider the whitening and coloring of the face. (Being a painter and an artist, I speak as an expert.) Japanese women apply cosmetics as grossly as a decorator slaps paint onto the crassest of theatrical sets. The women whitewash the face with something that resembles powdered oyster shell. Then they redden the lips in a carmine like our *Tassenrot* [a deep, dull red] except the fanatical lip-painters, who do them in dark blue. Young unmarried women usually stop there; at most perhaps some in the upper classes also rouge the cheeks. Married women, going further, not only pluck the eyebrows to the last hair but stain the teeth black.

The remarkable dental cosmetic comes as a grayish powder, about a dram in a little paper packet, sold in many shops. Thunberg claims that the stuff consists of iron filings, saki, and urine.[5] I could not verify the recipe, but I saw enough to convince me that the effect is frightfully corrosive. One of our cabin boys tested it. For eight days his mouth swelled like dough rising, and nearly all his teeth fell out.

On an earlier page describing male dress I said that priests shave the head clean and that other men cut the hair of the crown, braid the rest into a tuft three or four inches long, and wear the tuft thrust forward over the bare crown. Children's hair, trimmed only in spots, provides enough for five or six small tufts, usually gathered into one on top of the head. I observed a few children with some hair in tufts and the rest combed down on the forehead and cut straight across above the eyes.

It is well known that many a Japanese shears his tuft as a votive offering. The frequent occasions include his giving thanks that his life has been spared. In places of worship—the temples or chapels or *mia,* on hills or along the roads—I saw such tufts.[6] Under a painting of a junk in a dreadful storm they ranged, male and female, hanging row on row: male shorter, female longer; male above, female below. Bows, arrows, fans, and other things joined them, arrayed in the way the fisher folk and other seafarers of Catholic maritime lands offer sundry objects to God or the Virgin.

Pictures and drawings with allegorical themes also appear in the chapels. For example the rendition of the legend of the devil who lived by eating the hearts of young women. He enjoyed too many on one occasion, proving himself pernicious. Three brave and pious princes, having decided therefore to kill him, climbed to the top of a mountain and prayed together. God appeared in the form of an old hermit and handed them two jugs of saki. Disguised as pedlars, the princes set out on the road to hell. A woman bathing in a stream showed them the entrance. They gave a banquet. Demons served as waiters. (They were an astonishing green, all but the color of their hair: red.) The devil drank until drunk. The affair ended happily when, thus aided by the blessed saki, the princes cut off his head.

In another of these works, a naive representation of the creation of woman, several young men jump over spears. One jumper goes awry, a sharp edge slashes his crotch, and he is changed from male to female.

Most of these places of worship have a large copper bell. A tug at its straw rope is supposed to draw God's attention to a person at prayer. The popularity of a place can always be determined with considerable accuracy by observing the wear on the rope.

Priests typically wear long, pleated vestments of a crepelike material. The many colors include black, brown, green, yellow, and even rose-red. For proper attire during services, priests add a stole that crosses from the left shoulder to the right hip. I saw one dignitary in headgear that looked like a [Catholic] bishop's miter. These gentlemen, like the clergy of other lands, seem to regard gluttony, drink, and depravity as prerogatives of office. Frequently I witnessed the consequences of their passion for saki. Nor do they marry but delight in surrounding themselves with boys.

On one occasion I observed two mendicant nuns. They had cut off their hair, like priests, and wore black veils. One was still young and pretty. The other, older, carried a child on her back. We were told that these unusual religious beggars roved about the country, giving themselves to men for money and bringing back to the convent the proceeds of such perigrinations. I cannot swear that the allegation is true.

When the surveying was done, I occupied myself with drawing until my portfolio held renditions of the interesting subjects. Then I decided to turn my efforts to expanding my collection of stuffed birds. So one morning before daybreak I shouldered my gun and went hunting. I followed the river about six miles, then turned to climb into the mountains that enclosed the valley. The landscape resembles the Alps around Salzburg. Instead of alpine meadows and leas, however, these mountains offer a grassy-bushy terrain spotted with rocky debris. The many cattle scattered in the mountains often had calves at their sides. Nearly all the mature ones evidenced with galled backs their widespread service as pack animals to carry loads across the mountains. I also encountered various ginseng diggers looking for that valuable root.

Fog hung heavy that morning. On a bald peak at two thousand feet the dank clouds enveloped me. Near some houses secluded in a ravine I encountered something like a mendicant friar or hermit. Later I saw where he lived. The hermitage, in a lonely ravine, consisted of nothing but flimsy reeds. On a prior page I have described the rosaries used by such people. He held one in his hand the morning I met him. He carried suspended at his chest a small wooden box painted with Japanese characters. People he encountered would put food into the box: rice and other things for him to eat. He accepted reverently the money I gave him. He fondled the rosary in supplication, then signed for me that he had prayed for my success on the hunt. Did his prayer help? In time, fortune smiled and I shot beautiful pheasants.

Among the rocky debris of those mountains a berry flourishes and provides feed for pheasants. For a while I had been hearing pheasants call. But when the first burst into view, I was unable to aim fast enough. Indeed, the gorgeously colored bird so startled me that for a moment I did not think of shooting. Later I bagged several; with a good dog I could easily have got a dozen.[7] This common Japanese pheasant, basically silver-gray and rather large, shimmers at the neck, breast, and shank in dark green and gold; a golden brown touches the upper wing; and bright red circles the eye. Two of my birds weighed fifteen pounds. I saw mostly cocks in the open on the mountaintop; hens kept to the bushes and sat on their eggs. I managed to get one hen for my collection.

A few days later I went hunting again, this time with Lieutenants [Silas] Bent and [James W. A.] Nicholson. The weather favored us even less than it had favored me a few days earlier. But at least the pellucid air let us see across the dark blue ocean to the horizon, to the many groups of islands, and to Oshima and its smoking volcano, as well as to valleys green and fertile and beautiful coastlines rocky and indented, with tall massifs rising behind them. We could even view the handsome Fujiyama, plain to the eye and lifting its venerable white head above the clouds. What a charming prospect!

A golden pheasant took flight. My shot did not drop it, but it left its splendid tail behind. It was the first I had seen—they are extraordinarily shy and therefore hard to get—and I discovered it in a narrow ravine, a practically impenetrable place. Later a Japanese sold me a complete and more beautiful specimen, a gorgeous thing. I can compare the phosphorescent plumage only to transparent gold overlaid with cochineal. At such a bird's every move the twenty-four-inch tail wafts with grace.

A long day of hunting exhausted us. We intended to spend the night in the home of a local official, someone like a village judge or mayor. This one dreaded the consequences [of taking in foreigners] and asked us to leave. We headed back toward Shimoda by the light of the moon. We were following the river when I saw something clinging to a tree: a fox, light gray, half the size of ours in Germany, and not common in Japan. For, here as in our country, red-haired

Master Reynard holds office as the arch chicken thief. A Japanese with dogs had chased this gray up the tree. I bought him for the exorbitant price of—a button off my uniform.

At 11:00 A.M., dead tired, we reached a temple on the city's outskirts. We requested, and the priests granted, lodging for the night. Scarcely had we stretched out in bed when some twenty Japanese soldiers forced their way in and tried to get us to return to the ship. Unsuccessful, they left—to return in about a half hour with an interpreter and several Japanese military officers. Lieutenant Bent, senior in our party, spoke for us: "We need rest until daybreak." They pressed us harder. They brought a multitude of lanterns into the room to make sleep difficult. Lieutenant Bent rejoined the issue with the interpreter. Meanwhile a soldier held a lantern so close to my eyes that, overcome by anger, I shoved the lantern and its paper globe into his face. Lieutenant Nicholson had grabbed another soldier by the leg and shaken him. Now Nicholson gave him a kick in the ribs and he tumbled with us into a pile. You can imagine the ensuing uproar.

Bent had loaded his revolver before these Japanese appeared. We loaded our shotguns quickly now. With them and the revolver aimed and cocked, we spoke in firm tones: "Get out at once." The intruders got out at once. We slept undisturbed until morning, then returned to the ship.[8]

We, all the American party, assumed that the prefect Kunakawa-Kahai was behind the incident. Back at the ship we [of the hunting excursion] learned that shortly after midnight several Japanese had come aboard and asked to speak to the commodore and were refused. According to the detailed report submitted later Lieutenant Bent—chief of staff since Captain Adams left—donned full uniform and went to see the prefect. Bent took along the captain of marines and an entourage proper to such rank. The prefect, disclaiming responsibility, said his officers were at fault. The officers blamed the soldiers. Bent told the prefect that the commodore, in high dudgeon, considered the affair an insult to American officers and a violation of the treaty of peace. "The commodore had intended to land a detachment, arrest the rowdies who disturbed the peace, and deliver them to Edo for punishment. And they were not to be treated so kindly should something like this happen again." In conclusion Bent said: "Nothing but our remonstrances and our pleas changed the commodore's mind." The message astonished and bewildered the prefect. Eventually it brought from the Japanese a solemn apology to our satisfaction.[9]

We left Shimoda on the thirteenth of May in clear, beautiful weather. About 10:00 A.M. we stood within cannon shot of Oshima Island. Its tallest peak seemed to have collapsed into a kettle-shaped crater. Dense white smoke poured from it, cloud upon cloud without pause. The crater's rim looked black and charred. A stream of lava flowed southward from crater to sea, filling the south slope's valleys and hollows with grayish red ash. The rest of the slopes retained the green of their vegetation. Two or three small towns or large villages, picturesque on the cliffs, nestled half-hidden amid tall trees.

Noon found us off Cape King; late afternoon, Cape Blanco. (Captain Vancouver named Cape King in honor of his first lieutenant.) We sounded stretches off both capes with gratifying results.

CHAPTER FIFTEEN

HAKODATE

The Straits of Sanger.—Dangerous Fogs.—Yesso Island.—The Bay of Hakodate.—
Duplicate of Gibraltar. — Layout and Situation of the City. — Fisheries. —
Inhabitants' Fears.—Birds and Fish.—Quicksand.—Domestic Arrangements.—A
Similarity to Switzerland.—Fire Stations and Police.—The Old Soldier.—Amiability
and Kindness of the Japanese.—Temples.—Hakodate in Panorama.

Hakodate Bay, Yesso Island, May 1854

THE STRAIT of Sangar [Tsugaru Strait] divides the islands of
Yesso [or Ezo, now Hokkaido] and Nippon [Honshu]. At
noon on the sixteenth we rounded Cape Toriwi-Raki [Sirija-Saki,
now Shiriya], Nippon's northernmost point, and entered the
strait.[1] The cape terminates in a clutter of rocks and reefs, partly submerged, partly protruding jaggedly from the water. A strong current, about four or five miles per hour, runs northwesterly off the
southwestern coast and southeasterly off the northwestern.[2] This
current imperils seafarers ignorant of local conditions, especially the
thick fogs that blanket these waters in May, June, and July.

"Take bearings, crossbearings, and tangents as long as daylight
permits," the commodore ordered.[3] Lieutenant Bent, [Acting]
Master [Reigart B.] Lowry, and I busied ourselves at taking them as
long as daylight would permit. In May in these latitudes it lasts until
nearly 7:00 P.M. But today fog returned to end our work quickly
and abruptly even before sundown.

On the seventeenth the fog socked us in until nearly 8:00 A.M.
Bells rang, horns blared, and steam whistles blew—the usual precautions taken and retaken to prevent our colliding one ship with
another. When at last the fog began to lift, we saw the *Mississippi* a
half mile astern of the *Powhatan*.[4] "Follow the commodore," we signalled, and steamed full ahead up the straits.

Our ships of sail had preceded us. After an hour underway we sighted a huge, lone rock at the end of a level point of land and their masts behind the rock. The flagship fired a gun and hoisted a small American flag at the foremast, a signal for the pilots. We approached about three miles and saw three of our boats—[one each] off the *Macedonian,* the *Southampton,* and the *Vandalia*—being rowed toward us. Mr. [George A.] Stevens, [acting] master of the *Southampton,* commanded the *Southampton*'s boat. It arrived first [at the *Powhatan*]. The other two went to the *Mississippi* and [the crews] boarded. At midday we were in line and riding easily at anchor in the splendid Bay of Hakodate, the second Japanese port we would open by treaty.[5]

I know the port of Gibraltar only from pictures, descriptions, and maps, to my regret. Other officers, however, who had often called there, affirmed that Hakodate can almost be termed Gibraltar's twin. I have mentioned the narrow isthmus that completes the bay on its southeastern side. A huge rock stands at the narrows, like the rock of Gibraltar; the city, Hakodate, lies at the foot of the rock, like the city of Gibraltar.[6] Moreover, the bay is beautiful and spacious. It reaches a width of some six to seven miles and diminishes to an entrance of two to three. The viscous muck provides excellent anchorage. There are (so far as we have ascertained) no reefs or shoals. Everywhere, and as near as a scant three-fourths of a mile from land, depths admit even the largest ships. Meanwhile a north–south sandbar protects the entrance from heavy seas. (To my mind, though, the bar must be minimal here because the harbor's entrance lies perpendicular to the Strait of Sangar, hence the distance to the opposite shore is only about twenty-eight to thirty miles.)

Rough estimates put the recent population at some four thousand to five thousand houses and about twenty thousand people. The bay's shores extend inland five to ten level miles, partly stone-covered, partly of meadows. There a massif rises to peaks of 1,200 to 3,000 feet, to rim the whole [bay and shores] in a half moon. The whole, this is, except toward the western end, where the heights gently flatten and approach the shore. Snow still covered most of the peaks and, indeed, even the lower foothills. Five rivers and creeks flowed from various directions off the heights and down into the bay, where the ships therefore found the water crystal-clear. Many villages lie along the streams; fields and kitchen gardens sur-

round the villages. Fisher folk have settled, clustered, at the streams'
mouths. For, in the spring, shoal upon shoal of salmon go upstream
to spawn. In each fishing village or near it there is always a level place
for drying nets upon the sand or salmon on long wooden frames in
the sun. I saw vats close by, with fireplaces underneath. A species of
sorrel, cooked in them, stains dark and protects from rot the nets
dipped in the infusion. At that moment, fishing season imminent,
fishermen were busy at this task.

On a prior page I have mentioned the Rock [Hakodate's Gibral-
tar]. The city, unlike the villages, has two principal streets, which
parallel the coast. The city so crowds the Rock that, of the streets,
the [inland] one is thirty feet higher than the other, and from the
coast the many cross streets run uphill. The main temples, four large
affairs, thrust their roofs above the other buildings. Toward the
lower end of the city and near the narrow isthmus, several buildings
share a small island with a dockyard for junks.

Lieutenant Bent, then the commodore's adjutant, went ashore
with Mr. Wells Williams and several other officers. They would
return the visit of Japanese officials sent by the governor of Hakodate and arrange the talks preliminary to a definitive meeting. I felt
rather ill and did not go along, my first absence from such a mission
since the start of the expedition. Remaining on board, I occupied
myself with sketching a general view of the bay and environs.[7]

This work occasioned my noticing numbers of people hurrying
away from the city and across the isthmus. I saw several hundred
pack horses, loaded. "The imperial commissioners have not yet
arrived from Edo [with word of the treaty], so people here did not
expect us, and they've looked at how big our ships are, and they've
counted how many there are, and they've got so scared that many
are running away and trying to carry along the best of their things."

Lieutenant Bent had returned with that explanation, which
amounted to a riddle. The answer soon appeared. You will recall
that Captain Golovnin, of the Russian navy, had been taken prisoner, perfidiously, thirty-three years before. Captain Ricord then
tried to bombard the place, Kunashiri, located seventy to eighty
miles north of Hakodate. Later, in a similar incident in 1849, the
Japanese had seized the crew of an American ship driven ashore and
inflicted a long and harsh imprisonment in Matsmai [Matsumae],
some thirty miles west of here. Thus the people now probably

believed we had come for revenge. So as not to increase their fright, none of us (except Lieutenant Bent's delegation) went ashore the first two days.[8] On the other hand, to be sure, many Japanese, including the governor of Hakodate himself, visited us aboard. Everything therefore soon returned to normal.

As soon as good relations were restored, I obeyed the commodore's order and landed in a small boat to shoot specimens for my ornithological collection. In the worst month for hunting, May, my hunt proved quite successful, and I bagged several rare and beautiful birds. Indeed, I trust I provided scientists with examples of a few unknown, or little known, even down to the present time. I delighted in a gorgeous wild duck, crested in greenish-gold, with five curved feathers bending at each shoulder into a speckled arch of gray and white. There were a diving bird with a large horny growth above the bill, like that of the toucan, and a small but supremely lovely partridge. Fourth, an unusually large woodcock. And above all a very rare snipe, small (scarcely four inches long), with white breast, brown neck, black head, and silver-gray wings: to the best of my knowledge the smallest webfooted bird known even now.[9]

Meanwhile the cutter, sent daily to fish, had met equal success. We often caught magnificent salmon, weighing fifteen pounds. One day the abundance totalled thirty buckets of fish, including no fewer than twenty-three salmon.[10]

I crisscrossed the level areas of the countryside. On one occasion, out with a man of the ordnance corps, I happened onto quicksand and sank rapidly to the hips—and deeper. I would have perished but for his presence of mind. He grabbed solid ground in time and reached his gun to me. Let me therefore warn any passionate hunters who come after me: keep to the level areas [i.e., out of low places] and be vigilant; such traps abound hereabouts.

I visited fishing villages and found all houses locked; indeed, many doors nailed scrupulously shut and the Devil's picture posted: he of the horns and a big-pronged fork. Not a living thing showed itself except soldiers guarding the houses—and dogs. Soldiers and dogs in equal numbers.[11]

After three days the arrangements had been made for us to live among the Japanese. My colleague Mr. Brown and I moved into the place assigned us, a small temple, which was to be our daguerreotype studio and residence.

We usually came ashore at a pier and stairway of superior stone-work. The wooden guardhouse on the pier could accommodate about twenty soldiers in its several rooms. Junks anchored between there and the isthmus, about two hundred at that time. The typical number, said to be more than twice as many, had diminished because most had fled when we arrived. From the guardhouse—better to call it a customs house—a short side street leads to the first of the principal streets. It is exceptionally clean; it runs at a width of about fifty feet, parallel to the shore; solid, spacious buildings line it. Often of two stories, they then accommodate a retail business at street level. The side street continues, crosses the second principal street (higher than the first but parallel with it), and leads straight to our temple. From there, at that elevation, we enjoyed an unobstructed view of the city and the harbor basin. A little to the right of the temple, another street leads even higher and into a street where, it seemed to me, mostly well-to-do people lived.

How the architecture reminded me of Switzerland![12] The flat, shingled roof with long poles held down by stones: The poles would keep storms from ripping the shingles off.[13] (Similar conditions produce similar practices. On these shores the violent storms of spring and fall concede nothing to any foehn off Lake Lucerne. Likewise the bitterness of winter [in both places] makes it desirable to keep on the roofs the several feet of snow as cover.) On the second story handsome balconies project far out all around. Before the main door there is a small enclosed porch or exterior vestibule, of wood, with gables separate, thrust out, and supported by small pillars often decorated with elegant carving—all reminiscent again of the Swiss. (Yet again, a belt of trees about a hundred feet wide, extending along the base of the mountain and close behind the city, protects its buildings from avalanches that cascade off the steep slopes.) A big tub, filled with water, stands at the gable ends of a house, and beside the tub a long pole with a whisk of straw. (I never discovered the purpose of the pole and whisk.[14]) Others of these tubs often range along roofs and resemble from afar the chimneys I have failed to see anywhere in Japan. Still other and even bigger tubs of water, which bulk frequently before doors, serve (so to speak) as stand-ins for the wells of Switzerland. This last touch imparts a similarity nothing short of striking. (There *are* wells here but in the yards, open wells, each with its long pole and bucket hanging from it.)

I have been discussing precautions against fire.[15] Though numerous, they seem too few; for I noticed many a burned-out place; one was the size of ten houses. No doubt about the causes of this pestilence: buildings of wood; the ugly custom of lighting every fire without protection in the middle of the hall; and the widespread use of coal braziers, often put, not only directly on the thick mats of straw that carpet every room but also, yes, right next to partitions and windows. (And in Japan those parts of houses are of paper.) Fire stations and their firemen's quarters occur accordingly in every section of the city—they resemble the ones I described earlier in Shimoda—but seem organized more strictly and in greater detail here. Several watchmen patrol every street, and a board—two feet long, a foot wide, and two inches thick—hangs from a post on every corner. At the outbreak of fire the watchman sounds the alarm by banging the board with a short iron rod. Once a fire company commander, the first to arrive, plants his standard on the scene, no other company may help unless he expressly desires it, nor even enter the territory, as each commander begrudges others the honor of putting out the fire.

The watchmen, together with the police, enjoy abundant prestige. Both are organized along military lines and carry the usual two swords. These may be used only by specific order of the commanding officer. Each man therefore carries also an iron baton, twelve to fifteen inches long and an inch thick. The hollow curve at one end will intercept a blow from a sword. A stout silk cord and tassel serve as wristband to hold baton to hand. The men in question, like English and American constables, wield these batons masterfully against mobs and riots. Thus they cleared the way several times for us through the densest of crowds.

Two soldiers and a non-commissioned officer of some sort, billeted under our [temple] roof, remained with us during our stay in Hakodate, from start to finish. This "temple guard" was to guarantee the safety of our equipment. One of them, a venerable soldier (a good-natured old wag), demonstrated to me the art of Japanese fencing. (Yes, there is a Japanese book on the subject and of no fewer than twenty thick volumes profusely illustrated.) A sword had left an imposing scar across his forehead and cheek, and his comrades admired him as brave and good. He fenced superbly. I would attack, as ordered, with a stout club; time after time, using his iron baton, he wrested the club out of my hand. Serving as courier during our stay, he carried official messages to Matsmai on several occasions. He told me that in his youth he had been a capable warrior and a skillful hunter. But now "I'm too old." (He might have been in his late fifties.) "My lungs are shot." He nonetheless urged and goaded the workmen to the task of setting up our studio and arranging our quarters. Nor did his condition prevent his clearing the way for us through a thicket of a crowd in the streets several times; he parted them with a lion's roar. The roar often tickled us. He cheerfully joined our laughter.

He and his comrades, doing their duty, kept scrupulous watch on our studio and quarters. (We were completing portraits of ranking officials. How conscientious the guards when an official appeared!) Thanks to the guards, nobody entered without our permission. One day, indeed, a Japanese functionary, carrying some message or other, penetrated our quarters unnoticed. He was shown unceremoniously to the door and relieved of his message there.

The people of Hakodate, strikingly short, often barely reach five feet. Their respect for our officers and crews differed in proportion to height: the taller the man, the greater the respect. Japanese frequently asked me, very politely, "Could we be measured together?" Once during a visit to the governor of Hakodate—he is called the bungo here—some person went so far as to mark my height with a notch on a wooden post.[16] I signed my name under the notch as asked, and somebody captioned the signature in Japanese.

I must confess that, once I accustomed myself to some rather peculiar customs, I began to grow fond of the Japanese. Good manners grace their behavior toward others, manners in the best sense of the word. The Japanese also possess extraordinary self-control, a remarkable feature of the national character. In these respects the Prince of Matsmai's emissary, cultivated and well bred, proved a paragon. As host, as diplomat, and as guest, he conducted himself with endearing charm. Let the same be said for the bungo and vice bungo: the former an agreeable older man of fifty-odd years; the latter a small and amazingly robust one of thirty, who sat a horse superbly and in general exhibited many qualities of the prize athlete.

I noticed the lighter complexion of the people of Yesso compared to the Nipponese to the south. A notable example, a businesman of Kunashiri, visited us several times in our studio. (He was probably a Kurile, called *ainos* by the Japanese.) On the whole I saw fewer women here than in Shimoda, though several young ones came to the studio to be daguerreotyped: faces attractive, behavior fetchingly modest.

In addition to the city's many chapels and small temples, four principal centers of worship, large temples, abounded in beautiful wood carvings. One, particularly spacious at perhaps 200 or 250 square feet, bristled with carvings, adornments in bold relief, mostly cranes and turtles (symbols here for beauty and good fortune) but also other creatures, such as rabbits, bulls, horses, wild boars, dragons, and others, with the boars and the dragons especially plentiful as decorations along the eaves. In another temple, probably to a Japanese Aeolus, the god of wind sat enthroned to the left of the main entrance, the wind itself in a sack over his shoulder. And to the right the god of thunder amid flickering tongues of red lightning. In this temple, throughout a two-day blow during our stay, two priests prayed continually a kind of responsory recited in nasal voices. This big temple's altars consisted of a main and four subsidiaries, and many of their features resembled altars in our Catholic churches. Indeed, there was a tabernacle above the altars and in the middle a figure carved in wood: a woman in a veil, not unlike a statue of Saint Elizabeth.[17]

The mountain (the Rock) crowds the city at the rear and rises to about fifteen hundred feet. From its peak the observer looks out over a splendid panorama: to the north the Bay of Hakodate, and the city itself in the foreground; beyond the city, in the same direction, the valley begins, the broad one (which I have already mentioned), enclosed by the mountains on three sides; to the south, farther and on the other side of the peninsula, the Bay of Sangar, with its steep and rugged banks; and to the south and west, beyond the straits or narrows, Nippon's chief mountain range; and it losing itself in turn behind the tall, snow-covered mountains on a point of the island of Yesso, with Matsmai, Yesso's capital, at their feet.

A twelve-foot statue of the Buddha, representing him kneeling and asleep, occupies a shrine on the Rock's highest peak.[18] A well-maintained path zigzags up there: something like the Catholic stations of the cross. There is a small temple at about three hundred feet; another at two hundred beyond; and a third about four hundred to five hundred above it.

On the southwestern slope, facing the ocean, a cold sulphur spring offers purgative waters.[19]

I went up this mountain first to draw the bay and to depict the panorama of the environs. Later, making a map and needing the topography, I went up again with Lieutenant [William L.] Maury of the *Mississippi* and Lieutenant [George H.] Preble of the *Macedonian* to triangulate.[20] I climbed this beautiful height no fewer than five times in all. At the peak, and on two lower ledges, observation posts had been built: of matting, overlooking the sea, and now abandoned. From them the Japanese had spied on our ships. At the mountain's western foot, barracks and a magazine complemented a newly installed battery of two cannon. The cannon had been wrapped and then, yes, small houses constructed over them, enclosing them so well that I could not estimate their size. Not more than twenty-four pounders at any rate. They had been put there to guard the harbor. The light Japanese vessels would stop inside one of those north–south sandbars in the eastern and somewhat shallower part of the bay, finding a protected and secure anchorage there. The battery in question, and a second at the other end of the isthmus, were to protect that anchorage. They would of course have been next to worthless, wretchedly ineffective against our big-bored blasters.

CHAPTER SIXTEEN

DEPARTURE FROM JAPAN

Money and Exchange.—Timepieces and Musical Instruments.—The Japanese Love of Music.—Hopes Thwarted.—The Thief Caught Red-Handed.—Foxhunting.— Return to Shimoda.—Altered Aspect of the Place.—Last Meeting with the Councilors.—Dallying.—Graves.—Friendship with a Japanese.—Departure.—What Did We Want and What Did We Get?

Aboard the frigate Powhatan
June 1854

IT DID NOT take long to agree with the Japanese on something like a standardized rate of exchange to simplify our purchases. Gold on this exchange stood ten percent lower than silver. The American silver dollar, pegged at 4,800 *cash,* would buy forty-eight large, oval, copper coins pierced to be strung through a square hole in the center.[1] To carry ten dollars' worth a strong man would have had to labor like a railway porter.

I bought some lacquerwear, porcelain, pipes, and tobacco pouches; a variety of notions; and an exceptionally high-grade watercolor [pigment], superior by far to the Chinese article. One might suppose the wares for sale in such a provincial town to be sleazy, but my purchases excelled in price (low) and in quality (high).

Our pocket watches provoked an astonishment that far exceeded the interest they aroused in the Bay of Edo, where several high-ranking officials owned such watches. In turn a Japanese wall clock fascinated me. Its case measured two feet long and six inches wide. The mechanism, powered by the descent of a weight into the top part of the case, bore some resemblance to our famous clocks of the Black Forest. Sixteen copper butterflies, in two rows of eight, occupied the length of a recess in the lower part of the case. Proportionately

153

half the distance separated one butterfly from another in the upper as in the lower row. In a second recess to the left, another butterfly counted hours by moving up and down. The eight butterflies of wider spaces registered the hours of the day at this season; the eight of the narrower, the hours of the night.[2]

Thus was expressed the Japanese idea of a day of sixteen hours, eight longer and eight shorter; in summer the longer for those from sunrise to sunset, the shorter for those from sunset to sunrise, and the opposite in winter. What of the other seasons and their waxing and waning days? I never learned how the Japanese manage then; they must ignore two seasons, divide the year in half, and reverse the hour markers every six months.[3] It follows that no Japanese can accommodate himself to our conception of time, for we mark no distinction on the clock between day and night. Indeed, most Japanese use sun dials. The dials seem to keep fairly good time. Some Japanese carry in a small box at the belt a writing case, a sun dial, a compass, a kind of folding rule, and sometimes even a small quadrant.

I saw various musical instruments for sale in several shops: a kind of lute or zither; a simple, reedless flute, of the stem of the bamboo; as well as another sort of zither. Of the first, some came with three catgut strings, others with five, and all with the body covered, not in wood but with parchment, like the instrument of Latin American Negroes. The flute, despite simplicity of design, would have baffled our players; its mouthpiece and seven [finger] holes were so big. Some Japanese nevertheless brought from it a simple and fairly agreeable music. The third—with five metal strings, plucked with a wooden plectrum held between thumb and index finger—approximated the Tyrolean zither except for a much longer neck.[4]

With a passion the Japanese seem to love music. When the commodore brought our choir ashore at Shimoda, half the city assembled to hear them. The next time he landed, without the choir, many Shimodans followed him and by all sorts of signs let him know how much they liked the singing and how they wished he would bring the choir along again. The same sentiment prevailed here in Hakodate. We had with us a group of "Ethiopian minstrels," dilettantes who performed songs and dances of plantation blacks of the South.[5] The commodore threw a banquet on the *Powhatan* for the commissioners of Matsmai, the imperial councilors, the two bungos, and other ranking officials. A concert followed; the choir alternated with the minstrels, and our Japanese guests seemed delighted. They applauded in every possible way and shouted again and again: *"Kussi! Kussi!"* That word signifies the greatest degree of pleasure, mental or physical.

A few days later I went hunting in the mountains. As usual a Japanese soldier accompanied me. This one had picked up half the words and music of those songs and spent most of the time singing scraps of them. His renditions sounded ludicrous enough. When I corrected him and helped him learn more, he laughed with glee and shouted an ecstatic *"Kussi! Kussi!"*

I hunted over a distance up the largest of the four rivers. Having started early, I had already taken a handsome bag of snipe and partridge before 9:00 A.M. In a good-sized village at the foot of the mountains, both of us weary, my companion and I took a break in the house of the village's *camida* or chief magistrate. The amiable old man treated us to rice cakes, pickled radishes, smoked salmon (in thin slices and delicious), tea, and a sweet. I contributed wine out of our canteen. To our host the wine seemed to taste excellent.

My companion, the soldier, wanted to keep me from the mountain. The climb would be severe for one thing. Moreover, the gullies and ravines supposedly harbored many bears. For me the bears gave all the more reason to climb. I perservered. Horses were brought, and the camida picked four local men who knew the way. Each carried a long hunting knife. The many dogs number several to a house here because bears descend in droves upon the villages in winter, and bear hunts are a local delight. To our armory the camida added three large dogs. One big old black cur and I quickly became pals. It had lost an ear in one of its battles and exhibited scars as proofs of courage and determination. The other dogs, after but a sniff, seemed to take less pleasure in the foreigner.

After a climb of two strenuous hours we reached a plateau at last. It offered a magnificent prospect over the bay far below. My companions built a fire, two stayed with the horses, and the others followed me with the dogs into the thicket. I carried my shotgun, in each barrel a ball and three buckshot, the typical load on our ships. Thick forests invest these mountains, and narrow paths serve the pack animals that carry quantities of wood and charcoal down to the plain. (Charcoal-burning here, done in heaps in the forests, practically duplicates the way we do it.) The paths soon ended. An almost impassable thicket made further penetration harsh; rarely did we meet a tree whose size [suppressed the undergrowth and] eased our advance for a while. Again and again I saw that the bark of certain young trees had been gnawed. Our friend, Mr. Bruin, likes to indulge his sweet tooth. When he cannot find honey, he hunts up various sugary roots and the saplings of the bamboo. (Bamboo shoots, by the way, provide nourishment for people, a food not to be scorned. They have been served to me more than once as a delicious salad.)

We came upon spoor several times. A patriarch of the family Ursidae must have left his mark near a small spring: paw prints the size of my splayed hand. They quickened and sharpened my zeal for the hunt. Suddenly, after the dogs had been uneasy for a while, my one-eared old sourpuss of a friend pressed his nose to the ground. A brief growl, then he raised his hackles and a hue and cry; with the other dogs following, he drove into the thicket straight ahead. Loud rustle and rattle of underbrush. Agitated leaves registered the chase: It turned left. With unspeakable difficulty we all followed as fast as we could in pursuit of the bear, but it soon gained a long lead. When at last we reached a thinner part of the forest, we spied the dogs yelping and leaping about a dark hole under a tree on the side of a hill. This must be our shaggy fellow's headquarters. Abundant spoor proved it. But how to get at the beast? That *was* the question!

The den seemed to enlarge inside, and I thought initially that I would crawl in. Two obstacles. (1) As I started for the den, the dear Japanese, my companions, resisted—now by entreaty, now with force. "Something terrible might happen to you," they said in alarm. In that case, since they were responsible for me, I would in all likelihood cause those poor souls big trouble. I did not want to cause them trouble. (2) This was the season for cubs. According to the Japanese, ours could not be the small brown bear but must be the large, black, Russian one. Cubs would turn a beast of such size into the most dangerous of foes.

So my companions tried something else. Brushwood, heaped at the mouth of the den and ignited, was to smoke out the bear. I put little faith in the method. Indeed, as I had presumed, the bear did not come out. Perhaps the den was very deep or had another exit.

High time, now, that I thought of my return (I had arranged for my boat to meet me at sunset) and I started back at 3:00 P.M. The hunt had failed. I was depressed. The kind-hearted Japanese tried to cheer me up. "This," they strove to explain, "is the wrong season for bear." And "Come again in the winter. We want to go hunting with you then." I could shoot at least three in one day, they said. It sounded beautiful, consoling, cheerful. But chances remain slim that I shall return to Hakodate ever, least of all in winter.

Last February, by the way, although the weather had been fairly cold in the Bay of Edo, our ships had seen nothing more than a light frost. Here [in the mountains of Hakodate], however, snow still lay deep in many places. I had not set foot on snow for three and a half years. With peculiar delight I swept together a handful and devoured it. This refreshing coldness in the mouth brought a most agreeable sensation. But what an incomparably greater joy to stumble on, in a sunny spot, a great cluster of snowdrops. I picked a tuft and fixed it to my hat. At that moment this simple little flower, a kind we knew at home, seemed to have come to me as a greeting from dear friends far away!

We returned to our horses and by evening reached the village. After a cup of tea I set out for the bay. I had entrusted to the camida the birds I shot in the morning. Obviously embarrassed when I asked for them now, he said a dog ate them. I did not believe him, but I wanted to let the matter rest to avoid discord. Thereupon I observed my soldier-companion kindle a heated discussion with the camida, then mount one of the horses and gallop off. I reached the bay and found waiting for me not only my boat but the soldier and several of his fellows. The soldier forced another man, who kneeled in front of him, to hold up to me my missing birds. Meanwhile, at intervals, the soldier, with baton, applied a few emphatic admonitions—enough to send the thief (yes, he was a thief) to my feet, screaming. The scene revolted me; the soldier seemed bent, simply and without malice, on beating the fellow to death. I stepped between them, the soldier desisted, and the thief fled. He had got off cheap, which plainly delighted him. (Here in many cases the severe penalties for theft mean capital punishment. I wanted not at all to see more of Japanese justice.)

Now I must record that I could not force anyone to accept payment [for having helped me]. I had distributed a handful of small change among the children of the village, but I found even this pittance returned to my boat that evening by someone on the qt. A little powder and lead; a few shiny buttons off my jacket, much liked by the people; and a pencil—nothing else could I get them to take. And then, while showing me with distinct pride his little garden, my soldier gave me a big bunch of green onions and some garlic. A treat, especially for my sailors, long without fresh vegetables.[6]

Fog gathered in the evening of the same day—so thick that I could find my ship only with the aid of a compass. The fog remained dense upon the water the next morning. Welcoming the commodore's permission, I went with one of our engineers and a marine to the swamps to hunt ducks.

We shot plenty of them, and the fog prevailed, so we moved to the bay's west end. A scattering of dunes, partly covered with a brushy growth, crowded the shore and displayed fox tracks in abundance. We separated: the marine to the left, I in the center, and the engineer, Mr. [Henry] Fauth, on the right and a little ahead. Suddenly, from the left, a voice: "Mark!" It meant "Pay attention!" Sure enough, on the right, a few minutes later a shot rang out. The fox, emerging on the left, had tried to angle behind a dune and into the swamp but showed himself to Mr. Fauth, who fired. It tumbled head over heels but sprang to its feet and bounded off, tail in the air. While Mr. Fauth reloaded, we—the marine and I—followed the tracks of other foxes, I about two hundred paces in the lead. Presently a gray shadow flitted through the fog at short range.

"Bang!" went my gun.

A leap. A collapse. A recovery.

"Bang!" went my second barrel.

Friend Reynard rolled whining in the grass, snapping angrily at the bushes, clawing at the ground. At almost the same time another shot sounded far behind me. Mr. Fauth, having reloaded, had pursued his wounded fox as it tried to escape. I heard the shot that finished it. Meanwhile the marine flushed a third, but out of range unfortunately. We happened to have bagged a male and a female, each a lovely specimen in reddish yellow; larger than our German fox, a compromise, in build of body and shape of head, between the Latin American coyote and the common red fox. I hoped our beauties would be given to enrich the zoological museum [of the Smithsonian Institution] in Washington.

We took seats in triumph on the wet grass and ate our hard ships' biscuit and salted meat—devoured them with as much satisfaction as if they were pheasant and fresh white bread.

The fog held until nearly 3:00 P.M. When it dispersed at last, we saw before us, nearby, one of our boats out to fish, the crew only now eating the midday meal. Anyone can readily understand that we welcomed a pan of fresh fish added to our frugal lunch.

Fog during the following days cloaked everything. Leaving Hakodate, we had to anchor in the Strait of Sangar for more than two hours. Such fogs commonly occur here in May, June, and July; strong east winds typically announce and accompany them. Yet, all things considered, I declare the climate around Hakodate salubrious. I saw many healthy old people; let them evidence my claim.

We went back to Shimoda by the same course we had followed out: around Cape Sirija-Saki [Shiriya].

Aboard the Mississippi
28 June 1854

At noon on the seventh of this month we reentered the Bay of Shimoda—to find the town much livelier than during our first visit. For, in the meantime, the imperial councilors had returned from Edo and, as is the Japanese custom, brought with them an enormous retinue. It had taken up quarters in every part of the little town; each member had planted his colors at his door, and with these many flags and standards brightening everything, the place looked brisk and bustling.

Time-consuming negotiations followed, over weights and measures both sides could use, over the value of our money, over prices for wood, water, food, and so forth. Agreement must be reached—the results drawn up into a table—and it took time, because each day brought new difficulties. Everything ended happily, all problems solved, at last.

The commodore's final official meeting with the imperial councilors occurred on the fifteenth. We put ashore about three hundred men and four cannon; in glitter and pomp, everyone paraded to the meeting.[7] A scene of rare drama unfolded in the beautiful setting of the pleasant town amid picturesque mountains. Vivid and memorable groups moved along the street from the waterfront to the place of the ceremony: Shimoda Dio-Rengo, the main temple.

The ceremony so resembled the prior one that I should not trouble you with the description again. I also confess I was fed up with Japanese treats and entertainments. So I left the temple for the open air as soon as possible and relieved the officer in charge of the cannon. He, far more than I, wanted to get at the delights that crowded those tables. To me, God's outdoors offered far more pleasure and comfort.

The cannon had been drawn up in the shade of a group of beautiful trees. Three-quarters of the people of Shimoda, including many lovely young women, attended to the band's cheerful music. In the monotony of the sailor's life, chances are slim for gallantry toward the fair sex; therefore I seized this one. I had brought sweets and fine pastries from the banquet; when I shared them, gifts came to me in return: flowers and fruit. When I tried to put the same flowers into a pretty one's hair—or in fun, toss the fruit to another— flowers and fruit rebounded to me with interest. Thus I spent the time laughing and joking and much more agreeably than indoors at one of the ceremony's unpleasant tables.[8] When at last the drums called us back to station at the guns, I had enough problems rounding up my artillerymen. For they, too, had seized the chance to impress the ladies. Needless to say, despite the high jinks, nothing exceeded the limits of decency and decorum.

To conclude, we staged miniature maneuvers. The speed and precision of our artillery fire, and of our infantry exercises, evoked from the Japanese the maximum of admiration and applause.[9]

A few days later the commodore repaid his Japanese hosts with a farewell banquet aboard the *Mississippi*. She had been restored as flagship to the commodore eight days before, and I, therefore reassigned, had spent them aboard her. Our Japanese friends expressed their heartfelt regret to see us leave.

We had buried a marine and a sailor in Korsaki, and the commodore now sent me ashore one last time, on the twenty-fourth, to make a drawing of the graves. The sailor had slipped from the mainyard of the *Powhatan* and died of the fall. We lay in the Bay of Edo when brain fever claimed the marine. He, as I have mentioned, went to a temporary grave in Yokohama until the signing of the treaty. Then two sergeants, sent back on a Japanese junk, exhumed his body, put it into another coffin, brought it back to Shimoda, and reinterred it for good. As instructed I took along two of his messmates. We found the grave marked with a gray limestone of uncommonly neat workmanship. Graves and surroundings—a cemetery under beautiful trees—created a pleasant impression but also dignified.

The same day, in the afternoon, we sailed to the edge of the roads and anchored again. There our Japanese friends paid the last visit. They brought many of us little gifts as mementoes. I do not recall whether I have mentioned the cordiality between me and Gohara Isabura, the prefect's (or bungo's) lieutenant, a likeable, well-educated man, not yet thirty years old. He spoke Dutch with considerable fluency, and diligent study had advanced him notably in English. He had shown me much kindness and done me many favors. Now, in some measure of return, I gave him my big Streit atlas, which he prized.[10] I also gave him a Dutch-English dictionary and with it a little poem in German and an English translation of it.

> When your eye, dear friend, shall rove about these pages,
> Where all the Earth is plain to one quick glance,
> And your thoughts flash across oceans far and wide,
> To the other peoples of this grand and spacious world—
> Then think in friendship of him who gave this gift,
> Who came without notice, stayed a while, and disappeared!
> As the chain's each link clasps the other,
> So my people take yours by the hand.
> Think of me, therefore, as I here take leave of you,
> And may your Godspeed be mine when now I sail away.[11]

When Gohara said good-bye, he brought me gifts in return: a handsome, opulent tobacco pipe with companion pouch and a tea canister artistically crafted and inlaid with mother-of-pearl. He too had written a poem and accompanied the Japanese verses with a Dutch translation. They would sound odd were I to transcribe them literally, so I shall try in some degree to suggest their poetry thus:

> When through the crowns of pines the evening breezes rustle,
> And from your golden pipe curl little clouds of blue,
> Then take in hand a few of these green leaves
> And brew in the pot a drink of spicy good taste.
> One sip shall set your mind at ease,

But call your man, that he hand you a second, forthwith;
How fine it tastes upon the tongue, how it ennobles the heart,
What peace of mind it brings!
O tasty leaf that yields so much refreshment,
Let me be remembered as the one who gave these gifts![12]

—Gohara Isabura, to W. Heine, Farewell

The handsome gifts and the little poem's happy sentiment so pleasantly surprised me that I cannot help mentioning the incident.

On the twenty-fifth a stiff sou'wester bounced us around on our exposed anchorage. We must be patient and await fair skies, however, for the commodore still wanted to take soundings among the islands. Good weather arrived on the twenty-sixth. At dawn on the twenty-seventh we said good-bye to the shores of Japan, long in ill repute as inhospitable.

Thus our expedition must be considered finished. I cannot refrain from a brief statement by way of summing up. Why did we come? To what extent did we get what we wanted?

The United States sent a naval expedition to Japan to ensure that in the event of mishap American ships would receive aid and protection on those treacherous coasts; furthermore, that American ships in need of essentials could get water, wood, coal, and provisions; and that, if possible, at least one port [in the North Pacific] be secured between California and China, where the United States could erect a coaling station. Commodore Perry, one of the most distinguished officers ever to serve in the American navy, led the awe-inspiring armada to what had been one of the least accessible nations on earth. He presented his credentials to the emperor [through the emperor's representatives], together with a letter from the president; he compelled negotiations by virtue of a steadfast determination and a sober rationality simultaneously applied; and he achieved more than we had thought possible—without resorting to force.[13] Our shipwrecked mariners would get aid and protection now, regardless where they were wrecked in the Japanese empire. The ports of Shimoda, Hakodate, Naha, and a fourth (we could take up to a year to choose it) were open to American ships. Japanese pilots would guide them to a secure anchorage for a reasonable fee. Wood, water, food of all kinds, and enough coal would be provided in exchange for cash or goods. And Americans were to be allowed anywhere inside a ten-nautical-mile radius of the four cities. We also had buried our dead with Christian rites, while Buddhist priests mingled their prayers with ours. An American railroad, telegraph, and other machines had been put into operation on Japanese soil and aroused admiration and applause; and a law, at this moment being drafted by the imperial council, shall permit Americans to instruct the Japanese in the application and use of these practical contrivances. Japanese gifts in return loaded one of our storeships; it could barely hold them all. And the Japanese have promptly sent respectful letters in answer to the letter from the President of the United States.[14]

I have nothing to add to the bare facts; they speak for themselves. I need not raise my poor voice in praise of Commodore Perry; he has himself inscribed his name in history, in golden letters. I paid him the affection and respect due my commanding officer. And now I stand in awe. He compels my admiration.

CHAPTER SEVENTEEN

LAST CALL

AT LOO CHOO

The Island of Oshima—An Uncertain Rendezvous at Sea.—Return to Naha.—
Discord.—A Murder.—Legal Proceedings.—The Commodore and the Regent.—
Celebration of the Fourth of July.—A Penal Colony.—Dr. Moreton.—Departure
from Loo Choo.

In the Bay of Naha, July 1854

A F E W things remained to be settled at Loo Choo in connection
with the depot and the coaling station to be erected there. The
commodore accordingly decided on the return to Hong Kong to
call at Loo Choo one last time.

We intended to establish the facts on the geographical situation of
Oshima, the island about three hundred miles north of Loo Choo.
Therefore we hove to, lay for nearly a day, and landed two boats.
This effort would crown an endeavor that had been as difficult as it
had been important. For, from Formosa, a chain of islands stretches
along the coast of China and up to the southwestern point of Japan.
Until now, lacunae flawed the maps, and groups of islands had been
represented wrong. Consequently we, the ships of the Japan expedition, had taken various courses [among the islands], and the commodore himself had gone with the flagship a different way each
time. Data thus gathered could be assembled and collated, and fuller
and better results obtained than from all prior studies. Indeed, this
coastal survey at Oshima would be our last in these waters. This
island, after Loo Choo the most important in the group, constituted a benchmark; the observations and measurements could be
taken from shore.

The principal island affords a pleasant view: wooded in some places, productively cultivated in many others, and mountainous overall. Because of the narrow entrance, ships—at least those of the largest class—unfortunately use with difficulty the harbor at the island's north end. The inhabitants resemble those of Loo Choo; the two peoples practice almost identical customs and agriculture. Our boats returned with vegetables, including beans, radishes, and yams, among others. Toward evening we resumed our journey.

The *Southampton* left us in the morning and headed straight for Hong Kong. The *Mississippi* and the *Powhatan* meanwhile proceeded to Naha.

The same afternoon, immediately as we began to steam north in the channel between the islands of Endermo and Loo Choo, a foreign sail appeared, driving south toward us before the wind. Then, suddenly changing course about four miles away, the foreigner tried to round Endermo's western point. We of the *Mississippi* changed course. Drawing near, we fired a shot, and another, both ignored. The gun, readied at once to let go a third, this time would have put a ball through the foreigner's canvas. But he hove to—abruptly—and showed British colors. We hove to, in turn, at about half the range of the gun and lowered a boat in search of an explanation. She was the *Great Britain*, out of Shangai for London, with tea and silk. She had taken us for the Russian [Pacific] squadron and tried to escape. The captain sent us newspapers, and we got our first word that the English-French-Russian war [the Crimean War] had indeed broken out. No wonder the weak merchant vessel tried to elude us! A half-million-dollar cargo would have been too tasty a morsel for the enemy to have easily let slip through his clutches.

The *Lexington* had already left Shimoda for Naha in May, and now we arrived in Naha the morning of 30 June. We mingled again with the good-natured islanders but—for the first time—on other than the friendliest of terms.

Let me explain. I said on a prior page that during our second sojourn in Japan two officers and a few sailors had stayed in Loo Choo to guard our coal and other things left behind at our station. Soon after we had departed, the islanders began to exhibit a palpable mistrust [of those men] and to behave [toward them] with considerable reserve but without notable perturbation at first. When the Russian squadron called at Naha in April, its personnel did not deal directly with the local people but turned to our men. They helped them as much as they could, especially to buy the fresh fruit and vegetables the Russians sorely lacked. Our men also guided the Russian officers on brief walking tours. In short our men tried, in comradely fashion, to make things pleasant for the Russians while they stopped here. The Russian admiral [Eyfemii Vasilevich] Putiatin (if I am not mistaken) extended his warmest thanks and twice sent his band ashore [to play] on separate evenings.[1] The Russians soon went their way, whereupon tiffs began between our men and the local people. Complaints by our men followed, first to the prefect of Naha, later to the regent of Loo Choo himself.

Presently the *Lexington* arrived. One day, when a *Lexington* boat landed, its men went into Naha and quarreled in the marketplace with local people over the price of food. The quarrel ended in a brawl. Now I have mentioned the young interpreter Yusizado on a prior page and that a temple served as our billet here. Into it he stormed the evening of the brawl [12 June]. He asked one of our officers, Mr. B., to accompany him to the inner harbor: "An American sailor has drowned." Arrived there, our party did indeed find at water's edge the body of a sailor off the *Lexington*.[2] They prepared to carry it away, local people tried to stop them, but our party prevailed. An autopsy discovered three wounds to the head, of a kind caused by punches or blows. Local people ascribed them to a fall from the pier into the water. Evidence showed that the deceased had taken no part in the altercation; at that moment he had been on the opposite side of the river. Moreover, everyone knew him to be quiet, even-tempered, and peaceable. But, lacking proof positive of murder, a panel of *Lexington* officers ruled "death by unknown causes."

There the matter rested until we arrived. The commodore, having gotten reports, hurried a vehement message to the regent, urging that the city investigate. Local officials, now as on earlier occasions, tried every which way to duck it. Nothing worked; they were given three days to catch the criminals. This ultimatum got things moving. Investigations began. At the end of the three days, the prefect or hadji-madji of Naha came aboard. Yes, the sailor had been murdered. Could he, the prefect, have another three days to apprehend the murderers? We balked for a while, then he got his three days but with a stipulation. If these three end in nothing, the commodore himself would take over and devote every effort to the problem. To stiffen this warning, a captain and a detachment of marines were assigned to our station; and except for essential official messages, the strictest prohibitions blocked every communication with the countryside.

Things began to hum! Diligent investigations, arrests, and hearings took place. At the hearings the judges sat at the upper end of the courtroom, and next to them a clerk, keeping some sort of record. (Officers of ours were there; they told me what happened.) The individual in question answered from the other end of the room. A beadle flanked him on either side, each holding a pointed stick. The questioned must hold his hands above his head the entire time. Should he hesitate to answer, be it ever so slight, the beadles jabbed him in the ribs—a unique and foolproof way to make somebody talk.

Then it was the morning of the last day of grace. We were readying a sizeable force (two cannon had already been sent ashore) when a pair of large boats, one carrying the regent of Loo Choo, came out to our ship. He and his bigwigs were received with cold politeness and taken before the commodore. The regent reported that four men guilty of the lethal battery had been apprehended and that the ringleader would be handed over for punishment. Even as the regent talked, the criminal himself, escorted by four bailiffs, was being brought aboard from the second boat.

(I believe I have mentioned on a prior page [not included in this translation] the striking resemblance between a Chinese tailor in Queen's Road in Hong Kong and another tailor I knew in the Scheffelgasse in Dresden. I must likewise note here that—be they in cocked hats, spiked helmets, white constabulary caps, Chinese pigtails, Japanese bald pates, or, as here in Loo Choo, metal hairpins—policemen all over the world seem to belong to the same physiological family.) One of them held the criminal fast on a leash. The ship's provost marshal, sword drawn, took him and led him below. Hands and arms bound to his sides, walking his last mile, shivering, the poor devil looked devastated yet managed on the whole to be steady enough.

The regent spared no pains to right himself in the commodore's eyes. He blamed the delay on the prefect of Naha. "He gave me false reports. He has been stripped of his office. He has been disgraced. Commodore, punish the ringleader. Don't make the nation suffer for one man's crime."

After this *pater peccavi* the commodore moderated his stern tone.[3] "What is the punishment for murder in your law?"

"Exile for life," the regent said, "on an island that serves as a penal colony."

"Then take the criminal back. Punish him according to your law. Our country does not want revenge, only the strict administration of justice." The commodore pointed to the *Powhatan,* where a court martial sat at that moment. "See the blue flag at the foremast? It means, when it goes up and a gun is fired, that our court is in session. Any of our people found guilty in connection with that quarrel shall not escape the punishment provided by law. That's for sure."

This short speech seemed to make a deep impression. Every local person present, even the regent, threw himself to the ground and touched his forehead to it. All seemed to breathe easier. They tried, in one way or another, to express their gratitude. The prisoner especially seemed elated to be returned to the authorities ashore; his face and bearing stated how he felt.

After this incident, harmony reigned undisturbed. Indeed, a treaty, subsequently signed, served in its apt form as the basis for the agreement with Japan.[4] Thus the harbor of Naha has become ours as a port of entry for trade, and the trade no longer subject to restrictions. Should disputes occur or the law be broken, the parties shall be delivered each to their own authorities for legal action, and punishment likewise administered. The little cemetery of earlier mention in these pages shall remain in perpetuity a place of burial for all Christian foreigners. Any American shall enjoy free movement anywhere in these islands without the government's regarding him as a spy and without official interference. The local people behaved with less reserve after the signing, and we could buy without difficulty any little thing from the craftsmen and the merchants and at the public market.

On July fourth, the birthday of the United States, we staged an appropriate celebration on the *Mississippi:* flags and apt slogans on the quarterdeck and at the forecastle; a plain and homely speech to the assembled officers and men by our senior quartermaster; his reading of the Declaration of Independence; and the beautiful national anthem, "The Star-Spangled Banner," sung by another quartermaster with the assembly joining in the chorus, one and all.

Those events took place between 11:00 and noon. At the stroke of noon all our cannon together fired a salute to the birthday of our flag. Next a double ration of grog for the crew. Items distributed with largesse at the midday meal included some that had been stashed for six months—here and there even a bottle of wine, brought to light from the depths of a trunk. Individuals with will-power had kept them hid; for, as nothing new had gone into our private "cellars" since we left China, a state of depletion had pre-vailed there for a long time. How fortunate for me on this occasion to be able to present not only two bottles of madeira but a bundle of fine Manila cigars—in those circumstances an effusion of riches!

Two days before we left Loo Choo the commodore gave still another farewell banquet for Loo Choo's regent. Our "Ethiopian minstrels" put on an evening of theatrical entertainment afterward. The guests seemed well pleased—they laughed a lot—but why? Per-haps even they did not know. At any rate, they relished the refresh-ments, liquid and solid, served during the show. Champagne, pro-nounced "sampan" here, seemed to be their favorite drink. A wise government stateside had laid in our holds a supply of the juice of the Épernay grape. On this occasion only the most distinguished guests could enjoy it, however, because the Japanese had tried many times to civilize themselves with it, impoverishing our stocks. Lesser individuals must therefore take pot luck now among a variety of other wines, punches, and liquors.

Our band played dance music during and after the meal. Sud-denly the idea hit me: Take one of these lords of the realm by the arm and waltz him around the quarterdeck two or three times. I do not know where this idea came from, but His Excellency nonethe-less ventured for the first time into the province of Terpsichore. He contented himself to hold fast to me, and he weighed little, so I whirled him about with ease to the amusement of the esteemed guests looking on. My white-bearded "lady," offended not at all by my taking such liberty, relished the glass of punch and the pastry that I, in the manner of a grand cavalier, presented to "her" at the end of our number.

I have yet to mention an interesting excursion among the islands of Loo Choo. Several lie west of Naha, across the water about eight or nine miles: low islands and sandbars often scarcely visible in heavy seas or at high tide. The commodore, desiring that a closer look be taken at them, dispatched the cutter and a smaller boat. The *Mississippi*'s gunner commanded one, I the other. On our way before dawn, we reached the first island before 8:00 A.M. We took soundings all around, found the water too shallow near shore, anchored the cutter a half-mile out, went in with the smaller boat, and followed a channel that bisected the island at high tide. Mr. B., left behind to command our station at Naha [when we went to Japan], had from there undertaken several expeditions himself during that six months. He arrived one day to find nine or ten women who (he was told) lived in exile on this island. We had been ordered to learn the particulars of their situation during this visit. Accordingly we divided into two parties, one to circle the island's south side, one the north.

Every inch of its length added up to about a mile and a half. Width? A half-mile at most. Except for a ribbon of sandy beach, thick brush covered everything. The channel [at high tide] cut off the western end or about a third of the island's length, but at low tide the channel could be crossed with dry feet. A reef, also dry at ebb, surrounded the island with about a half-mile of coral.

Our parties met at the other end. Having found no trace of habitation, we formed ourselves into a line [across the island] and again traversed the length, through the brush. A most difficult enterprise, the growth being so rank. Holly, pandanus, aloe, and artemesia asserted a thick, almost impenetrable mass; we could only hack our way with knives [or machetes]. At last, near the channel, we discovered four or five miserable huts, hidden deep in the bush and half buried in the ground. Each had beside it an earthenware tank, also half-buried, holding about fifty to sixty gallons of water. There were outdoor fireplaces. Broken cups and the remains of potatoes showed that the place had been lived in. A careful search convinced us that, as of the moment, not one person remained on the island.

We sent several men back in the smaller boat while we took the cutter farther west to a second island very much like the first. We searched it in the same way and found identical huts and eight or nine women. At the sight of us they fled in terror. Conversely, a few men approached us from fishing boats near shore. They accepted a little gift of ship's biscuit and tobacco, in return gave us a few fish, and grew friendlier. It seemed to me the men had brought food and water for the women; we had spied not a hint of those essentials on any of the islands. Perhaps the people in fact were fisher folk who lived on one of the islands.

But why would anyone choose a home whither even the water must be hauled ten or twelve miles? In Naha, when I asked our interpreter about this miniature Botany Bay, the evasive answers convinced me all the more that the island was indeed a penal colony.[5] The people of Loo Choo do not suffer adultery, as everybody knows. Nor do they permit capital punishment. Therefore I think it likely that those female exiles were convicted adulteresses. Why did we find the first island deserted? The second, like the first, has a coral reef around it. When Mr. B. visited the first, the convicts were perhaps transferred to the second.[6]

We returned to where we had stopped at the first and anchored the cutter outside the reef in order to walk on its coral, high and dry, to shore. Meanwhile several fishing boats had landed. Men had been left with them. We exchanged tobacco and biscuit for fish, a tolerable meal. But we would enjoy neither convenience nor comfort. The heat grew so oppressive in the bushes, and the mosquitoes and stinging flies swarmed in such clouds there, that we preferred to pitch on the beach a tent of one of our sails: a little shelter from the blazing sun. Exile in this wretched wilderness certainly seemed to me the equal of death as a capital punishment.

The islands' only permanent dwellers appeared to be flocks of wild pigeons. I shot a good many and took them back to my boat.

Dr. Bettelheim had abandoned his Naha mission after eight years. Beginning with our initial call he had always done us kind service as interpreter and as agent in the purchase of provisions.[7] His successor, Dr. [E. H.] Moreton, will replace him permanently: a modest, gentle young man, here since April with wife and child. Dr. Bettelheim had arrived under severe circumstances and been forced long to struggle against the insurmountable suspicion of the local people. Only in the last days had he been allowed to preach and been heard with forbearance. His family had already gone to Shanghai with the *Supply* at the end of March. He followed now [with us] in the *Powhatan*.[8] Leaving Naha for this our last time, we saw Dr.

Moreton and his people waving farewell. In truth we all regretted not only leaving those dear folks behind but saying good-bye to a place so often a hospitable port, where we had so liked to call.

Officers and men of the *Mississippi,* the *Powhatan,* and the *Lexington* had taken up among themselves a collection of several hundred dollars.[9] They gave it to Dr. Moreton for his mission, with a multitude of other things that might be of use to him and his family in their isolation, their loneliness.

CHAPTER EIGHTEEN

HOMEWARD BOUND!

A Sad Good-Bye.—Setting Out for Home.—Once More in Shimoda.—Good
Results of the Treaty. — A Young Lady Plays the Zither. — Mild Climate. —
[Good-Bye at Last].

On Board the Mississippi
At sea, October 1854

ON THE twelfth of last month Commodore Perry said farewell
to us. Accompanied by Lieutenant Bent, he left for home via
the Isthmus of Suez and Europe. What a sorrowful separation, especially for me. I had spent nearly two years in close company and intimate association with the beloved commander-in-chief. He had
become a second father to me, and now for the first time [on this
expedition] I must go to sea without him and without my dear
friend Lieutenant Bent. How I should have liked to accompany
them and with them to have seen the fields of my homeland [Ger-
many] once more!

But my situation [as official artist of the expedition] meant that I
take the longer way home, on the *Mississippi,* across the Pacific to
New York. All my [ornithological and other] collections, all my
paintings and drawings, now aboard her, must be organized and finished. Even on that extended voyage it would be all I could do to
complete the task before we reached the United States. We were to
call at the Sandwich Islands, California, Panama, Valparaiso, and
Robinson's famous island, Juan Fernández.[1] People would be cele-
brating Christmas at home and we probably rolling and pitching in
the Straits of Magellan. And then up the east coast of the Americas,
via Rio de Janeiro and the Gulf of Mexico, to New York—a long,
long voyage home, about twenty thousand miles. Indeed, after we
had negotiated the huge Pacific and reached San Francisco, we

173

would be as far from where we were going [New York] as whence
we had come, Hong Kong. Much beauty awaited me, therefore,
and many an interesting thing or a fascinating experience to be
exploited.

The day of the commodore's departure, 12 September 1854, I
too separated from various friends made here [Hong Kong]. In all
probability, indeed, I said good-bye forever. I spent the last evening
in the home of brave and worthy countrymen, Herr Meier and Herr
Scheffer.[2] On the morning of the thirteenth the *Mississippi* left China
to begin the voyage home.

"Homeward bound!"—a phrase to please every sailor.[3] As his
keel cuts the broad seas inch by inch, the distance lessens between
him and wife, child, relatives, and friends. He watches the weather
impatiently, he welcomes every favorable wind joyfully, and to
reduce the time between now and reunion, he hoists every scrap of
canvas.

My mood (I must admit, unfortunately) did not exactly match
that exuberance. True, I had joined the expedition with the enthusiasm of a youth thirsty for knowledge. The expedition had succeeded, and I deserved a modest but nonetheless worthy share of
the credit. But when the enterprise ended happily, my interest
largely vanished. I had longed for this moment; yet, on the verge of
it, with everything nearly done, I almost regretted the end in sight.
The time had practically come when I must look elsewhere for occupation. To my good fortune now, however, I had yet to do an honorable duty, and the obligation comforted me. That is, a long interval stretched ahead, of the agreeable, satisfying, rewarding work
with my assembled abundance. I had sown but given not a thought
to the golden harvest.

Now we must call at Japan a third time. The *Susquehanna* and the
coal-laden storeship *Supply* preceded us. At noon on the twenty-
third, with nothing more of interest occurring meanwhile, we
anchored in the Bay of Shimoda, to find both ships there. On the
twenty-sixth the *Susquehanna* left us again, for the Sandwich Islands,
our next stop.

Shimoda this time looked in many respects very different from
the Shimoda we had seen earlier. The retinues and soldiers had disappeared; no abundance now of them that had come from Edo with
the councilors. And then Shimoda's inhabitants had returned to

their usual way of life. Moreover, our putting in an appearance had lost the charm of novelty; we no longer constituted an object of their gross and often onerous curiosity; and our presence in houses did not cause confusion among the dwellers. Yet I believe I can rightly assume that the people were glad to see us again. Thus we could already witness the abundant results of Commodore Perry's intelligent and moderate procedure. We had done more than overcome the Japanese. We had made them our friends.

During our last call I had met numbers of local people. Many recognized me now. What a delight, their warm welcome! Many called to me on the streets. Others invited me into their homes and plied me with tea and pastry of every sort. Fellow officers met the same reception. The old priest, the one whose temple Mr. Brown and I had used as a studio, could scarcely tell me often enough how sad he had been when we left.

We saw notably better goods to be bought this time than in times past. Two large trader junks, arriving from Edo while we lay in the harbor, delivered many items for sale, including a great lot of superbly handsome lacquerware. Shops had nearly doubled in number in the interval; shopkeepers' profits from us had obviously quickened the entrepreneurial spirit. Prices at the same time had dropped as competition increased. Only let enough American ships visit the ports we have opened, and the Japanese get used to trade with us, and both sides (I feel sure) will enjoy a brisk trade.

Visiting many homes, I became more and more familiar with local customs. I met universally a deep desire to learn the English word for every last thing. As a result many people besides the interpreters have grown notably more fluent in our language. Already most shopkeepers make themselves understood quite well. Prices are in *cash* [the local unit of exchange] but nearly every shopkeeper quotes them in English.

One day, strolling through the streets, I saw a young blind woman playing one of those three-stringed zithers I described on a prior page: an instrument with an ususually long neck; plucked not with the fingers but with a small piece of wood like a wide but stubby painter's knife; and the upper and lower strings pitched in the eighth chord, the middle string in the fifth. The compositions—music entirely in flat—combined snatches of rhapsody that would vanish in sudden retreats to shrill regularity. Unknown to the blind lady-musician I stood a long time and listened to her remarkably odd interpretations. At last some women came by who told her about me. She broke into bitter tears and would hear nothing to comfort her.

On another occasion I heard a young man play one of the flutes, the rather primitive instrument with big finger holes and large mouthpiece. Again very simple renditions, little more than runs up and down the scale, sometimes without connection of one run to another.

Our call coincided with the new moon. Therefore I could observe a singular form of divine worship, performed in most homes, by the women, at the altar of the household god. Each woman holds a small metal dome in her left hand and a small wooden hammer [in her right]. The women form two groups; and these alternate—now one, now the other—in a monotonous chant, while the women accompany themselves with regular beats of hammer on dome.

Only the chilly and windy twenty-fourth and twenty-fifth deviated from the mild and pleasant weather, the warm and sunny days, that prevailed now. The bitterness of winter seems scarcely known here. We had arrived the first time in April to a lush, green world. When we left [for this, the last time] at the end of September, the landscape beamed, happier and more verdant than ever. The second crop of rice verged on harvest. (The first had been harvested as early as the beginning of June.) We tasted all sorts of delicious fruit, such as pears, apples, persimmons, and even grapes. The grapes, however, were somewhat costly; they had been brought from Kiu-Siu.

When we left Shimoda this time, three new graves had been added to the American cemetery, [the third being] Dr. Hamilton off the transport *Kennedy*.[4] He had taken passage as an invalid in the *Susquehanna,* died at sea, and was buried there.

On October first, at 2:00 P.M., we weighed anchor. I said farewell to Japan. In all likelihood, forever.[5]

Homeward Bound!

1540s

Japanese ships have gone as far as India and perhaps America's northwest coast, but Japan and the West know little of each other. Shipwrecked Portuguese, followed by other European merchants and traders, land in the feudal Japan of a weak emperor unable to control quarreling warlords.

1549

Francis Xavier and other Jesuits begin work in Japan. By 1579 they will claim to have converted a hundred thousand Japanese.

1600

The Tokugawa shoguns come to power; they will rule for the next 250 years or so before abdicating in 1868. During this time Christians are persecuted and foreigners driven out except the Dutch, who are restricted to Deshima and a few enclaves on the main islands.

1791

The *Lady Washington* (Captain Kendrick) and the *Grace* (Captain Douglas), American traders, visit Japan. They offer sea otter pelts but are refused. American ships will fly the Dutch or the British flag when calling at Japan until 1837.

1797

The *Eliza,* the first American ship to dock in Japan, arrives under Dutch charter.

1811

Captain Vasilii Golovnin, in the Russian sloop-of-war *Diana,* surveys the Kurile Islands and then begins several years of incarceration in Japanese prisons.

1825

The Japanese issue *shinron,* the edict against foreigners: death to any seeking to land, destruction of their ships, "smash the barbarians whenever they come in sight."

1827

Peter Bernhard Wilhelm Heine is born near Dresden, Saxony, 30 January.

1836

Edmund Roberts, appointed by President Jackson in 1832, heads the Embassy to the Eastern Courts and concludes the first American treaty with Siam, but dies before he can do the same with Japan.

1837

The *Morrison* is fired on while trying to land missionaries and return shipwrecked Japanese. This driving-off of a private vessel flying the American flag so touches a nerve in the United States that "the subject of opening up [Japan] was never suffered to drop out of sight."

1838

Captain Charles Wilkes commands the century's greatest scientific expedition of exploration to the Pacific and the South Seas, returning in 1843.

1839

Aaron Haight Palmer, director of the American and Foreign Agency (commission agents in overseas trade), after securing from the Republic of Central America a concession for an Isthmian canal, begins to study Asian markets and launches his campaign to open Japan to American commerce.

1841

John Quincy Adams favors Britain in the Opium War. According to Adams, it is a war against Oriental despotism, which demands the lives and property of the English and Americans: "The cause of the war is the *kotow!*" Adams "urged the right, and even the duty, of Christian nations to open the ports of Japan, and the duty of Japan to assent on the ground that no nation has a right more than any man has to withdraw its private contribution to the welfare of the whole."

1843

The *Manhattan* is repelled at Edo Bay while trying to return shipwrecked Japanese.

1844

Caleb Cushing, first American commissioner to China, signs the Treaty of Wanghia, resulting in China's opening of five ports and granting other trade concessions to the United States. Later, at his own suggestion, Cushing will receive from Secretary of State John C. Calhoun " 'full power' to treat with the Japanese."

1845

The Pratt resolution in Congress urges President Tyler to open trade and secure friendship with Japan and Korea, February.

Secretary of State James Buchanan authorizes U.S. Commissioner to China Alexander H. Everett to negotiate a treaty with Japan, April.

The *Manhattan* (Captain Cooper) of Sag Harbor is met kindly but allowed to stay only a few days at Edo, 17 April. Commodore Perry will later consult Cooper on Japan.

1846

The whaler *Lawrence* (Captain Baker) of Poughkeepsie, wrecked in the Kuriles, gives up seven survivors to be imprisoned and one to be killed before repatriation through the Dutch at Deshima, May.

Bernard Jean Bettelheim, a Protestant missionary, arrives to begin work at Naha, Loo Choo, 1 May.

Senator John A. Dix of New York lays before the Senate a proposal for a mission to Japan, signed by presidents of marine insurance companies, shipbuilding firms, and firms manufacturing steam engines, 8 June. Dix will be Heine's commanding officer in the Civil War.

Commodore James Biddle and the *Columbus* and the *Vincennes* arrive at Edo Bay to request a treaty of amity and commerce, 20 July. This is an official attempt, using the navy, to establish relations and begin trade.

1848

Secretary of the Treasury Robert J. Walker says that Japan and its commerce, "separated but two weeks from our western coast, . . . can be secured to us by persevering and peaceful efforts."

The whaler *Lagoda* (Captain Brown) of New Bedford is wrecked on a shoal in the Sea of Japan. The Japanese confine and mistreat the survivors.

1849

Captain James Glynn arrives in the *Preble* for a week's conference at Nagasaki, securing release of the captives off the *Lagoda,* 17 April.

1851

Daniel Webster, President Fillmore's Secretary of State, sends Captain John H. Aulick to Japan to demand a treaty that will include permission to buy coal, "a gift of Providence deposited by the Creator of all things in the depths of the Japanese islands for the benefit of the human family." Aulick, recalled because of ill health and accusations that he abused his office, never reaches Japan.

1852

Steamships begin regular runs up the coast to San Francisco from the terminus of the newly completed Trans-Isthmian Railroad.

Matthew Calbraith Perry is named commander-in-chief, United States Naval Forces, East India, China and Japan Seas, 24 January. He receives written orders and begins eight months of preparation (24 March), traveling the eastern seaboard to learn of Japan, assembling equipment, and collecting gifts for the Japanese.

Perry arrives in Washington for final talks with Secretary of State Charles M. Conrad and Secretary of the Navy John P. Kennedy, September. He leaves Annapolis for Norfolk in the *Mississippi,* 8 November.

Edward Everett, the new secretary of state, drafts the letter from the president to Japan's emperor and sends it to President Fillmore, 13 November.

Perry, China bound, leaves Hampton Roads and heads across the Atlantic in the *Mississippi,* 17 November.

Perry in Madeira, 11–15 December.

1853

Perry in St. Helena, 10–11 January; Capetown, 24 January–3 February; Mauritius, 18–28 February; Ceylon, 10–15 March; Singapore, 25–29 March; Hong Kong, 7 April.

Samuel Wells Williams receives "a request from Commodore Perry to accompany him to Japan as interpreter," 9 April.

The *Plymouth,* the *Saratoga,* and the *Supply* join the *Mississippi* at Macao. The skeleton squadron moves to Shanghai, 28 April.

Perry transfers his command to the *Susquehanna* (10 May) before the squadron departs Shanghai, 16–17 May.

The *Mississippi* and the *Susquehanna* arrive at Naha, Loo Choo, 26 May; the *Supply* arrives, 28 May.

The regent of Loo Choo meets Perry aboard the *Susquehanna*, 30 May; a day later an exploring party is dispatched to gather information on Loo Choo.

Perry and a large escort, on parade to and fro, visit the royal palace, 6 June.

The *Mississippi* and the *Supply* remain at Naha while the *Susquehanna* and the *Saratoga* leave with Perry for the Bonin Islands, 9 June.

Commander Cadwalader Ringgold and five ships depart Hampton Roads on the United States Surveying Expedition to the Pacific, 11 June. They will return in 1856. Heine will later translate the expedition's report into German and expand it.

Perry arrives at Port Lloyd, Bonin Islands, 14 June.

Having returned from the Bonins, Perry leaves Naha, the *Susquehanna* towing the *Saratoga*, the *Mississippi* towing the *Plymouth* (2 July), and anchors off Uraga, Edo Bay, 8 July.

Perry goes ashore to present his credentials and Fillmore's letter at the Kurihama meeting house, 14 July.

Perry's men take soundings of Edo Bay, 9–16 July.

The squadron sails for China via Loo Choo, 17 July.

Perry tells the regent that Loo Choo must remain open to American use, 28 July.

Perry arrives at Hong Kong and prepares to winter there and at Macao; the *Vandalia*, the *Macedonian*, and the *Southampton* join him, August and September. He transfers his command back to the *Mississippi* (30 September) and then back to the *Susquehanna*, 19 December.

Storeship *Lexington* reaches Hong Kong with the printing press and gifts for the Japanese, 26 December.

1854

Word reaches Perry that Russia is trying to negotiate a treaty with Japan, early January. He will sail from Hong Kong via Loo Choo for Japan (14 January) and arrive with seven ships at Edo Bay (13 February), transferring his command to the *Powhatan*, 19 February.

The squadron—the *Mississippi*, the *Susquehanna*, the *Powhatan*, the *Vandalia*, the *Macedonian*, the *Lexington*, and the *Southampton*—assembles off Kanegawa, near Yokohama, 25 February.

Kanegawa is agreed on as the meeting place, 27 February; a meeting house is built, 7 March.

Negotiations open, 8 March.

Private Robert Williams, USMC, dead on the *Mississippi,* is buried ashore, 9 March.

Japanese gifts to the Americans are delivered, 13 March. Four days later Perry and the Japanese negotiators will agree on Shimoda as the port to be opened to American ships and trade.

American gifts to the Japanese are delivered, 24 March.

Having seen the shogun, the Japanese negotiators return from Edo and report to Perry that Shimoda and Hakodate will be opened, 26 March.

The "Ethiopian Minstrels" perform in blackface aboard ship to celebrate various occasions in several places off Japan, 26 March, 29 May, 22 June, 15 or 16 July.

The Minstrels entertain the Japanese negotiators at a party aboard the *Powhatan,* 27 March.

Shimoda is declared open, 28 March.

The Treaty of Kanegawa is signed, 31 March.

Commander Henry A. Adams leaves in the *Saratoga* for Washington with the treaty for ratification, 4 April.

Perry and the squadron approach Edo for a view of the capital, 10 April.

The *Macedonian* departs for the Bonins while the rest of the squadron heads for Shimoda and Hakodate, 18 April; Perry goes ashore at Hakodate (20 May) before departing, 3 June. He will return to Shimoda for final negotiations (7–8 June) before leaving Japan, 28 June.

Perry arrives in Naha, Loo Choo, to negotiate a treaty similar to the Treaty of Kanegawa, 1 July.

The Treaty of Naha is signed, 11 July.

The last ship of the squadron departs Naha, 17 July.

Perry arrives at Hong Kong (22 July), leaving for New York via Ceylon, Suez, and Europe, 11 September. He will arrive at The Hague and the home of his son-in-law August Belmont, the American ambassador to the Netherlands, 20 November.

Perry departs Liverpool, 30 December.

1855
Perry arrives at New York, 11 January.

The *Mississippi* arrives at New York via the Pacific with expedition records and memorabilia that Perry will use to compose his report and with Heine and his collections of art and natural history, 23 April.

1856
The *New York Times* reports that Heine's lecture on Japan "in the German course" at Clinton Hall was delivered "to an appreciative audience," 11 January. Later in the year Heine's memoir of the expedition (in German and Dutch editions) and the first volume of Perry's report, *Narrative of the Expedition of an American Squadron,* will be published. The second volume of Perry's report will appear in 1857, the third in 1858.

Heine becomes an American citizen in the New York Court of Common Pleas, 4 May.

1857
Perry finishes his work on the *Narrative,* 28 December.

1858
Perry dies, 4 March.

1859
Heine's memoir of the expedition is published in French. A second edition will appear in 1863.

Heine lectures before the Geographical Society of Berlin, 7 May. "Germans have gone around the world, to explore and trade, without protection or aid. Send the flag and guns after them, that they enjoy the rights and privileges befitting citizens of a great power."

1860
The Prussian East Asia Squadron arrives at Edo, 4 September. Heine, who has piloted the flagship *Arcona* into the bay, will spend five months in Japan, studying, photographing, painting, and drawing the land and the people, gathering material for his later books.

1861
Heine begins seven months in China, February.

He enters service as captain of topographical engineers, Army of the

Potomac, with the Maryland infantry, near Washington, D.C., December.

1862

Heine is taken prisoner in Richmond (30 June) and later exchanged, 15 August. A shoulder injury will cause him to resign his commission and seek treatment in Germany, 1 December.

1863

Heine returns to the United States to accept a colonelcy in the 103d New York, a German-speaking regiment, February. He will hold three commands before the end of the Civil War.

1865

Heine is breveted brigadier general, 13 March, mustered out, 17 March.

1865–1869

In Germany and the United States Heine works as an artist, illustrator, and teacher of art.

1869–1871

After joining the diplomatic corps Heine serves as a consular clerk in Paris and Liverpool.

1871–1885

Heine settles near Dresden, where he lectures, works as an artist and teacher, and publishes his last books.

1885

Heine dies where he has lived since 1871, in Lossnitz, near Dresden, 5 October.

NOTES

PREFACE

1. "The famous phrase of Robert Frost's—'Poetry is what gets lost in translation'—doesn't cover the situation. If something is lost, something is also recovered [of an original, universal language, an archetypal message]." Octavio Paz, quoted in Edwin Honig, *The Poet's Other Voice: Conversations on Literary Translation* (Amherst: University of Massachusetts Press, 1985), 154, 157.

INTRODUCTION

1. Quoted by Johnson, *Far China Station,* 42. See also Griffis, "Millard Fillmore and Japan," 71, and Doenhoff, "Biddle, Perry, and Japan," 80–81.

2. Taylor, *India, China and Japan,* 364.

3. King, *The Claims of Japan* 1:174–175, 179–180, cited by Sakamaki, "Western Concepts," 3, 7–8.

4. Palmer, *Documents and Facts,* 13.

5. Johnson, *Far China Station,* 45.

6. Morris, "Bamboo Curtain," 178–179.

7. On the changes of policy and the preparation to advance on Japan, see Rayback, *Millard Fillmore,* 293–315.

8. Guest, *Yedo,* 39.

9. Doenhoff, "Biddle, Perry, and Japan," 81; Rayback, *Millard Fillmore,* 315–316; and Dennett, *Americans,* 260–265.

10. F. Wells Williams, *Life and Letters,* 193.

11. Dennett, *Americans,* 262. On Perry's desire for a grand expansion into the Pacific basin, see ibid., 270–277. Perry's was the prophetic foresight to advocate "a doctrine of benevolent imperialism . . . still somewhat new for an American citizen." Dulles, *America in the Pacific,* 67.

12. "Japan. Commodore Perry's Expedition," *New York Tribune,* 4 Nov. 1853, 3.

13. "An act of . . . war": Hale, "When Perry Unlocked the Gate," 94. See also Cole, "Background to the Surveying Expedition in *With Perry in Japan,*" 3–5; and Dennett, *Americans,* 265–267. "Broke . . . arena": Redman, "New Editions," 63. Perry "brought [Japan] to agreement by a demonstration of power." Sansom, *Western World and Japan,* 277. The United States so craved this treaty that as soon as it was signed, Commander Henry A. Adams left Edo Bay with it for Washington as fast as sails and steam could carry him. The Senate ratified it immediately and unanimously, and Adams returned as fast as he had come. He carried, as an instrument of ratification, "one of the most elegant and costly documents ever to have emanated from the United States Government." As if a triumphant

nation lavished its joy on this proof of success, the ratification sported a binding of "stamped dark blue velvet. American eagle in center, surrounded by corner decorative motifs. 14¾ × 10½. Silver skippet with the Great Seal of the United States in relief. 5 inches in diameter. Silver metallic cords [and] enclosed in a gold-fitted, velvet-lined, rosewood box. . . . The bill of Samuel Lewis, Washington jeweler, was paid in August 1854 in the sum of $1,220.52." National Archives, *"Art" of Diplomacy*, 26.

14. Cole, Introduction to *Scientist with Perry*, xiv–xv; and Perry and Hawks, *Narrative* 1:75–76. See also Neumann, "Religion," 255–256 passim; and Griffin, *Clippers and Consuls*, 39.

15. On prejudice see Dower, *War Without Mercy*, 33, 60, 73, 145–146, 148–154. See also Horsman, *Race*, 1–2 passim. "Such phrases as the 'nobler principles' [and] the 'better life' of a 'higher civilization' [are mentioned throughout] the private records of the [Perry] expedition." Sansom, *Western World and Japan*, 277. The Japanese entertained equally profound racial prejudice toward Westerners. Dower, *War Without Mercy*, 239.

16. "Perry's attitude and action . . . give indications of the compelling influence that the concept of manifest destiny had upon American foreign policy." Borton, Review of *Narrative of the Expedition*, 626. See also Phillips, "Some Forces," 434–435; Griffin, *Clippers and Consuls*, 9–12; and excerpts from newspapers of the time in Greene, "The Japan Expedition," 92–104.

17. Coal, provisions, and good treatment for Americans are "our ostensible reasons" for "this great outlay and sending this powerful squadron." The "real reasons are glorification of the Yankee nation, and food for praising ourselves." F. Wells Williams, *Life and Letters*, 197.

18. "I am sure that the Japanese policy of seclusion is not in accordance with God's plan of bringing the nations of the earth to a knowledge of His truth, and, until it is broken up, His purposes of mercy will be impeded—for His plan is made known to us." Ibid., 192–193.

19. Phillips, "Some Forces," 440–441. See Palmer's own story in *Documents and Facts*.

20. Henderson, *Yankee Ships*, 220.

21. S. Wells Williams, *Journal*, 50.

22. Stuart, *Naval and Mail Steamers*, 36.

23. Perry, *Personal Journal*, 9.

24. Plath, "Pictures from an Exploration," 13.

25. Commission des sciences et arts, *Description de l'Égypte*, 21 vols.

26. Perry, *Personal Journal*, 6, 8. See also Perry and Hawks, *Narrative* 1:88–89.

27. Cole, Introduction to *Scientist with Perry*, vii, ix, xvi–xvii.

28. F. Wells Williams, *Life and Letters*, 195.

29. Hansen-Taylor and Scudder, *Life and Letters* 1:251. See also Perry and Hawks, *Narrative* 1:152.

30. Plath, "Pictures from an Exploration," 13.

31. Schiff, "More than 200 Years," 79. Cook set the pattern but did not begin the practice. A man in ship with Sir Francis Drake said that Drake "kept a book in which he . . . delineated birds, trees and sea lions." Drake also "carries painters

who paint for him pictures of the coast in its exact colors." Klinkenborg, "The West Indies," 92.

32. Hunt, "Artists of the Western Surveys," 57.

33. Lindsey, "Perry in Japan," 45–46.

34. "Japan. Commodore Perry's Expedition," *New York Tribune,* 4 Nov. 1853, 3.

35. Shimazaki, *Before the Dawn,* 96.

36. Ibid., 21.

37. Naff, Introduction to *Before the Dawn,* xi.

38. S. Wells Williams, *Journal,* 61.

39. Shimazaki, *Before the Dawn,* 22.

40. Taylor, *Japan in Our Day,* 21. "The Tycoon is their king. There is another chap somewhere to the west. The Mikado. We think he is a spiritual ruler. A pope, perhaps. But Yedo is the seat of government and we deal with the Tycoon's councillors." Sir Radley Ferrier to Pev Fitzpaine in Guest, *Yedo,* 61. On this confusion in national affairs and the uncertainty of leadership, see also Naff, Glossary, *Before the Dawn,* s.v. "shogun" and "Tokugawa"; Adams, *History of Japan* 1:106–107; Benedict, *Chrysanthemum and Sword,* 68–69, 125–127, 309; and Nitobe, *Intercourse between the United States and Japan,* 58–59.

41. "The Yedo government" of the shogun was "a usurpation" and "a sham." The mikado at Kyoto was "the only real and permanent source of authority." This "truth [was] not fully discovered until ten years later." Taylor, *Japan in Our Day,* 21. Tension between shogun and emperor had so increased that American interposition "saved the Empire from civil war." Griffis, *The Mikado,* 65.

42. Baba, *Japan* 1:5–8. For a discussion acknowledging and exploring the complexities between "exclusionists" and "accomodationists," see Beasley, *Select Documents,* 3–45 (esp. 5–25), 102–119. See also Adams, *History of Japan* 1:110–113. On artists and their scrolls, see Shaw, "Japanese Picture Scrolls," 136; and Perry and Hawks, *Narrative* 1:237. See chap. 7, nn. 14, 18 below on how the Japanese felt despite having met Perry and agreed to meet him again, and after an exchange of courtesies. "Perry in a memorable display of gunboat diplomacy kicked open Japan's closed door. The Japanese promptly sent a delegation of Samurai warriors to America, not to fight but to fathom the ways of the 'red-faced' foreigners. Present-day descendants of these early observers are still at it." Pfeiffer, "How Not to Lose the Trade Wars," 146. Japan asked itself such probing questions, subjected itself to such frank analysis, and reached such radical conclusions because at a "critical moment in their development," nations ask themselves: "What are we, and how can we fulfill our obligations to ourselves as we are?" Answers "differ in different situations, and the national character, which was thought to be immutable, changes with them." Paz, *Labyrinth of Solitude,* 9. The Black Ships produced the critical moment leading to imperial restoration in 1868. Japan, once inward-turning, turned outward and applied Western drill and tactics to expansion that ended in defeat in World War II. Today, as Pfeiffer notes, Japan wages war in a different way.

43. F. Wells Williams, *Life and Letters,* 211.

44. S. Wells Williams, *Journal,* 59, 60.

45. Lewis, in Graff, *Bluejackets*, 139.

46. F. Wells Williams, *Life and Letters*, 196.

47. Doenhoff, "Biddle, Perry, and Japan," 87.

48. F. Wells Williams, *Life and Letters*, 229, 231.

49. Heine's help seems probable. They worked at the American Bible Society in Astor Place. Heine lived at 48 Bible House, Astor Place, in 1856. Cowdrey, *Exhibition Record* 1:221.

50. Instances of the interpretations are scattered through the volumes. See for example 1:3–5, 75–79 (advancement-and-progress interpretation), 1:225 (oppression), 1:248 (intemperance), 1:398 ("great licentiousness"), 1:405 (economic injustice, lewdness), and 1:406 ("political intrigues of the Roman priesthood").

51. Hawks, Introduction to *Graphic Scenes*, no pagination.

52. On the influence of Oriental upon Western art, begun by the return of the Perry Expedition, see, for example, Roberta Smith, "When Japan Captured the French Imagination." *New York Times*, 7 Aug. 1988, sec. 2.

53. Heine, *Die Expedition*, ix–xi.

54. Heine, "Einleitung," 65–66.

55. Moore, "More about the Events," 82–85.

56. They and other letters form much of his military, diplomatic, and pension records in the National Archives.

57. "General Peter B. W. Heine," *Deutsche Pionier*, 48.

CHAPTER ONE

1. Alexander von Humboldt, to whom Heine dedicated this book, said in 1846 that Central American cultures originated in Asia. See Jairazbhoy, *Asians in Pre-Columbian Mexico*, 7–8; and Shao, *Origin of Ancient American Cultures*, v.

2. Marco Polo wrote about Cathay, a grand province of China, and about Zipangu, an island of great wealth and fabulous sights in the "eastern ocean." *Book of Marco Polo*, bk. 2, chaps. 1, 7, 17, 23 passim (Cathay) and bk. 3, chaps. 2, 3 (Zipangu). Columbus, seeking China and Japan, thought he had landed somewhere in the Indies. He impressed Caribbean natives to guide him to Zipangu and Cathay and followed them to Cuba. Morison and Commager, *American Republic*, 18.

3. The *Mississippi* as flagship would have been flying the "*broad pennant* or *bougee* at the main, in token that [she] carried a commodore—the highest rank of officers recognized in the American Navy." Melville, *White-Jacket*, 21 (chap. 6). The expedition was a long while preparing, and Heine able to catch it, because "the mismanagement in the equipment of the vessels" delayed their departure "more than nine months." Perry and Hawks, *Narrative* 1:77–78. Had preparations kept to schedule, Heine would have missed his adventure, the expedition have lost his services, and posterity be poorer without his visual and written record of this momentous event in Pacific affairs.

4. "An American commodore [the highest rank of officer recognized in the American navy], like an English commodore, or the French *chef d'escadre*, is but a

senior captain, temporarily commanding a small number of ships, detached for any special purpose." Melville, *White-Jacket,* 21–22 (chap. 6).

5. Heine has confused Perry with his brother Oliver Hazard Perry, the hero of Lake Erie.

6. Nobody could accompany the expedition "except in some naval capacity. Everybody has been refused. English noblemen, German barons, and American scholars have applied in vain." Bayard Taylor to his mother, 8 May 1853, *Life and Letters* 1:250. Perry did accept a few civilians, but some had to join the Navy, notably Heine and Taylor. See Perry and Hawks, *Narrative* 1:78–79.

7. The rank was *acting* master's mate perforce because it had been resurrected for the purpose of attaching artists and scientists to the expedition. Warranted mates remained obsolete. Rank and uniform were that of a passed midshipman, but pay—twenty-five dollars a month—less than half a midshipman's, was about enough for the mess bill. The rank had been left vacant for "artists and naturalists," that they "belong to the service and be under the control of its officers." Taylor says he joined Heine, Draper the telegraph engineer, and Brown the daguerreotypist. Portman the clerk and interpreter would soon follow as the fifth. The five constituted a separate mess with their own steward and cook. Taylor, *India, China and Japan,* 363. Perry and Hawks' *Narrative* lists twelve master's mates (2:414). The rank "imposed upon me no higher obligation in reality, than that of conforming in all respects to the etiquette of the service. I was attached to the corps of artists, who held the same rank, and were especially subject to the Commodore's orders; and when not employed on explorations—a branch of duty of which I was never weary—occupied myself with making sketches of birds, flowers, fish and landscapes, and with keeping a faithful record of our experiences. The fact that I messed on the orlop deck, went up and down the port ladders, and smoked forward of the main shaft, did not exclude me from the hospitalities of the ward-room and the commanders' cabins. . . . The only ship's duty I was called upon to perform, besides taking charge of a boat now and then, and keeping a two-hour watch in Japan, was to appear at 'general quarters,' which were beaten quite frequently previous to our arrival in the Bay of Yedo." Taylor, *India, China and Japan,* 457–458.

8. Buttoned to the throat, the blue jacket would display "eighteen gilded eagles and anchors." Taylor, *India, China and Japan,* 362.

9. Heine thus enacted Perry's assertion of "no room to spare after the proper officers of the vessels were accommodated. Scientific men, accustomed to the comfort of a shore life and abundant space for their instruments and books, would find themselves constantly annoyed by the confinement to narrow uncomfortable quarters." Perry, *Personal Journal,* 6. Heine was one of the "young and adventurous men" who would accept "those terms" of low pay, minimum prestige, and crowded conditions. Morison, Introduction to *Personal Journal,* xvi–xvii. Heine did get a permanent, custom-built studio after a while, proving that Perry wanted to advance knowledge as much as possible within the limits imposed by an expedition "altogether of a naval and diplomatic character." Perry, *Personal Journal,* 8.

10. "The dinner-table is the criterion of rank in our man-of-war world." All

ranks "respectively, dine together [each in its own mess], because they are respectively on a footing of equality." Melville, *White-Jacket,* 30 (chap. 6).

11. Perry spent from 31 July to 1 September on this "Down-East interlude." He learned the nature and extent of the problem, cautioned Yankee fishermen not to exceed limits imposed by the Anglo-American Convention of 1818, conferred with British and Canadian officials, and, successful, returned with "one more diplomatic mission to his credit." Morison, *"Old Bruin,"* 280–282.

12. Trinity's "famous notes" began when "the first 'Ring of Bells', a gift from London, was received in 1797." Others were added later. Federal Writers' Project, *New York City Guide,* 311.

13. A "new, and in this country untried, plan had been adopted" in the construction or arrangement of the *Princeton*'s boilers. "The experiment caused the expedition the loss of a year." Indeed, the *Princeton* "never formed part of the squadron"; the *Powhatan* "was substituted for her." Perry and Hawks, *Narrative* 1:78.

14. The Mexican Monument commemorated not two but four midshipmen—Clemson, Hynson, Pillsbury, Shubrick—killed at Vera Cruz. The Japanese Bell, given to Perry by Japan before he left in 1854, was installed on the academy grounds. Writers' Program, *Maryland,* 192, 194.

15. Under normal circumstances, Fillmore as a president would be due twenty-one guns, Kennedy as a cabinet secretary nineteen, with seventeen being the number for a general or an admiral. This is the first of several times that Heine may have miscounted a salute or been misinformed.

16. The granite dock was completed in 1834, exterior dimensions 100 by 341 feet, at a cost of $943,676.73. Stuart, *Naval Dry Docks,* 60, 66.

17. Melville's *White-Jacket* from start to finish describes life aboard such a vessel as Heine refers to here.

18. Perry headed the squadron but not any ship of it. A diplomat besides, he may have done less than the usual in running a squadron. The expedition would prove him not the navy's best sailor but "the Navy's most brilliant diplomat." Lewis, "Matthew Calbraith Perry," 211.

19. See Melville, *White-Jacket,* 30–33 (chap. 7).

20. On this sort of housekeeping, cf. ibid., 89–93 (chap. 22).

21. "In the American Navy, the law allows one gill of spirits per day to every seaman. In two portions, it is served out just previous to breakfast and dinner. At the roll of the drum, the sailors assemble round a large tub, or cask, filled with the liquid; and, as their names are called off by a midshipman, they step up and regale themselves from a little tin measure called a 'tot'." Ibid., 56–57 (chap. 14).

22. "Once a week [in the *Mississippi*'s sister frigate the *Susquehanna*] the whole ship's company are beat to general quarters, when the magazines are open, the powder-boys busy in passing and repassing cartridge-boxes, the guns are cast loose and worked by their crews, boarders are called away, pikemen are posted to repel boarders, marines are stationed near them, &c.; the master gives his orders for sail-trimmers to put stoppers on such portions of the rigging, as an active imagination suggests must have been shot away, and all the evolutions of an actual engagement

at sea are gone through; together with exercise at fire-quarters, when an alarm with the ship's bell is rung, at which sentinels are placed at the falls of each boat, so that in an actual emergency there could be none of the inhuman desertion and infamous flight. . . . All of these exercises . . . increase the discipline of a crew and the efficiency of a ship." Spalding, *Japan*, 29. See also Melville, *White-Jacket*, 68–75 (chap. 16); and Taylor, *India, China and Japan*, 458.

23. "The entire abolition of corporeal punishment in the Navy, without authorizing some effective substitute, was one of those mistaken acts of philanthropy which are founded on abstract ideas of humanity rather than a practical knowledge of human nature." Taylor, *India, China and Japan*, 463. See Taylor's discussion of punishment, 461–465.

24. Johnston calls it the "Episcopal Church service," read by Reverend Henry Wood, chaplain of the *Powhatan*, 2 Aug. 1853. *China and Japan*, 140. Mr. Whiting, "our 2nd Lieutenant, read the services of the church of England, they being the most appropriate for ship use as they are all printed [and] required nothing extemporaneous." William B. Allen, cabin boy, the *Vandalia*, 20 March 1853, in Graff, *Bluejackets*, 79. "When their captain would read the Church of England service to them, [the crew in question] would present a congregation not to be surpassed for earnestness and devotion by any Scottish kirk." However, "a remarkably serious, but bigoted seaman" said to the captain: " 'Sir, I am a Baptist; the chaplain is an Episcopalian; his form of worship is not mine. . . . May I be allowed, sir, *not* to attend service on the half-deck?'—'You will be allowed, sir!' said the captain, haughtily, 'to obey the laws of the ship. If you absent yourself from prayers on Sunday mornings, you know the penalty'." Melville, *White-Jacket*, 164, 166 (chap. 38).

25. The description of the storm, in this and the subsequent three paragraphs, has been inserted here from Heine, *Reise um die Erde* 2:118–120. "Our frigates" are the *Mississippi* and *Susquehanna*. Cf. the description of this storm, "The Cyclone of the *Mississippi*," in Perry and Hawks, *Narrative* 2:347–349.

26. See Heine's picture, " 'Mississippi,' October 7, 1854," a mast broken, decks awash, as if about to sink in a tempest. Perry and Hawks, *Narrative* 2:347.

CHAPTER TWO

1. The skeleton squadron—*Saratoga, Mississippi, Susquehanna, Plymouth*—raised the islands on the twenty-sixth, made Great Loo Choo in the rain in the afternoon, felt its way into the harbor of Naha before dark, and anchored. "When the next morning dawned, bright and clear, I thought I had never seen a more lovely landscape." Taylor, *India, China and Japan*, 365–366.

2. Perry and Hawks' *Narrative* does not mention a compensatory gift and cites "the practice of our government not to accept such presents for her ships" (1:155) as if no gifts were exchanged. See also Perry, *Personal Journal*, 83. According to Reynolds, Perry wanted no obligation to his hosts nor an advantage to them in negotiations. *Perry in Japan*, 6. Kerr says that the rejection of customary hospitality offended the islanders, and that Perry did it because he wanted to maintain an

imperious attitude to people he saw as too low in social and official station to welcome him. Kerr, *Okinawa*, 307–308.

3. Probably coral fish. See S. Wells Williams, *Journal*, 39–40.

4. He commanded the *Alceste* and Captain Basil Hall the *Lyra*. In these waters in support of the British embassy to China in 1816 they were using available time to survey and explore the coasts of Korea and Loo Choo. Hall wrote *Account of a Voyage* and *Alceste*'s surgeon John M'Leod *Narrative of a Voyage:* Heine's and Perry and Hawks' sources for some of their discussions of Loo Choo. See also *Dictionary of National Biography*, s.v. "Maxwell, Murray," and "Hall, Basil."

5. The founder of the mission was not Maxwell and Hall but Herbert John Clifford in 1843. Clifford, an officer of Maxwell's *Alceste* in 1816, founded it to repay the hospitality of the people of Loo Choo—a repayment "in strange coin," according to Kerr, *Okinawa*, 279. See also 256–257. Bettelheim was a Hungarian Jew who took a medical degree in Italy and became a Christian and, after 1838, a British subject. In 1845 he accepted the mission's appointment as medical missionary to Loo Choo. Heine's discussion of him, generally accurate as to fact, takes a sympathetic view of him here and especially in chaps. 10 and 17. (So do Perry and Hawks, *Narrative* 1:225; Smith, *Lewchew*, iv–vi; and Bull, "Trials.") Heine differs from Kerr on Bettelheim as much as one can differ from another on anything. To Kerr, Bettelheim was of less-than-flawless character and "more than a little mad," 287. He behaved to the people of Loo Choo so as to deserve their ill will. What seemed to Heine to be his generous aid and cordial hospitality to ships calling at Loo Choo was, to Kerr, his way of advancing his own interests and enriching himself. Kerr, *Okinawa*, 279–296, 337–341. For Bettelheim's relation to the Perry expedition see ibid., 295–341. Kerr levels equal reproach at Perry, whose "policy in Okinawa was throughout based on coercion." Ibid., 311.

6. Cf. "a very neat cottage furnished him by the authorities of Loo Choo, on a slope behind Capstan Rock." Taylor, *India, China and Japan*, 369.

7. In fact the bishop tried to "secure a better position" for Bettelheim but the government, not wanting him and disliking what he did, continued its "passive resistance" to him, and to baffle "his attempts to hold intercourse with the natives. . . . His bodily safety was insured, but all intercourse with the people was effectually stopped." Smith, *Ten Weeks in Japan*, 339, quoted in Kerr, *Okinawa*, 294.

8. Perry and Hawks' *Narrative* confirms this hostility (1:225). Bettelheim "made one convert who on acknowledgeing [*sic*] it in public was immediately stoned to death, & has himself been several times sent to his bed, by drubbings received on his Mission." McCauley, *With Perry*, 72. See also Kerr, *Okinawa*, 286–288.

9. The interpreter was probably not the American S. Wells Williams but Ichirazichi the interpreter for Loo Choo. See S. Wells Williams, *Journal*, 12–13.

10. Loo Choo was an hereditary monarchy, which, like most monarchies, took a regent when the would-be ruler could not or would not rule. The expedition arrived when the queen dowager was ill and the king a boy. See Kerr, *Okinawa*, 310.

11. The squadron's Chinese served as stewards, some blacks as deckhands and

cooks. See Taylor, *India, China and Japan,* 363. Six blacks, servants to Perry, escorted him, armed, when he landed at Edo Bay in 1854. Sproston, *Private Journal,* 5. Blacks also held responsible positions in this navy, such as "the captain of the gun—a fine negro." He named the gun Black Bet "in honour of his sweetheart, a coloured lady of Philadelphia." Melville, *White-Jacket,* 71 (chap. 16).

12. Probably "government deputies" who always kept "unsolicited company" with the Americans. Spalding, *Japan,* 106. They were "unarmed Okinawan officials ordered to follow" the Americans, according to Kerr, *Okinawa,* 311. "Their faces exhibited considerable surprise and alarm, as they beheld eight armed men, with the cool assurance natural to Americans, taking the direct road to Shui, their capital." Taylor, *India, China and Japan,* 372. A "system of spying" operated not only against strangers "but also among [the local people] themselves, every man being a spy on his neighbour, so that every thing that passes is known to the mandarins." McCauley, *With Perry,* 71. "Secret espionage forms a distinguishing feature" of "the system of government." Perry and Hawks, *Narrative* 1:160.

13. Efforts to evade them proved futile. Taylor, *India, China and Japan,* 375.

14. As there is "little travelling, inns are not known in this country." But, for the few VIPs and government employees, "Kung-Kwas, or government houses, are erected at certain distances." The traveler might not be aware of one "till he enters the yard" as "stone walls, hedges, or earthen embankments, enclose and often hide a Kung-Kwa." Native watchmen kept the curious away—the "rabble" in Heine's view—while his party was there. The party slept on straw mats on the floor but were comfortable. Heine, *Graphic Scenes,* captions to pictures 4 and 5, no pagination. Picture 5 is of the *kunk-kwa.*

15. Probably just north of Barrow Bay, where Heine climbed a tree "to obtain a view." Perry and Hawks, *Narrative* 1:177.

16. See reports by Jones and Taylor, in Perry and Hawks, *Narrative* 2:51–63, 65–71.

17. The party would hoist a flag on the roof and post a guard, another manifestation of the Americans' aggressive behavior. Local people would mount a counterwatch and seize the chance to gratify their curiosity. "We frequently saw hundreds of dusky heads peering at us through the gloom." Taylor, *India, China and Japan,* 377. Hence the native watchmen mentioned in n. 14 above.

18. This reference remains unexplained. Heine may have misunderstood what he saw and what the interpreter told him.

19. Nagagusko or Nakagusuku, described in Perry and Hawks, *Narrative* 1:169–171. Probably built in feudal times, before the fifteenth century.

20. Therefore the castle would not repel cannon balls but be more susceptible to their force. But the castle, built before the days of cannon, might have been shaped the best against weapons then. See ibid., 1:171.

21. Heine never offers the opinion. In fact there was no "vanished race." Okinawans began as migrants in prehistoric times. They maintained ethnic integrity, though under Chinese and Japanese influence and despite some intermingling with the Chinese and Japanese. Kerr, *Okinawa,* 15–82, esp. 15–17.

22. They had circled about two-thirds the island, missing only the northeastern and southwestern ends.

CHAPTER THREE

1. The commodore's chair, a "dignified vehicle" and the object of talk and attention on the expedition, "became the occasion, large and stately, deeply indebted to paint and putty," a "feature in the procession." Perry and Hawks, *Narrative* 1:188. Perry, implementing in Asia what he had learned at home about dealing with Asians, tried to strike a pose of dignity and stature, of the man in charge. "It would have been very undignified for me to have walked," he said, and took "the precaution to have a comfortable sedan chair made on board ship." *Personal Journal,* 67. It may be the most famous sedan chair in American history, after Franklin's at the Constitutional Convention.

2. There were about 215 Americans in all, 32 officers, 122 sailors and marines, and 30 musicians. Spalding mentions twenty-three brasses and winds, directed by an old Italian who kept both ears stopped with wool yet retained a "nice 'ear for music'." *Japan,* 13.

3. Perry and Hawks' *Narrative* agrees that the commodore expected "a reception as became his rank and position," therefore, *"at the palace"* (1:156). Kerr suggests that the other side, thinking him too high-handed, asked—begged—that he not expect to be received there. The Englishmen had forced their way in. Hence the locked doors and a deserted palace and the chary reception for Perry when he got in at last. Merely "tea and pastries were served," in contrast to the feast at the regent's, where Perry was expected in the first place. Bettelheim may have been behind Perry's breach of gates and etiquette. Kerr, *Okinawa,* 309–318.

4. Here and in Japan, sugar was not used directly but in candy in various forms. See Perry and Hawks, *Narrative* 1:191, 2:20.

5. However aggressive, overbearing, high-handed, imperious, domineering, and tactless Perry may have been, here and in Japan, his methods worked at least to the extent that the other side not only gave him what he wanted but also stated officially and publicly, as in this toast, that they approved of him and desired friendship with the United States.

6. Heine depicted this scene in a watercolor complete with Perry in sedan chair. See the best published copy in Reynolds, *Perry in Japan,* 58–59. See also Perry, *Personal Journal,* facing 93.

7. A purpose for stopping here had been to test, in a dependency of Japan, the reception in Japan itself. Reynolds, *Perry in Japan,* 58. Perry's methods had been tried and found effective.

8. See n. 6 above.

CHAPTER FOUR

1. As Perry had gone to Loo Choo, so he went to the Bonins as part of his "Japan Strategy." In Loo Choo (a nominal Japanese protectorate) he wanted to learn of Eastern diplomacy, prompt Loo Choo to send word to Japan that he came in peace but with a sword, and establish a base for himself near Japan. The Bonins, virtually uninhabited, would play a lesser role. He expected at best to establish a base for himself now and the United States henceforth. To that end he first bought

as a private purchase a frontage of 1,000 by 500 yards on the harbor at Port Lloyd. Later he claimed for the United States the southern cluster of Bonins. Head and Daws, "The Bonins," 64, 65.

2. Perry "saw at once the advantages of Port Lloyd as a station for steamers, whenever a line shall be established between China and California" and bought one thousand yards of waterfront "admirably adapted for a coaling station." Taylor, *India, China and Japan*, 395, 396.

3. In point of fact a vaguely British expedition, which included an American named Nathaniel Savory, landed from Honolulu in 1830. Head and Daws, "The Bonins," 62. Cf. Perry and Hawks, *Narrative* 1:200.

4. Savory was here when Perry called. Perry and Hawks, *Narrative* 1:199.

5. On the history of the Bonins, cf. Head and Daws, "The Bonins," 60–64.

6. Residents did not honor these English names but kept the old. Goat and Hog instead of Buckland and Stapleton, for example. Perry and Hawks, *Narrative* 1:199–200.

7. See for example Heine's dramatic woodcut of the natural tunnel at Port Lloyd. Ibid., 1:201.

8. Perry, here to raise the American flag and claim possession, must have had a similar eye to fortification and defense, should this become an outpost and haven for American shipping.

9. Selkirk spent 1704–1709 in Juan Fernández, off Chile, not Peru.

10. Bayard Taylor: "There have been moments when I have coveted such a lot [the easy, quiet life of this island and its genial climate]; but now, nothing could have been more terrible than the prospect of being left among [the settlers here]. While I inhabit the world, let me be borne on its most crowded stream, and feel the pulses of its deepest and most earnest life!" *India, China and Japan*, 395.

11. Taylor joined the expedition in Shanghai and the "artistic mess" of Heine, Brown, and the other master's mates. See Perry and Hawks, *Narrative* 1:iv, 152, 154; Taylor, "An Exploring Trip through Peel Island," *India, China and Japan*, 398–409; Taylor, "Report upon the Exploration of Peel Island" in Perry and Hawks, *Narrative* 2:65–71; and Charles Fahs, "Report Made to Commodore Perry of an Exploration of Peel Island" in Perry and Hawks, *Narrative* 2:73–78.

12. Pandanus (genus *Pandanus*), or screwpine, a source of fiber and edible fruit, and pineapple *(Ananas comosus)* occur on Pacific islands and resemble one another when the pandanus is in shrub, but the plants are not the same.

13. Heine, an avid hunter here and elsewhere on the expedition, hunted also on the Prussian East Asia Expedition, and shot buffalo in the American West. Heine, *Eine Weltreise* 2:267.

14. The party did not leave until "Mr. Heine had made a sketch of the bay." Taylor, *India, China and Japan*, 406.

15. "Though I suffered less, I believe, than most of the others, it was certainly the hardest day's work of my life." Ibid., 409.

16. "Some of these immense armor-plated beasts were four, five, even six feet long." One was "enough to make turtle soup for the whole ship's company for weeks. . . . We carried [two or three] to sea with us, and when the men were holystoning the decks in the early morning it was a favorite amusement with them

to trot out the turtles and have a ride or rather a crawl on their backs." Sewall, *Captain's Clerk,* 130.

17. The names of the places have been eliminated.

18. Fresh meat and fish were always welcome to sailors long on ship's biscuit and salt pork or junk [beef]. Turtles provided meat where no other offered itself, and they could be kept alive for a long time at sea. See pictures and text of fishing, turtle-killing, and turtle-eating in Statler, *Black Ship Scroll,* 48–49, 58–59, 75.

CHAPTER FIVE

1. The new regent had been installed before the twenty-third of June. Perry and Hawks, *Narrative* 1:215. Heine suggests what Perry and the other American officers believed: A new regent had been installed for "a more vigorous hand in control at a time of unparalleled crisis for the kingdom." Kerr, *Okinawa,* 320.

2. Heine—not at the main table but at a smaller one with O. H. Perry II (the commodore's son, serving as his secretary on this voyage), Portman, and Taylor—from this vantage "was making a sketch" of the scene. Perry and Hawks, *Narrative* 1:217. See the sketch as a woodcut/engraving, ibid., 1:216.

3. In fact there was no "civilization lost in the mists of time," only a time in history when nobles built castles. See chap. 2, n. 21.

4. See chap. 2, nn. 20, 21.

5. Captain Murray Maxwell (1775–1831) in the *Alceste,* with Captain Basil Hall (1788–1844) in the *Lyra,* explored the coasts of Korea and Loo Choo after they delivered the British ambassador to China. Maxwell published nothing about it, however. Hall published the *Account of a Voyage,* which may have been one of Heine's sources. Heine may also have gotten information orally from Bettelheim or from something Bettelheim wrote. (George Smith in *Lewchew and the Lewchewans* used "a MS. drawn up a few months previously [before Smith's visit in 1850] by Dr. Bettelheim" [59] for his description of Loo Choo.) John M'Leod (1777?–1820), an officer on Maxwell's *Alceste,* described the Maxwell and Hall expedition in *Narrative of a Voyage.* That book (see 69–87) provided Heine with Su-Poa-Koang's account of the history of Loo Choo. From it Heine never departs further than a close paraphrase. Heine's spelling of names, followed here, differs from M'Leod's but never so much that one cannot be identified as the counterpart of the other.

6. Heine's discussion of the relation of the spelling to German pronunciation has been omitted.

CHAPTER SIX

1. Perry, having hoped in vain to have a squadron enlarged by vessels promised him, set out with this "inferior force, which he trusted would so far answer his necessities as not to interfere seriously with the great object of the expedition." Perry and Hawks, *Narrative* 1:228–229.

2. These junks performed better than those of the Chinese. Spalding, *Japan,* 169–170.

3. "Guns [were] run out into position and shotted." Ibid., 143. Perry, having

weighed the seriousness of his mission, decided to do what no others had done before. He would demand courtesy as the right of a civilized nation, not solicit it as a favor; he would brush aside the "petty annoyances" showered upon his predecessors; he would uphold the dignity of the American flag; and he would let events decide whether he would land by force. Accordingly "I caused the crews to be thoroughly drilled and the ships kept in perfect readiness as in time of active war." Perry, *Personal Journal,* 92. He thought rightly that the Japanese would consider resisting, and might resist, and he would be ready for it. See ibid., 183. To at least some Japanese it seemed he would get what he wanted or he would shoot his way in. Shimazaki, *Before the Dawn,* 91–92.

4. This agitation, and that seen ashore later, were probably part of the alarm produced by the Black Ships. A surprised and aroused populace erupted in "wild confusion," and the authorities took measures for defense of the coasts. Shimazaki, *Before the Dawn,* 21–22. Perry's ships, and those of other nations later, were called Black Ships not only because of the color of their hulls but because the steam-powered belched smoke of that color. Statler, *Black Ship Scroll,* 33. Smoke and paddlewheels impressed the Japanese. Shaw, "Japanese Picture Scrolls," 137. In Edo, civil and military preparations caused such uproar and tension that "it is like wartime. . . . The overwhelming first impression made by the Black Ships was not quickly forgotten." Statler, *Black Ship Scroll,* 79, 100.

5. "Continued action of the sculls—instead of rowing at their sides" drove them "with greater speed than the boats of the celestials." Spalding, *Japan,* 169. "Merrily as the oars of our men dipped the waves, it required their utmost to keep pace with the athletic scullers of Japan." Taylor, *India, China and Japan,* 427.

6. Asians revered rank, Perry believed, so he would not diminish himself by dealing with anyone lower than himself: a direct representative of a head of state. Perry, *Personal Journal,* 92. See also Reynolds, *Perry in Japan,* 60. His was "a policy of magnifying his own office and dignity" by surrounding "himself with a majesty which the Oriental always recognizes and appreciates." Dennett, *Americans,* 265. See also Bennett, *Steam Navy,* 130.

7. According to Spalding's *Japan,* a letter warning them to advance at their peril, had been thrown onto the *Plymouth.* One boarder had been repelled by pikes and others kept off by the motion of the paddlewheels (145). Heine's "earlier occasions" probably refer to former calls at Japan, such as those by the *Morrison.*

8. He may even have threatened that the boats "would be fired into." Spalding, *Japan,* 146. See also Perry, *Personal Journal,* 93; and Sewall, *Captain's Clerk,* 145.

9. This "lord mayor" was Eizaemon Kayama, a slightly higher functionary than had come the day before. Heine, like Perry, was fooled into thinking him a man of rank. Perry thought he was the governor. *Personal Journal,* 94.

10. According to Perry, Commanders Buchanan and Adams, and Lieutenant Contee, met him. Ibid.

11. "Even in winter every person in Japan has a fan." Morrow, *Scientist with Perry,* 116.

12. Not the emperor but the Tokugawa shogun is the authority represented, his colors and "coat of arms," or crest, being displayed: three stylized leaves of the hollyhock. Sproston, *Journal,* 8 n. 21, 9 n. 30.

13. The commodore's policy "was to assume a resolute attitude" and to fore-

stall what had been "visited upon those who preceded him." Ships were "kept in perfect readiness" and the crews "drilled as thoroughly" as in "time of active war." Perry and Hawks, *Narrative* 1:235. "Steam [was] kept up, and every suitable person on board ship directed to stand strict guard" armed "with cutlass, carbine, &c." Also "blue and red signal lights" were "to be hoisted upon the appearance of any burning junks sent down upon us." Spalding, *Japan,* 146.

14. Golovnin, captured at Hokkaido in 1811 and freed in 1813, wrote a memoir, translated as *Narrative of My Captivity* and probably read by Perry and others of the expedition.

15. Probably signs of the uproar of terror and preparations for trouble. Sewall, *Captain's Clerk,* 143–144.

16. The Japanese observed that "a gun is fired from the ships each morning and evening." Shimazaki, *Before the Dawn,* 79. The guns probably increased Japanese fright. See Adams, *History of Japan* 1:110–111.

17. "The Tokugawa leaders demanded that each daimyo [feudal lord] and a large retinue spend every other year in expensive palaces in Yedo." Guest, *Yedo,* 7. Cf. Naff, Glossary, *Before the Dawn,* s.v. "Alternate attendance." The cost dissipated their wealth and "rendered them less likely to indulge in adventures." Ibid., 762.

18. The Japanese who met the expedition had sent to the shogun at Edo word of what Perry wanted and desired time for a reply. See Adams, *History of Japan* 1:110–111.

19. Perry wanted and got a peaceful opening but probably would have shot his way in had he not been let in. He would have loosed all his firepower in self-defense. Here as at other points Heine's narrative makes clear that the expedition "was at bottom an act of aggression and a virtual challenge to war." Hale, "When Perry Unlocked the Gate," 94.

20. In 1851 at the World's Fair, or the Great Exhibition of London, Colt's revolver, Hobb's lock, and especially McCormick's reaper were the most popular of the American exhibits. Fay, *Palace of Industry,* 88–89. The revolver displayed at the fair and worn by Perry's officers was probably the Navy Model 1851, which Colt began to make in late 1850: a 36-caliber, 6-shot, percussion type with octagon barrel. See Carey, *American Firearms Makers,* 21. "Sam [wanting to open an Asian market for his guns] provided [Perry] with a generous supply of gift revolvers, graded in quality from those of which a colonel might not be ashamed to magnificent specimens of the gunsmith's art, of which even a king might be proud." Rohan, *Yankee Arms Maker,* 225.

21. Cf. Adams, *History of Japan:* "The military class had during a long peace neglected military arts; they had given themselves up to pleasure and luxury, and there were very few who had put on armour for many years" (1:111).

22. "Mr. Heine, the artist, obtained a panoramic sketch of the shore, with the batteries, villages, and other objects in detail." Taylor, *India, China and Japan,* 420.

23. The whistle repelled the last of the half-hearted, uncoordinated demonstrations against the Americans. Henceforth American-Japanese relations would go smoothly enough, and the Americans would get what they wanted within reasonable time and after reasonable effort. Though he did not express in the memoir the significance of this moment, Heine must have understood it. For he titled his pic-

ture of this dramatically decisive moment "Crossing [sometimes given as Passing] the Rubicon," reproduced in Perry, *Personal Journal,* following 156. The nearby geographical feature was named Point Rubicon after this incident. It guarded the end of the narrows, where the bay opens clear and wide to Edo, as such the last place the Japanese could have stood with maximum aid from topography against the American advance on their capital.

24. Not the commodore but lower-ranking officers received them. Perry and Hawks, *Narrative* 1:243–249. On what was said in the afternoon, 12 July, see ibid., 1:245–247.

CHAPTER SEVEN

1. Heine, like Perry, thought they were dealing with the emperor when they were in fact dealing with the shogun.

2. The *Morrison,* under David Ingersoll, with Samuel Wells Williams as interpreter, arrived at Edo Bay on 30 July 1837 to return seven Japanese castaways. Gunfire drove them off. Williams described the incident in detail, including the "strips of cloth, blue and white in bars," "officers on horseback," and persons "beyond the cloth" with "flags and guns." F. Wells Williams, *Life and Letters,* 97. See also 93–100.

3. According to Perry and Hawks' *Narrative,* "ornamental screens of cloth had been so arranged as to give a more distinct prominance, as well as the appearance of greater size to the bastions and forts" (1:252). Spalding's *Japan* calls them "long striped-cloth curtains" (147). The screens occurred so often that the Americans came to disregard them but for the "amusing" reports of quartermasters gravely reporting: "Another dungaree fort thrown up, sir!" Taylor, *India, China and Japan,* 419.

4. "The commodore, who had studied the customs and traditions of the Far East as thoroughly as it was possible at this period, succeeded by firmness, inscrutability, and impressive pomp to break the resistance of the Japanese." Shaw, "Japanese Picture Scrolls," 135. To make him look the leader on this occasion, and to protect the others from hot weather, Perry wore full dress buttoned up, the others undress and unbuttoned, so the Japanese could "see who is the high officer." Junior officers, happy to escape the torment of tight collars, pitied Perry nonetheless. Lewis, *Buchanan,* 138–139. Heine's picture (see Perry, *Personal Journal,* following 156) captures in grand panorama the event in all details: coastline, harbor, ships, boats, American forces, Japanese forces, and even the boxes containing Perry's credentials. This and every picture of the marines shows the trim order inculcated by Zeilin. At any port of call he would want "to see a level place where he could drill his marines." S. Wells Williams, *Journal,* 11.

5. Perry and Hawks' *Narrative* has Toda-Idzu-no-kami and Ido-Iwami-no-kami (1:255) and Kayama Yezaiman, the governor of Uraga (1:250).

6. The Dutch had been allowed to remain at Deshima after other foreigners were expelled. Annually a Dutch envoy, in audience with the shogun, had to kneel, crawl, kowtow, then retire without looking up or uttering a word. He and his suite might also have to sing, dance, make music, and play the buffoon for the entertainment of the shogun and his court. Reynolds, *Perry in Japan,* 31–32. As for

the Russians, Heine may be referring to Golovnin and the other captives of 1811–1813. See chap. 6, n. 14.

7. This sentence reports exactly what the Japanese felt. See Shimazaki, *Before the Dawn,* 93–94.

8. See Perry, *Personal Journal,* 92.

9. This vague sentence probably means that the Americans were not forced to humiliate themselves in Japan. "I have never recognized on any occasion the slightest personal superiority, always meeting the Japanese officials, however exalted their rank, with perfect equality." Perry, *Personal Journal,* 159. To the Japanese, however, he may have conveyed the impression that he knew little of Japan and thought the Japanese an inferior civilization. See Shimazaki, *Before the Dawn,* 110.

10. The Japanese "made signs about the enormous size of our guns and expressed great dread and apprehension of them." Morrow, *Scientist with Perry,* 117.

11. Perry and Hawks' *Narrative* does not mention this document.

12. Perry may have spoken ironically here. The Japanese had said, "No decision could be arrived at without mature deliberation"; he had "better go away" and would "get a definite answer" in "a short time." Adams, *History of Japan* 1:111. Thus the Japanese, though no longer belligerent since the standoff in the bay shortly before this meeting, remained haughty enough. Perry may have wanted to assert American strength in what he said then, as well as flaunt it later by moving the squadron up the bay and sending out more survey parties. See Reynolds, *Perry in Japan,* 81.

13. Heine's statement of Japanese astonishment is problematic. The Japanese wanted Perry to leave. Were they astonished that he so readily consented, or that he so boldly declared his return, acting as if he, not they, were in charge?

14. But Spalding saw "many a scowling fellow meanwhile looking daggers at us," their officers "perhaps thinking how agreeable a thing it would be, to hold one of those Americans on the end of one of their blades, as a fork, and hack him with the other as a knife; if they only dared try." *Japan,* 165–166. The Japanese saw these foreigners as greedy conquerers who forced their way in and cared nothing for the culture but everything for the goods and minerals of Japan. The foreigners thus left an unfavorable impression with the Japanese, who "looked upon the visitors with such revulsion." Shimazaki, *Before the Dawn,* 93, 94. The Japanese would sign the treaty when Perry returned; not because they wanted amity and commerce but because it had been forced upon them. They intended to change things as soon as they could. See introd., n. 42.

15. The knowledge gained in this inspection may have further nudged the Japanese to yield to a superior force.

16. Yezaimon wanted "to examine a revolver." Commander Buchanan "fired off all the chambers of a genuine 'Colt,' from the quarterdeck," to Yezaimon's "great astonishment." Taylor, *India, China and Japan,* 435.

17. Since 1644 the Dutch at Deshima had been teaching the Japanese languages and informing them on technology, history, scientific inquiry, and current events. Reynolds, *Perry in Japan,* 32–34. If the Dutch, semiprisoners of the Japanese, did

not show them modern firearms, it may have been out of self-preservation. Most expedition memoirs note the Japanese curiosity about things American and the Japanese awareness of international affairs, including what was happening in the West. "Dutch learning" probably prompted Japanese desires to cease isolation and if not to reach out to foreign and especially Western nations, at least to allow foreigners and "Western learning" in. See Shimazaki, *Before the Dawn,* 48–49; and Naff, Glossary, *Before the Dawn,* s.v. "Dutch learning."

18. Cf. Shimazaki on American "goods in bottles, boxes, and cans" burned because "they might be carrying a curse." *Before the Dawn,* 96.

19. Despite the chill of the last meeting, Japanese-American relations had taken a turn for the better and would improve. They would be almost warm when the Americans returned the next March. Liberal elements in Japan had gained influence; they favored contact with the world, hence negotiations and a treaty. See Reynolds, *Perry in Japan,* 90–97.

20. The Japanese and the foreigner shared tobacco. "Kansai found that this Westerner, the first he had observed at close range, had hair and eyes of a different color but was in no way the terrifying apparition associated with the Black Ships. He was neither a ghost nor a demon. He was, after all, another flesh and blood human being." Shimazaki, *Before the Dawn,* 98.

21. The islands of various sizes south-southwest between Japan and Okinawa and between the Pacific and the East China Sea.

22. "Those upon the land" declared it "one of the severest" they "had ever experienced." Perry and Hawks, *Narrative* 1:275.

23. Cf. the more complicated nature of these negotiations, according to ibid., 1:275–279. See also S. Wells Williams, *Journal,* 74–79. Perry had "toughened his attitude" and forgotten the instructions "to act only with the consent of the natives." He "remembered rather the 'broad discretionary powers'." Kerr, *Okinawa,* 323. He demanded and got a station, a coal shed, an end to spying that had dogged the Americans, and an understanding that Loo Choo could expect to be put to American purposes in the years ahead. Ibid., 323–325.

24. Perry had threatened force, should this or any objection stand between him and an American station. Reynolds, *Perry in Japan,* 83. See also Perry, *Personal Journal,* 108.

25. "The building is 50 by 60 feet in dimensions, with a water-tight thatched roof, with the eaves projecting beyond the sides, which are boarded up more than half the distance from the ground to the roof, leaving an open space sufficient for purposes of ventilation"; thus of five hundred-ton capacity and capable of being enlarged by adding "a wing to each side." Perry and Hawks, *Narrative* 1:282.

26. This sentence is ironic, or Heine failed to see that "friendly relations" had been thrust upon "those good-natured people."

CHAPTER EIGHT

1. That is, Perry sailed with the *Mississippi* and the *Susquehanna,* leaving the *Plymouth* behind at Loo Choo to maintain relations there and to survey some of the Bonin Islands. Perry and Hawks, *Narrative* 1:282–283.

2. The *Mississippi* went to Whampoa to protect American interests from possible revolutionary uprisings in the Taiping Rebellion. (The *Susquehanna* had been called away earlier for the same reason.) The *Supply* went likewise to Canton. The *Susquehanna* went to Cum Sing Moon to rendezvous with the rest of the squadron, absent for the first visit to Japan but arriving and gathering at last for the second. At Cum Sing Moon, ships were to be repaired and crews rested. Ibid., 1:288. See also McCauley, *With Perry,* 72–77; and Reynolds, *Perry in Japan,* 83. These places cluster on China's southeast coast around the estuary of the Pearl or West River: Canton, farthest inland; downriver, its port, Whampoa; on an island on the southwest side of the bay, near the South China Sea, Cum Sing Moon and Macao; and northeast across the bay, Hong Kong.

3. Literally "Golden-sun-born-pass." Spalding, *Japan,* 186. "A devil of a name truly." McCauley, *With Perry,* 72.

4. Cum Sing Moon—the large port between Hong Kong and Macao, used by opium ships of Canton—now served as the Japan expedition's rendezvous. Morrow, *Scientist with Perry,* 276–277, n. 14. "We [of the *Powhatan*] found the Susquehanna with the broad pennant, the Mississippi, Vandalia, Macedonian, Southampton, and shortly after the Supply and Caprice came in." McCauley, *With Perry,* 73. The squadron proceeded to conduct drills and extensive target practice. Allen, in Graff, *Bluejackets,* 92.

5. "A large building which [Perry] has hired as an hospital for seamen," a "fine old Portuguese mansion, in the highest part of town, and we find it an airy and agreeable residence for a tropical summer." Taylor to George H. Boker, 18 Aug. 1853, in Hansen-Taylor and Scudder, *Life and Letters* 1:258. The hospital served Americans, perhaps Perry himself, who caught the dysentery raging in Macao. Morrow, *Scientist with Perry,* 277–278, n. 21. Cf. Morison, *"Old Bruin,"* 345.

6. Coasting vessels called *lorchas,* under Portuguese and other flags, plied these coasts in mid-century trade. Fairbank, *Trade and Diplomacy,* 325–328. They were indispensable at Macao for the shallow draft that let them into the inner harbors. Perry and Hawks, *Narrative* 1:299.

7. Heine's prior reference to Macao occurs in a part of the memoir not included here.

8. Work continued apace on apparatus and records. The survey section, never slackening on hydrography, prepared "fair copies of charts" made "during the last cruise. The artists and draftsmen were constantly engaged in making and completing their sketches and drawings," more than two hundred. Perry and Hawks, *Narrative* 1:289. See also Morrow, *Scientist with Perry,* 277–278, n. 21; and McCauley, *With Perry,* 73.

9. What with Heine's statements below and his condescension to the Chinese, these gatherings were probably not among Chinese workers and merchants but among the idle Portuguese "living upon the remnants of the once princely fortunes of their ancestors" and still occupying "in beggarly poverty, the stately mansions erected in the olden time of Macao's splendid prosperity." Perry and Hawks, *Narrative* 1:297–298. The Chinese ranked the Macao Portuguese "somewhere between a 'Chinaman' and a 'barbarian'." Macao's "population [of Portuguese

and other non-Chinese] were in fact interbred with Chinese." In 1853–1854 Macao was "a backwater, where a previous century was preserved" and only beginning to participate in the "western penetration of China." Fairbank, *Trade and Diplomacy*, 325.

10. A "pleasant foreign society" that "presented many attractions." Perry and Hawks, *Narrative* 1:300.

11. She was "an American lady, whom he married while secretary of legation at Washington." Ibid.

12. Cf. Perry and Hawks, *Narrative* 1:501–504; and Morison, *"Old Bruin,"* 343.

13. Russia had been trying to do what Perry had done in Japan. Shimazaki recreates what happened in a Japanese village when reports were received of Russian Black Ships in Nagasaki. *Before the Dawn*, 28, 29–30, 33. A Russian expedition had been negotiating with the Japanese, who broke off negotiations on 1 Feb. 1854. See Lensen, *Russia's Japan Expedition*, vii, 7–34, esp. 29–30. Lensen does not mention a "three-year period of mourning."

14. Not the emperor but shoguns of the house of Tokugawa had run Japan since 1615. Not the emperor but the ruling shogun Ieyoshi died ten days after Perry's visit, 27 July 1853. His son Iesada took office on 22 Nov. 1853 without incident. Profound changes were occurring at the same time that would affect the government, but nothing had happened to change anything so far as the outside world was concerned. Negotiations with the Americans proceeded as they might have had Ieyoshi not died. Not only Heine but Perry himself believed throughout that he dealt with the representatives of an emperor who ruled Japan. Barrows, *Great Commodore*, 309; and Perry, *Personal Journal*, 91 (esp. n. 7). See also Preble, *Diary*, 109.

15. This paragraph's mixture of fact and error, wisdom and folly, shows Heine's ignorance of Japan's internal affairs, a condition shared with other Westerners, Perry included.

16. She had been left behind to maintain relations with Loo Choo and to survey the Bonin Islands.

17. Carlo Gozzi, the Italian playwright, wrote *Re Turandot*. Karl Maria von Weber, Ferruccio Benvenuto Busoni, and notably Giacomo Puccini based operas on it. Friedrich Schiller, the German man of letters, translated the play into German.

18. The troubles are probably those Heine discusses two paragraphs later.

19. Amaral became governor in 1846, after decades of trouble for Portugal in Macao. Britain had twice threatened to take it over, while China threatened to reassert control. In 1842 the Treaty of Nanjing gave Britain Hong Kong, and Britain abandoned Macao. Amaral arrived to reaffirm Portuguese authority. He proceeded to annex the island of Taipa; force Chinese fishermen to pay taxes; extend the city's developed areas by clearing what had been in the way, including graveyards, farms, and squatters' shacks; and expel China's customs officials, the *Hoppo*. Guillen-Nuñez, *Macau*, 41–44. Chinese authorities accused him of "desecrating their ancient burial places" with his energetic building of carriage roads "through

and about" Macao's "limited space." Perry and Hawks, *Narrative* 1:302. But it was the expulsion of the Hoppo that brought out the assassins. Guillen-Nuñez, *Macau,* 45.

20. Guillen-Nuñez cites "seven assassins disguised as beggars." *Macau,* 45.

21. According to Guillen-Nuñez, Lieutenant Vicente Nicolau de Mesquita led a contingent of thirty-six men from a larger force at Porta do Cerco, rushed a mile against a barrage from a garrison of two thousand, captured Passaleong, and blew it up. Ibid.

CHAPTER NINE

1. To Perry, the Chinese, "probably the most knavish" of races, cheated and robbed and practiced "with consummate skill and audacity" the "art of deception and trickery." *Personal Journal,* 55.

2. This squad from "the watch" was probably made up of American marines of the hospital guard, for Heine refers to them as "my soldiers" *(Soldaten),* a corporal leads the squad, and they seem to speak English.

3. Shortly before leaving the expedition, Bayard Taylor tried opium at Canton, found it a delight that increased toward perfect happiness with each pipe, and woke the next morning "feeling stronger and brighter than I had done for weeks past." *India, China and Japan,* 492–494.

4. "There is no part of the world where piracies are more open or more frequent." Perry, *Personal Journal,* 55.

5. The speech is in English in the original. The speaker is probably the Dick Short mentioned later.

6. Morison's numbers differ from these. *"Old Bruin,"* 356.

7. This was Ringgold's North Pacific Surveying Expedition, later led by John Rodgers. Not intended, strictly speaking, as a reserve to Perry's, the Ringgold-Rodgers expedition was to follow Perry's, gather additional information, chart trans-Pacific steamship routes, and implement Perry's diplomatic accomplishments, especially the treaty with Japan. See Cole, "Background of the Surveying Expedition in *Yankee Surveyors,*" 4–8.

CHAPTER TEN

1. American officers invariably received courtesies "from the British authorities abroad" and "in no instance during a long service in foreign countries have I experienced any want of hospitable attention [from them]. . . . The English at large are in all their social relations hospitable." Perry, *Personal Journal,* 53. Sir Fleetwood Broughton Reynolds Pellew was a rear admiral and the commander-in-chief of the East India and China station, appointed in 1852. He took command of the *Winchester* in April and had been in Hong Kong since September 1853. *Dictionary of National Biography,* s.v. "Pellew, Fleetwood."

2. Maxwell, Cecille, *Preble,* Adnet: For Maxwell, see chap. 2, n. 4; Rear Admiral Jean-Baptiste Cecille tried to get a treaty for France with Japan in 1846; Mathieu Adnet was the French priest and missionary on Loo Choo; the *Preble,* not

small but in the largest class of sloops-of-war, arrived under Captain James Glynn to join the East India Squadron in 1849, stopping at Nagasaki for imprisoned Americans. Johnson, *Far China Station,* 44–46.

3. This was the International Cemetery at Tumari. The neglect mentioned below remained in 1925. Bull, "Bettelheim," 54. Spalding called it "the foreigners' grove at Tumai." *Japan,* 174.

4. On Bettelheim and family, see Schwartz, "Commodore Perry," esp. 262–263. Cf. Schwartz's Bettelheim, Heine's sympathetic profile here and elsewhere in this book, and Kerr on Bettelheim, *Okinawa,* 279–296, 337–341.

5. The Americans wanted to find coal, "essential for steam communication [but] commercially scarce in the Pacific." The search for coal was a reason for the expedition. Cole, "Background of the Perry Expedition" in *With Perry,* 19.

6. Jones was not only a geologist but also an astronomer and a chaplain.

7. The expedition gained "much new information" about "a singular people" little known before and about their products and the botany and other aspects of their island. Perry and Hawks, *Narrative* 1:319.

8. But marines accompanied the commodore in his sedan chair. McCauley, *With Perry,* 80.

9. Fifteen soups, according to McCauley, who "recognized the taste & flavor of cat, dog, rat & snake, but I cannot vouch for Hedgehog, ant or Buzzard." Ibid., 81.

10. "We find that keeping a ship anchored in the bay during the summer has had a very good effect, the spy system has diminished, on account of so many of them having been knocked head over heels, and the natives buy and sell freely, that is to say comparatively so." Ibid.

11. The question is in English in the original. "Some of them have already picked up a good deal of English." In the streets "we hear from time to time: 'How do you do?' 'Good-morning', 'American', and other phrases chirruped out by little boys, who then hop quickly back into the dirt and oblivion they emerged from." F. Wells Williams, *Life and Letters,* 207.

12. This paragraph contradicts Perry, who says he did not dispatch the *Susquehanna* to China but left with her, the *Powhatan,* and the *Mississippi* for Edo Bay, 7 February. *Personal Journal,* 138, 147. See also his letter of a few days later from the "United States Flagship *Susquehanna* / At sea, 9 February 1854 / Latitude 30° 13′ N, longitude 132° 15′ E." Ibid., 149. The change to the *Powhatan* and the dispatch of the *Susquehanna* to China, according to Perry, took place off Uraga after 13 February. *Personal Journal,* 157.

13. The *Saratoga* had been expected from Shanghai, where she had been "protecting American interests." She was now being recalled for the more important mission. See Morison, *"Old Bruin,"* 344; and Perry and Hawks, *Narrative* 1:324.

CHAPTER ELEVEN

1. "A perfect gale of wind which together with the darkness, rain, and snow and hail make our situation very dangerous." Lewis, in Graff, *Bluejackets,* 115.

2. This was the American Anchorage, so named on the prior visit. Perry and

Hawks, *Narrative* 1:327–328. The headland of Point Rubicon was given its name because survey boats, after some Japanese opposition, had gone beyond the point, continuing the survey and crossing "as it were the Rubicon." Ibid., 334 (footnote).

3. This was the famous scene of the Black Ships before Kanegawa, often depicted visually by the Japanese and the Americans. See for example Reynolds, *Perry in Japan*, 84–87.

4. Perry did not receive the embassy directly. Captain Adams met them on the *Powhatan* and acted as intermediary. See Perry and Hawks, *Narrative* 1:328. Perry had concluded, from his prevoyage study of Japan, that to get respect from the Japanese he ought to hold himself above ordinary people and humdrum events and meet only Japanese equal to him. "It seemed to be the true policy . . . rather to establish for myself a character of unreasonable obstinacy than that of a yielding disposition. . . . I have succeeded far beyond my expectations in maintaining this extreme point of diplomacy, and, as I believe, to very great advantage." Ibid., 338–339.

5. For these discussions, and as a corollary to the rest of this chapter, see S. Wells Williams, *Journal*, 100–119.

6. Of these names only Boncraft does not appear on Pineau's list of officers. Nor is there a Bancraft. Perry, *Personal Journal*, 226–232.

7. The *Powhatan* left Shimoda with the Treaty of Kanegawa consummated on Washington's birthday, 1855. "As we trust, enduring friendly relations with Japan are thus associated, in date at least, with the name of Washington." Perry and Hawks, *Narrative* 1:513.

8. Although the Japanese had taken military measures with an eye to resisting the Americans this time, "the Tokugawa government could not deal with the situation by military means." Shimazaki, *Before the Dawn*, 47. The Japanese were too weak militarily, and too many Japanese wanted contact with foreign, especially Western, nations. Pro-Western feeling must have strengthened by November. For, rather than rejoice at Russian plans to leave, the Japanese made a "paradoxical change" and showed anxiety at the prospect. Lensen, *Russia's Japan Expedition*, 32.

9. Judging from Heine's verbal picture of the scene, his woodcut/engraving (see Perry and Hawks, *Narrative* 1:334) does not do it justice.

10. " 'Two hundred sail' bearing the American flag" helped convince the Japanese of American greatness. "Of course they must have counted the same whaler over many times" as it cruised for whales, but "every time she repassed, she was as good as another ship." McCauley, *With Perry*, 90. See also Morrow, *Scientist with Perry*, 179, 219.

11. "They are without exception the most polite people on the face of the earth, not only on board here, but also in . . . their intercourse with one another." McCauley, *With Perry*, 85.

12. Heine's report is a loose paraphrase embellished. See the message as found in the letter reprinted in Perry and Hawks, *Narrative* 1:337–338.

13. That is, Adams perhaps thought that the translation could be improved and sent changes.

14. Negotiations with the Russians had stalled at Russian objections to places

named by the Japanese. Lensen, *Russia's Japan Expedition,* 34. Perhaps Perry's "I don't know what it means to turn back," on top of the American show of strength and grit, were enough for the Japanese to ask Captain Adams "to pick the place."

CHAPTER TWELVE

1. There were 160 marines and 224 sailors, armed with musket, pistol, and cutlass. Sproston, *Journal,* 5.

2. "I have adopted the two extremes by an exhibition of great pomp when it could properly be displayed, and by avoiding it when such pomp would be inconsistent with the spirit of our institutions." Perry, *Personal Journal,* 159. Perry displayed a flair for the dramatic in staged landings with music, cannon, flags, ships and boats in formation, and bodies of marching men. Statler, *Black Ship Scroll,* 40–43.

3. According to Sproston, there were thirty boats in all, with twelve launches at center. *Journal,* 4.

4. The position of the ships meant that their batteries had been brought "to bear on the shore [to] cover our landing in case of an attempt of treachery on the part of the natives." Allen, in Graff, *Bluejackets,* 126.

5. That is, "square," *Quarré,* in the military sense, after the French *carré.*

6. This closed formation guarded against possible hostilities, as the landing party did not know whether they would be met "as friends or as enemies." Allen, in Graff, *Bluejackets,* 127.

7. See Heine's picture "Commodore Perry Comes Ashore at Yokohama." Perry, *Personal Journal,* following 156.

8. This "soup of eel" may have been Sproston's "snake chowder," called "fish chowder" by Sproston's editor. Sproston, *Journal,* 7.

9. The dessert included "heavy sponge cake and striped candy like that sold in the U.S." McCauley, *With Perry,* 95. According to Morrow, none of the Americans liked the "sackie" for its "sweetish and peculiar taste." *Scientist with Perry,* 126.

10. "A rather tall and gaunt Japanese that sat next to me drank them all [champagne, sherry, port, whiskey, punch, . . . every kind and quality of wine or liquor] and was, of course, rather merry afterwards." Sproston, *Journal,* 15.

11. The meeting is reported in eight pages in Perry and Hawks, *Narrative* 1:346–353.

12. Walks into the countryside were common among the Americans. See McCauley, *With Perry,* 108–110. See also Johnston, *China and Japan,* 284; and Lewis, in Graff, *Bluejackets,* 153–155, 160–161.

13. Perry negotiated long and hard for the resting place. *Personal Journal,* 165–166. This public burial with honors dramatized Perry's insistence that Americans valued every human life. Reynolds, *Perry in Japan,* 99. The United States would also have a kind of claim on Japan, having buried American dead there.

14. Afterward the Japanese "enclosed the grave neatly with stone and built a bamboo fence around it and placed a guard over it." Morrow, *Scientist with Perry,* 124. "The settled oppugnation to Christianity, of more than two hundred years,

was broken through with this burial from an American man-of-war." Spalding, *Japan,* 235.

15. See Perry, *Personal Journal,* 176.

16. See the picture of this event, by Peters in ibid., following 156. Many of the people "appeared interested in their manipulations. The most of these machines are far too expensive and complicated, I fear, for the majority of the agriculturists and gardeners of Japan," their enterprises being "on too small a scale for them to afford the cost, and human labor for these same too abundant to need such implements." S. Wells Williams, *Journal,* 141. See also F. Wells Williams, *Life and Letters,* 211–212.

17. Cf. Shimazaki: "The day after Perry left, these gifts [the goods in bottles, boxes, and cans] were all burned. . . . It was feared that they might be carrying a curse." *Before the Dawn,* 96.

18. The locomotive and tender "went scudding round and round the circus like a Shetland pony, to the great pleasure of every spectator. The Japanese are, I think, more pleased with this thing than anything else we have given them." S. Wells Williams, *Journal,* 143. "Commander Adams [returning in 1855] found that they had learned to manage the locomotive. . . . They had also the life-boat afloat with a trained crew, but the magnetic telegraph they said was too hard for them yet." Perry and Hawks, *Narrative* 1:512.

19. "One of our mechanics" was Morrow and the apparatus not one expressly for firefighting but a "garden engine" or an all-purpose water pump. Morrow, *Scientist with Perry,* 133–134.

20. Heine's list differs from that in Perry and Hawks, *Narrative* 1:356–358. See also S. Wells Williams, *Journal,* 131–134.

21. Samuel Colt gave a generous number of revolvers, hoping to create a market in Asia. Rohan, *Yankee Arms Maker,* 225.

22. "Finally" signifies the length and difficulty of the negotiations, with each side exchanging gifts and bestowing hospitalities as if to influence the opponent. See Reynolds, *Perry in Japan,* 99–118. The treaty was, strictly speaking, one of amity and commerce. The signers were "ministers plenipotentiary" in a broad sense: Perry as special envoy for the United States and Prince Hayashi as head of the council.

23. See Heine's picture of the scene aboard the *Powhatan.* Perry, *Personal Journal,* following 156.

24. Heine, like the rest of the expedition including Perry, seems to have labored under the illusion that they were dealing with the representatives of the emperor. Yet here his language—"of the shogun (the present emperor)" ("*des Sziogoun* [*jetzigen Kaisers*]")—suggests that he may have understood a de facto emperor or shogun ruling instead of the mikado. The role and power of the shogun and the emperor seems to have been hazy to the Japanese as well as foreigners, a relationship "in some ways analogous" to "the European separation of spiritual and temporal powers." Naff, Glossary, *Before the Dawn,* s.v. "Emperor." Yet the emperor retained such temporal power that it was unusual to open ports to the Black Ships "without waiting for the emperor's approval." Indeed, "there were those who ground their teeth as they maintained that the opening of the ports . . . constituted an act of

lèse majesté against the imperial court itself." Shimazaki, *Before the Dawn*, 100–101, 109.

CHAPTER THIRTEEN

1. The Japanese had opened Shimoda because it lay at the end of the mountainous Izu peninsula, where the "disturbing" Americans would be 110 miles from Edo and could most easily be kept out of the rest of Japan. See Statler, *Black Ship Scroll*, front endpaper.

2. The approach of the Americans to Edo became a matter of mortal dread for reasons and under conditions not perfectly clear. Heine may be suggesting that high-ranking officials, even members of the imperial commission, were aboard an American ship at the approach. According to Perry and Hawks' *Narrative*, only interpreters as commission emissaries came aboard and at the last minute. They confirmed the commission's wishes that the squadron not approach and expressed the danger of "possible injury and probable death" for the commission if the squadron did approach. The lives of the interpreters also "depended on the issue" (1:398–399). It would be the interpreters as commission emissaries that Heine describes, then, and not the commissioners themselves. As to why neither the squadron should approach nor the Americans enter Edo as tourists, Heine implies that the Japanese saw the Americans as unworthy, not having shown obeisance. Perry and Hawks' *Narrative* says that a popular excitement would have endangered the emperor and his household (1:399). Spalding offers the same interpretation. *Japan*, 260. Neither Perry and Hawks nor Spalding nor any other source explains why at the sight of the squadron the populace should rise against the emperor.

3. According to Perry and Hawks' *Narrative*, Perry turned back to cooperate with the commissioners (1:399). Graff says that tides prevented anchoring near Edo. Having told the commissioners that he wanted but a brief look at Edo, Perry turned back without loss of prestige. *Bluejackets*, 143, n. 405.

4. Any of several reasons could prompt *hara-kiri*, ritual suicide by self-disembowelment, called *seppuku* in Japan. See Naff, Glossary, *Before the Dawn*, s.v. "seppuku." Here it would probably have been to "register a protest" or "atone for an error or a humiliation."

5. Heine refers to the squadron's having found safe haven here the year before. See Perry, *Personal Journal*, 100.

6. Perry was sending with Adams the treaty just signed and other communications to Washington, where officials would want to know of an agreement of such importance. See Perry and Hawks, *Narrative* 1:393.

7. All dates in this paragraph differ from those usually given for the respective events.

8. Perry wanted and strove to sound and survey everywhere and to incorporate the findings in new charts. Throughout his career Perry was driven by a desire to aid navigation worldwide. See Morrow, *Scientist with Perry*, 290, n. 113. See also Maury, *Sailing Directions*.

9. Gates at intersections "may be easily closed in the event of any *émeute*." Spalding, *Japan*, 264.

10. "Judging from their carelessness in knocking fire from pipes &c I should say that conflagrations are by no means scarce." McCauley, *With Perry*, 95.

11. The reference is to one of several statues (third century B.C.) of the Roman goddess of love and vegetation, Venus. Heine's remark suggests the statue in the pose of modesty. Others of the expedition saw immorality in this public bathing. "Passing through the village of Simoda we saw more of the licentiousness and degradation of these cultivated heathen that we had seen before. It is common to see men, women and children,—old and young, married and single—bathing in the same large open bath house." Morrow, *Scientist with Perry*, 175. When Johnston saw men, women, and children of all ages mingling in a public bath, "Adam and Eve style—minus the fig leaves," his "nerves were terribly shocked" and he left "a wiser, but a much disgusted man." *China and Japan*, 139–140. See also S. Wells Williams, *Journal*, 183–184; and Preble, *Diary*, 181, 183.

12. "The village [of Yokohama] was rendered unsavory by the numerous vats, thatched over to retain urine, compost and other manuring substances from evaporating, which lined the waysides." S. Wells Williams, *Journal*, 115.

CHAPTER FOURTEEN

1. Cf. Johnston, *China and Japan:* "The upper part of these garments is thrown off in warm weather, and confined to the waist by the girdle alone. . . . [The women] do not appear in the slightest degree abashed at this partial exposure of their persons, and make no attempt to conceal themselves from the gaze of strangers" (105).

2. Photographing in Shimoda took place in a temple, probably as part of assembling the record of the expedition. See the Japanese picture of Americans, probably Heine and Brown, photographing "a courtesan to show the American king." Statler, *Black Ship Scroll*, 56.

3. Perry says the *dairi* is the "ecclesiastical emperor." *Personal Journal*, 102. Perry and Hawks' *Narrative* describes Miako as the chief seat of learning (1:58). Miako or Miyako was also known then, and is better known now, as Kyoto, meaning "capital city." *Japan: The Official Guide*, 677. The word *dairi* can refer to the emperor. Ibid., 55. In 1854 Kyoto was still the emperor's seat and the emperor more an ecclesiastical than a secular ruler.

4. The Japanese wanted to exchange cards and seemed "anxious to get at each of our names." Morrow, *Scientist with Perry*, 116.

5. Karl Peter Thunberg (1743–1828), Swedish scientist and traveler, was "first among scholars to contribute substantially to the American conception" of Japan. Graff, *Bluejackets*, 15. Graff cites Thunberg's travels published by the Royal Society of London as the work that informed Americans on Japan. It is more likely that Americans learned of Japan from reading the third volume of Thunberg's four-volume work translated as *Travels in Europe, Africa, and Asia, 1770–1779*, which appeared in at least three editions. Heine might also have read the German translation. Townsend Harris, too, saw the "abominable mixture, which permanently blackens" the teeth of the Japanese female, "& is so acid, that it destroys a large portion of the mouth gums, and the mouth is so much inflamed that the lips fre-

quently remain permanently swollen." *Some Unpublished Letters,* no pagination. Harris' editor contends that the mixture of "powdered gall-nuts and iron [and] a little water and vinegar" retained its efficacy "only a few days, and it is absolutely harmless." Ibid.

6. See a picture by Heine of a *mia* in *Graphic Scenes,* No. 6, no pagination.

7. The Japanese said that the Americans shot birds with a "thunder tube" emitting many pellets, its thunderous report evidencing its effectiveness. Statler, *Black Ship Scroll,* 50.

8. The Perry and Hawks report of this incident (*Narrative* 1:425–426) has fewer personal details and lacks the names of the Americans involved. In other respects the accounts agree. Perry and Hawks explain the cause as a misunderstanding over the right of Americans to stay ashore overnight without the permission of the authorities.

9. McCauley, *With Perry,* in general confirms this account (110–111).

CHAPTER FIFTEEN

1. The squadron came here because Hakodate was the other port besides Shimoda to be opened to American ships.

2. See the discussion of currents in Perry and Hawks, *Narrative* 1:427–430.

3. "Bearings" and "crossbearings" are in English in the original.

4. The flagship changed from the *Mississippi* to the *Powhatan* on 19 February 1854, the fourth change since 10 May 1853. Perry, *Personal Journal,* 157. Heine and the rest of the master's mates, a special staff to Perry, went where he went.

5. "Jack" or "Jack Tar" (meaning the sailors) called the place " 'Hack yr. daddy'—not quite so euphonious, but a deal more interesting" than Hakodate. McCauley, *With Perry,* 112. McCauley also called it "Hakky" (113).

6. See Sproston's crude but effective drawing. *Journal,* facing 42. See also Preble, *Diary,* 187–188.

7. See Heine's "Hakodate from Snow Peak," Perry, *Personal Journal,* following 156; and Perry and Hawks, *Narrative* 1: facing 430. See also his "Hakodadi from the Bay," "Hakodadi from Telegraph Hill," and "Fishing at Hakodadi," Perry and Hawks, *Narrative* 1:431, facing 447, and 451, respectively.

8. Bent's delegation, or perhaps one that went ashore to arrange for discussions with Bent's, informed the authorities of the treaty and of the reason for the Americans being there. See Perry and Hawks, *Narrative* 1:434.

9. The birds and the locations of their descriptions in ibid.: duck (the falcated duck), 2:231; diving bird (the horn-billed guillemot), 2:233; partridge (the Japanese quail), 2:227; and snipe (perhaps the northern phalarope), 2:230–231.

10. Shellfish were also taken, and "some very good wild game was killed on the opposite shore from the town." Spalding, *Japan,* 299.

11. Perhaps because enough of the initial "perfect panic" at sight of the Americans still prevailed. See ibid., 298.

12. For the architecture, especially the roofs, see Itoh, *Traditional Japanese Houses,* 52, 58–59, 73, 111, 124, 146–147, 207, 234, 329, 342.

13. "Flat" means not horizontal but unbroken by dormers or other projec-

tions. See Perry and Hawks, *Narrative* 1:438, which compares this architecture not to the Swiss but to the Dutch. Cf. Preble's description of houses here and in Shimoda. *Diary,* 218–219.

14. The whisk or broom would be used to sprinkle the roof against fire. Perry and Hawks, *Narrative* 1:438.

15. Heine must mean the tubs and the well, since he did not recognize the purpose of the whisks.

16. On Heine's pension application of 1885, he is six feet one, "very tall."

17. Sproston observed in the same temple: "The whole scene reminded me forcibly of a Catholic church, and I doubt not the same has been the impression of many." *Journal,* 46. McCauley saw "a very near approach to the images of the Virgin Mary as it is exhibited in Italy." *With Perry,* 115. See also Preble, *Diary,* 194.

18. The Americans found the Buddha depicted in many poses, but asleep was unusual. See Perry and Hawks, *Narrative* 1:407–408.

19. "A fine mineral spring of strong sulphur and limestone water. . . . The fisherman told me that the sick washed in it for their diseases . . . no doubt beneficial to them in curing those cutaneous diseases with which almost every other person we saw in Japan seemed afflicted." Morrow, *Scientist with Perry,* 188.

20. See Preble, *Diary,* 197–198.

CHAPTER SIXTEEN

1. Cabin boy Allen of the *Vandalia* describes the coin as round with a square hole in the center, an amalgam of copper and brass, the unit of exchange in China, Macao, Loo Choo, and Japan, and exchanged at 3,600 to the dollar in Japan. Graff, *Bluejackets,* 101. On the rate of exchange, cf. S. Wells Williams, *Journal,* 175–176, 190, 208–211, 221. Preble's *Diary* cites the rate as 4,800:1 at Hakodate but no more than 1,600:1 at Shimoda (205).

2. This was a pillar clock or a miscellaneous variation thereof. Heine's description corresponds to pictures of such clocks, with the important exception that his double row ("two rows of eight") seems to have been rare. See Mody, *Japanese Clocks,* 38–39, plates 71–84, 107 passim.

3. Except for reporting the day as sixteen hours, Heine seems right about the basics of reckoning time in Japan. See ibid., 25–26. But there was much more to it than Heine discusses. See ibid., 26–29. Cf. Naff, Glossary, *Before the Dawn,* s.v. "clocks."

4. Perry and Hawks' *Narrative,* in an unsatisfactory discussion of Japanese music, speaks only of the *samsic* or "guitar" (1:59). In fact each of the stringed instruments was probably a variety of the samisen, which indeed resembled the banjo. See Guest, *Yedo,* 12. The word *samisen* entered English in 1864, perhaps because relations with Japan brought the instrument to Western attention after 1853. For a Japanese drawing of a samisen, see Statler, *Black Ship Scroll,* 42.

5. For the program of the minstrel show on the *Powhatan* (at the banquet Heine describes below), see Lovett, "Japan Expedition Press," 246–247. McCauley mentions "a serenade of pseudo darkies," as if the performance was of whites in blackface. *With Perry,* 77. He also calls it an "Ethiopian performance"

(101). See also Sproston, *Journal*, 16. Perry and Hawks' *Narrative* calls the performers regular sailors, therefore probably white, who improvised a show to rival Christy's (1:470). Perry "and a number of Japanese nobles attended the performance expressing themselves much pleased with the efforts of these sable vocalists which for sailors on boa[r]d ship was highly creditable." Allen, in Graff, *Bluejackets*, 166. Cf. Melville, "Theatricals in a Man-of-War" in *White-Jacket*, 94–101 (chap. 23). Morison, in "Perry's Japan Expedition Press and Theatre," decides that the "shows were played partly by Negroes, of whom there were a considerable number in Perry's squadron, but mostly by black-faced white sailors" (39).

6. Vegetables tended to be in short supply, even in Japan, where they should have been available. Statler, *Black Ship Scroll*, 49.

7. Glitter and pomp included " 'present arms' and 'Hail Curlumby' " with field pieces, "band, tars, marines, Commo and suite." McCauley, *With Perry*, 123.

8. The Americans "teased and sported with young girls, [but] behaved with propriety toward married ladies," perhaps "put off by the artificially blackened teeth of married women." Statler, *Black Ship Scroll*, 65.

9. "We scampered back leaving traces of our wheels . . . that will last a long day." McCauley, *With Perry*, 124. See also S. Wells Williams, *Journal*, 204–205.

10. Probably Friedrich Wilhelm Streit and Wilhelm Fischer, eds., *Historischer und geographischer Atlas von Europa* (Berlin: Natorff, 1834).

11. In the interests of preserving meaning without distortion, the poetic features of the original have been abandoned in favor of this "semiprose."

12. See n. 11 above.

13. "To this [mixture of firmness, dignity and fearlessness on our side, against which their artful and dissimulating policy was powerless], and to our material strength, I attribute the fact of our reception having been so different from that of other embassies." Taylor, *India, China and Japan*, 417–418. Again we see that the Americans did not understand who spoke for Japan.

14. Cf. the more elaborate evaluation by Williams, which says about the same, except that Williams the Christian missionary saw much of the hand of God in this mortal work. S. Wells Williams, *Journal*, 222–226.

CHAPTER SEVENTEEN

1. "Putiatin was in command of the Russian squadron that visited Japan at about the same time as Commodore Perry—and for more or less similar purposes." Lensen, *Russia's Japan Expedition*, vii.

2. "A man named Board." Perry and Hawks, *Narrative* 1:492. On the "Board incident," cf. Heine, Perry and Hawks, *Narrative* 1:492–494, and Kerr, *Okinawa*, 330–333. Kerr bases his interpretation on S. Wells Williams, *Journal*, 228–242.

3. *Pater peccavi*, literally, "Father, I have sinned." Less familiar than the *mea culpa* of prayer and the confessional but meaning the same: a frank admission of guilt without excuse.

4. Heine's book was published in 1856. By "the agreement with Japan" Heine therefore cannot mean Perry's Treaty of Kanagawa (already signed), nor the one concluded by Townsend Harris, the first American representative in Japan, in

1858. It remains unclear which agreement with Japan Heine means. On the treaty with Loo Choo, see Kerr, *Okinawa,* 341.

5. Botany Bay is often named as Australia's famous penal colony, but the colony was at Port Jackson near Sydney.

6. These last three sentences, unclear in the original, seem to mean that the reef would serve at the second island the purpose its counterpart served at the first and that the people of Loo Choo were ashamed enough of their adulteresses to want to hide them from foreigners.

7. Through Bettelheim "we got all our provision as it had to go through a regular form." Lewis, in Graff, *Bluejackets,* 106. That is, purveyors would "receive lists from Bettelheim only." S. Wells Williams, *Journal,* 14. See also Schwartz, "Perry at Okinawa," 265–267.

8. Cf. Kerr's hostile summing up of Bettelheim's career. *Okinawa,* 337–340.

9. Bettelheim was leaving with the furniture and other chattels. His claim of these as perquisites hurt Moreton's feelings and prompted American sympathy for Moreton. The Americans had been leaning toward Moreton anyway, since Perry had caused the removal of Bettelheim. The collection, about $240, was to help Moreton re-equip himself. Barrows, *Great Commodore,* 340. Kerr's *Okinawa* takes a dim view of Bettelheim's motives and says Bettelheim made off with much that was not his (340).

CHAPTER EIGHTEEN

1. The Pacific island west of Chile where Alexander Selkirk, Robinson Crusoe's prototype, was marooned.

2. Probably two of the many German businessmen in China.

3. "Homeward bound" is in English in the original.

4. He remains unidentified. Perhaps he fell ill or was injured when with the *Kennedy* in the Far East.

5. He would return as an artist with the Prussian East Asia Expedition and, by virtue of experience with Perry, pilot the first German ship into Edo Bay in 1860.

BIBLIOGRAPHY

BY HEINE
Entries marked with an asterisk contain illustrations by Heine

Wanderbilder aus Central-Amerika: Skizzen eines deutschen Malers. Leipzip: Costenoble, 1853.

Graphic Scenes of the Japan Expedition. New York: Putnam, 1856.

Die Expedition in die Seen von China, Japan und Ochotsk unter . . . Ringgold und . . . Rodgers . . . 1853 bis 1856. 3 vols. Leipzig: Costenoble, 1858–1859.

Japan und seine Bewohner: Geschichtliche Rückblicke und ethnographische Schilderungen von Land und Leuten. Leipzig: Purfürst, 1860.

Eine Sommerreise nach Tripolis. Berlin: n.p., 1860.

"Einleitung." In *Die westliche Welt: Reise,* by Alexander Mackay. Translated from the English by Marie Heine. Leipzig: Kollmann, 1861.

Reise um die Erde nach Japan . . . unter Commodore M. C. Perry. . . . 2 vols. Leipzig: Costenoble; New York: Günther, 1856. Translations: *Reis om de wereld naar Japan . . . onder Commodore M. C. Perry. . . .* Rotterdam: Nijgh, 1856. *Voyage autour du monde. Le Japon. Expédition du Commodore Perry. . . .* 2 vols. Brussels: Dumont: 1859–1860. 2d ed. Brussels: Lacroix, 1863.

Eine Weltreise um die nördliche Hemisphäre . . . Ostasiatischen Expedition in . . . 1860 und 1861. 2 vols. Leipzig: Brockhaus, 1864.

Japan Beiträge zur Kenntniss des Landes und seiner Bewohner. Dresden: Selbstverlag des Verfassers, 1873.

Yeddo: Nach Original-Skizzen. Dresden: Gilbers, [1876].

Report to Major General John A. Dix, 21 August 1862. War Records Office. *War of the Rebellion: A Compilation of the Official Records of the Union and Confederate Armies.* Ser. 1, vol. 11, pt. 2, 920–921. Washington, D.C.: Government Printing Office.

Letters and other holographs (military records, pension applications, notes, consular dispatches, communiqués, etc). National Archives, Washington, D.C.

ILLUSTRATIONS BY HEINE:
PUBLICATIONS AND ARCHIVES

Christie's [Art Dealership] New York. Advertisement for "Perry's Expedition Encamped on Hako Date" (1856). *Apollo,* n.s. 111 (May 1980): 64.

Franklin D. Roosevelt Library, Hyde Park, New York.

Holland, Josiah Gilbert. *Illustrated Library of Favorite Song.* New York: Scribner, Armstrong & Co.; Chicago: Hadley Brothers & Kane, 1873. Illustrated by Heine.

Huth, Hans. "Poetry of Traveling." Includes "woodcut from drawing ['Trenton Falls'] by W. Heine." *Art Quarterly* 19 (Winter 1956): 357–377.

Library of Congress, Washington, D.C.

Mackay, Alexander. *Die westliche Welt: Reise.* Translated from the English by Marie Heine. 2 vols. Leipzig: Kollmann, 1861. Illustrated by Heine. Published, without illustrations by Heine, as *The Western World; or, Travels in the United States in 1846–47.* 3 vols. London: n.p., 1852.

Mariners' Museum, Newport News, Virginia.

Maritime Museum, Philadelphia, Pennsylvania.

Mystic Seaport Museum, Mystic, Connecticut.

National Museum of American Art, Smithsonian Institution, Washington, D.C.

New-York Historical Society, New York, New York.

New York Public Library, New York, New York.

Old Print Shop. Advertisement for four Heine lithographs of the Japan expedition. *Antiques* 63 (Feb. 1953): 84.

Peabody Museum, Salem, Massachusetts.

Peters, Harry T. *America on Stone.* Garden City, N.Y.: Doubleday, Doran [1931].

Rutledge, Anna Wells. "Cumulative Record of Exhibition Catalogues, Pennsylvania Academy of the Fine Arts." American Philosophical Society *Memoirs* 38 (1955): vi + 450.

United States Naval Academy Museum, Annapolis, Maryland.

Washington Art Association. Catalogues of the First, Second and Third Annual Exhibitions. Washington, D.C.: Polkinhorn, 1856, 1857; Moore, 1859.

Willis, N[athaniel] Parker. *Trenton Falls: Picturesque and Descriptive.* New York: Putnam, 1851. Illustrated by Heine.

Winchester, Alice. "Maxim Korolik and His Collections." Includes Heine's "Crossing the Rubicon." *Art in America* 45 (Fall 1957): 34–41, 70.

OTHER WORKS

Entries marked with an asterisk contain illustrations by Heine

Adams, Francis O[ttiwell]. *The History of Japan.* 2 vols. London: Henry S. King, 1874.

Akagi, Roy Hidemichi. *Japan's Foreign Relations, 1542–1936.* Tokyo: Hokuseido Press, 1936.

Alden, Caroll Storrs, and Earle, Ralph. "Matthew Calbraith Perry." In *Makers of the Naval Tradition,* by C. S. Alden and R. Earle. Boston: Ginn, 1942.

Allen, William B. See Graff, *Bluejackets.*

Allgemeine Deutsche Biographie 50:135–141.

Baba, Bunei. *Japan 1853–1864, or Genji Yume Monogatari.* Translated by Ernest Mason Satow. Tokyo: n.p., 1905.

*Baldridge, Harry A. "Perry's Pandora's Box." *American Collector* 11 (August 1942): 6–7, 20.

Barnaby, Nathaniel. *Naval Development in the Century.* London: Linscott, 1902.

Barrows, Edward M. *The Great Commodore: The Exploits of Matthew Calbraith Perry.* Indianapolis: Bobbs-Merrill, 1935.

Baylen, Joseph O. "Focus on the Pacific: A Note on Russia's Reaction to the Perry Expedition." *Pacific Northwest Quarterly* 46 (January 1955): 19–24.

Beasley, William G., ed. and trans. *Select Documents on Japanese Foreign Policy, 1853–1868.* London: Oxford, 1955.

Benedict, Ruth. *The Chrysanthemum and the Sword: Patterns of Japanese Culture.* Boston: Houghton Mifflin, 1946.

Bénézit, E[mmanuel], ed. *Dictionnaire . . . Peintres. . . .* New ed. 10 vols. Paris: Librairie Gründ, 1976. s.v. "Heine, Peter-Bernhard-Wilhelm."

Bennett, Frank M. *The Steam Navy of the United States.* Pittsburgh: Warren, 1896.

Boatner, Mark Mayo. *The Civil War Dictionary.* New York: McKay, 1959. s.v. "Heine, Wilhelm."

Boetticher, Friedrich von. *Malerwerke des neunzehnten Jahrhunderts.* 2 vols. Dresden: Schmidt & Günther, 1891–1901. s.v. "Heine, Wilhelm."

Borton, Hugh. Review of *Narrative of the Expedition of an American Squadron,* by M. C. Perry and F. L. Hawks, edited by Sidney Wallach. *American Historical Review* 58 (April 1953): 626.

Brewington, Dorothy E. R. *Dictionary of Marine Artists.* Mystic, Conn.: Mystic Seaport Museum, 1982. s.v. "Heine, Wilhelm."

Bull, Earl R. "Trials of the Trail Blazer, Bettelheim." *The Japan Evangelist* 33 (1925): 50–59.

Callahan, James M. *American Relations in the Pacific and the Far East, 1784–1900.* Johns Hopkins University Studies in Historical and Political Science, vol. 19. Baltimore: Johns Hopkins University Press, 1901.

Carey, A. Merwyn. *American Firearms Makers.* New York: Crowell, 1953.

Cole, Allan B. "Background of the Perry Expedition." In *With Perry in Japan.* See McCauley.

———. "Background to the Surveying Expedition." In *Yankee Surveyors in the Shogun's Seas.* See Rodgers et al.

———. Introduction to *A Scientist with Perry in Japan.* See Morrow.

Commission des sciences et arts d'Égypte. *Description de l'Égypte. . . .* 21 vols. Paris: Imprimerie impériale, 1809–1828. 2d ed. 25 vols. Paris: Panckoucke, 1821–1829.

*Cowdrey, Mary Bartlett. *National Academy of Design Exhibition Record.* 2 vols. New York: New-York Historical Society, 1943.

———. *Exhibition Record: American Academy of Fine Arts and the American Art Union.* Collections of the New-York Historical Society 77 (1944). New York: New-York Historical Society, 1953.

Dana, R[ichard] H[enry], Jr. *The Seaman's Friend.* 1845. Reprint. New York: Library Editions, 1970.

Davis, George. *Paper on the Origin of the Japan Expedition.* (Read before the Maryland Historical Society, 7 May 1857.) Baltimore: Murphy, 1860.

Dennett, Tyler. *Americans in Eastern Asia: A Critical Study of the Policy of the United States.* New York: Macmillan, 1922.

Dictionary of American Biography, s.v. "Hawks, Francis L."; "Jones, George"; "King, Charles William"; "Squier, Ephraim George"; "Williams, Samuel Wells."

Dictionary of National Biography, s.v. "Hall, Basil"; "Maxwell, Murray"; "Pellew, Fleetwood"; "Smith, George (1815–1871)."

Doenhoff, Richard A. von. "Biddle, Perry, and Japan." *U.S. Naval Institute Proceedings* 92 (November 1966): 78–87.

Dower, John W. *War Without Mercy: Race and Power in the Pacific War.* New York: Pantheon, 1986.

Dulles, Foster Rhea. *Prelude to World Power: American Diplomatic History, 1860–1900.* New York: Collier, 1965.

———. *Yankees and Samurai: America's Role in the Emergence of Modern Japan.* New York: Harper & Row, 1965.

———. *America in the Pacific: A Century of Expansion.* 2d ed. 1938. Reprint. New York: Da Capo, 1969.

Fairbank, John K. *Trade and Diplomacy on the China Coast: The Opening of the Treaty Ports, 1842–1854.* 2 vols. 1953. Reprint (2 vols. in 1). Cambridge: Harvard University Press, 1964.

Fay, C. R. *Palace of Industry 1851: A Study of The Great Exhibition and Its Fruits.* Cambridge: Cambridge University Press, 1951.

Federal Writers' Project, Works Progress Administration. *New York City Guide.* American Guide Series. New York: Random House, 1939.

"General Peter B. W. Heine." *Deutsche Pionier* 17 (1885): 48.

Golovnin, Vasilii M. *Narrative of My Captivity.* . . . 2 vols. London: Colburn, 1818.

Gordon, Leonard. "Early American Relations with Formosa, 1849–1870." *The Historian* 19 (May 1957): 262–289.

Graff, Henry F., ed. *Bluejackets with Perry in Japan: A Day-by-Day Account . . . by . . . John R. C. Lewis and William B. Allen.* New York: New York Public Library, 1952.

———. "He Came Bearing Guns and Gifts." Review of *Narrative of the Expedition of an American Squadron*, by M. C. Perry and F. L. Hawks, abridged by Sidney Wallach. *New York Times Book Review*, 21 Dec. 1952, 6.

Greene, Laurence. "The Japan Expedition." In *America Goes to Press: The News of Yesterday*, edited by Laurence Greene. Indianapolis: Bobbs-Merrill, 1936.

Griffin, Eldon. *Clippers and Consuls: American Consular and Commercial Relations with Eastern Asia, 1845–1860.* 1938. Reprint. Taipei: Ch'eng Wen, 1972.

Griffis, William Elliot. *Matthew Calbraith Perry: A Typical American Naval Officer.* Boston: Cupples & Hurd, 1887.

———. "Millard Fillmore and Japan." *Buffalo Historical Society Publications* 9 (1906): 54–79.

———. *The Mikado, Institution and Person: A Study of the Internal Political Forces of Japan.* Princeton: Princeton University Press, 1915.

———. *Millard Fillmore.* Ithica, N.Y.: Andrus & Church, 1915.

Groce, George C., and Wallace, David, eds. *The New-York Historical Society's Dictionary of Artists in America.* New Haven, Conn.: Yale University Press, 1957. S.v. "Heine, Peter Bernard William."

Guest, Lynn. *Yedo: A Novel.* New York: St. Martin's Press, 1985.

Guillen-Nuñez, Cesar. *Macau.* Hong Kong: Oxford University Press, 1984.

*Hale, William Harlan. "When Perry Unlocked the Gate of the Sun." *American Heritage* 9 (April 1958): 12–23, 94–101.

Hall, Basil. *Account of a Voyage of Discovery to the West Coast of Corea, and the Great Loo Choo Island.* London: Murray; Philadelphia: Small, 1818.

Hansen-Taylor, Marie, and Scudder, Horace E. *Life and Letters of Bayard Taylor.* 2 vols. 2d ed. Boston: Houghton, Mifflin, 1885.

Hariot, Thomas. *A briefe and true Report of the new found land of Virginia.* . . . 1590. Reprint. New York: Sabin, 1871.

Harris, Townsend. *Some Unpublished Letters.* Edited by Shio Sakanishi. New York: Japan Reference Library, 1941.

Hawks, Francis L. See Perry and Hawks.

———. Introduction to *Graphic Scenes of the Japan Expedition,* by Wilhelm Heine. New York: Putnam, 1856.

Head, Timothy E., and Daws, Gavan. "The Bonins: Islands of Contention." *American Heritage* 19 (February 1968): 58–64, 69–74.

Henderson, Daniel M. *Yankee Ships in China Seas: Adventures of Pioneer Americans in the Troubled Far East.* New York: Hastings House, 1946.

Horsman, Reginald. *Race and Manifest Destiny: The Origins of American Racial Anglo-Saxonism.* Cambridge: Harvard University Press, 1981.

Howe, Henry. *Life and Death on the Ocean: A Collection of Extraordinary Adventures in the Form of Personal Narratives.* Cincinnati: Henry Howe, 1857.

Hunt, David C. "Artists of the Western Surveys." In *Reader's Encyclopedia of the American West.* New York: Harper & Row, 1977.

Itoh, Teiji. *Traditional Japanese Houses.* Edited and photographed by Yukio Futagawa. Translated by Richard L. Gage. New York: Rizzoli, 1983.

Jairazbhoy, R. A. *Asians in Pre-Columbian Mexico.* London: By the Author, 1976.

"Japan. Commodore Perry's Expedition. Extracts from a letter written by a prominent and distinguished officer of the United States Navy, to his estimable wife, resident in this city." *New York Tribune,* 4 Nov. 1853.

Japan: The Official Guide. Tokyo: Tourist Industry Bureau, 1957.

Johnson, Robert Erwin. *Far China Station: The U.S. Navy in Asian Waters, 1800–1898.* Annapolis, Md.: Naval Institute Press, 1979.

Johnston, James D. *China and Japan: A Narrative of the Cruise of the U.S. Steam-Frigate Powhatan.* . . . Philadelphia: Desilver; Baltimore: Cushing & Bailey, 1861.

Jones, George. *Observations on the Zodiacal Light, from April 2, 1853, to April 22, 1855, Made Chiefly on Board the United States Steam-Frigate Mississippi . . . by Rev. George Jones.* Vol. 3 of *Narrative of the Expedition of an American Squadron to the China Seas and Japan,* by M. C. Perry and F. L. Hawks. Washington, D.C.: Nicholson, 1856.

*Kerr, George H. *Okinawa: The History of an Island People.* Rutland, Vt.: Tuttle, 1958.

King, Charles William. *The Claims of Japan and Malaysia upon Christendom.* New York: French, 1839.

Klinkenborg, Verlyn. "The West Indies as Freshly Seen in the Sixteenth Century." *Smithsonian,* January 1988, 88–98.

Kojima, Matajiro. *Commodore Perry's Expedition to Hakodate.* 2 vols. Hakodate: Hakodate Kyodo Bunkaki, 1953.

Leithauser, Brad. "Black Ships." Review of *Before the Dawn,* by Shimazaki Tōson. *New Yorker,* 3 Aug. 1987, 72–76.

Lensen, George Alexander. *Russia's Japan Expedition of 1852 to 1855.* Gainesville: University of Florida Press, 1955.

Letters and other holographs (military records, pension applications, notes, consular dispatches, communiqués, etc.). National Archives, Washington D.C.

Lewis, Charles Lee. "Matthew Calbraith Perry and the Awakening of Japan." In *Famous American Naval Officers,* by Charles Lee Lewis. Boston: Page, 1924.

———. *Admiral Franklin Buchanan.* Baltimore: Norman, Remington, 1929.

Lewis, John R. C. See Graff, *Bluejackets.*

*Lindsey, David. "Perry in Japan." *American History Illustrated* 13 (August 1978): 4–8, 44–49.

Lovett, Robert W. "The Japan Expedition Press." *Harvard Library Bulletin* 12 (1958): 242–252.

McCauley, Edward Yorke. *With Perry in Japan: The Diary of Edward Yorke McCauley.* Edited by Allan B. Cole. Princeton: Princeton University Press, 1942.

McClellan, Edwin. "The Shogun Wasn't the Problem." Review of *Before the Dawn,* by Shimazaki Tōson. *New York Times Book Review,* 18 Oct. 1987, 44–45.

M'Leod, John. *Narrative of a Voyage, in His Majesty's Late Ship Alceste, to the Yellow Sea, Along the Coast of Corea, and . . . to the Island of Lewchew. . . .* London: Murray, 1817; Philadelphia: Carey, 1818.

McLeod, Julia H., ed. "Three Letters Relating to the Perry Expedition to Japan." *Huntington Library Quarterly* 6 (February 1943): 228–237.

Mattice, Harold A. "Perry and Japan." *New York Public Library Bulletin* 46 (February 1942): 167–184.

Maury, William L., comp. *Sailing Directions and Nautical Remarks: By Officers of the Late U.S. Naval Expedition to Japan under . . . M. C. Perry.* Washington, D.C.: Nicholson, 1857.

Maury, William L., and Bent, Silas. "Chart of the Coast of China and of the Japan Islands. . . . Compiled by Order of Commodore M. C. Perry." 2 views. [Washington?] 1855.

Melville, Herman. *White-Jacket or The World in a Man-of-War.* 1850. Edited by A. R. Humphreys. London: Oxford University Press, 1966.

Mody, N. H. N. *Japanese Clocks.* 1932. London: Kegan Paul, Trench, Trubner & Co., [1969].

Moore, Merl M., Jr. "More about the Events Surrounding the Suppression of *Harper's Weekly,* April 26, 1862." *American Art Journal* 12 (Winter 1980): 82–85.

Morison, Samuel Eliot. "Commodore Perry's Japan Expedition Press and Shipboard Theatre." *American Antiquarian Society Proceedings* 77 (1967): 35–43.

———. *"Old Bruin": Commodore Matthew C. Perry.* Boston: Little, Brown, 1967.

———. "Introduction." See Perry, *The Personal Journal of Commodore Matthew C. Perry.*

Morison, Samuel Eliot, and Commager, Henry Steele. *The Growth of the American Republic.* 3d ed. New York: Oxford University Press, 1942.

Morris, Richard B. "The Decision to Raise the Bamboo Curtain." In *Great Presidential Decisions: State Papers that Changed the Course of History,* by Richard B. Morris. Philadelphia: Lippincott, 1960.

Morrow, James. *A Scientist with Perry in Japan: The Journal of Dr. James Morrow.* Edited by Allan B. Cole. Chapel Hill: University of North Carolina Press, 1947.

Naff, William E. Glossary. See Shimazaki.

———. Introduction. See Shimazaki.

National Archives. *The "Art" of Diplomacy.* Washington, D.C.: National Archives, 1971.

National Cyclopedia of American Biography, s.v. "Tomes, Robert."

Neumann, William L. "Religion, Morality, and Freedom: The Ideological Background of the Perry Expedition." *Pacific Historical Review* 23 (August 1954): 247–257.

New York City Directory, 1850.

New York, City and County of. Court of Common Pleas. [Citizenship records, 1855, 1856.] Bundle 143-D, record 243.

Nitobe, Inazo Ota. *The Intercourse between the United States and Japan: An Historical Sketch.* Johns Hopkins University Studies in Historical and Political Science, vol. 8. Baltimore: Johns Hopkins University Press, 1891.

*"Notes on Painters. Peter Bernard Wilhelm Heine." Isaac Delgado Museum of Art *Bulletin* 2 (July 1927): 4.

*Old Print Shop. "Perry in Japan." *The Old Print Ship Portfolio* 1 (January 1942): 11–15.

*———. "Biddle and Perry in Japan." *The Old Print Shop Portfolio* 8 (January 1949): 98–102.

Palmer, Aaron Haight. *Documents and Facts Illustrating the Origin of the Mission to Japan. . . .* 1857. Reprint. Wilmington, Del.: Scholarly Resources, 1973.

Paullin, Charles Oscar. "Early Voyages of American Naval Vessels to the Orient." U.S. Naval Institute *Proceedings* 36 (1910): 429–436.

———. *Diplomatic Negotiations of American Naval Officers.* 1912. Reprint. Gloucester, Mass.: Peter Smith, 1967.

———. *American Voyages to the Orient, 1690–1865.* Annapolis, Md.: Naval Institute, 1971.

Paz, Octavio. *Labyrinth of Solitude.* Translated by Lysander Kemp. New York: Grove Press, 1985.

*Perrin, Noel. "The Epic Novel of 19th-Century Japan." Review of *Before the Dawn,* by Shimazaki Tōson. *Washington Post Book World,* 23 Aug. 1987, 11, 13.

*Perry, Matthew C. *The Personal Journal of Commodore Matthew C. Perry.* Edited by Roger Pineau. Introduction by Samuel Eliot Morison. Washington, D.C.: Smithsonian Institution, 1968.

*Perry, M[atthew] C., and Hawks, Francis L. *Narrative of the Expedition of an American Squadron to the China Seas and Japan. . . .* 2 vols. Washington, D.C.:

Beverley Tucker, Senate Printer, 1856. *Vol. 1 edited and abridged, with introduction and notes, by Sidney Wallach. New York: Coward McCann, 1952.

Pfeiffer, John. "How Not to Lose the Trade Wars by Cultural Gaffes." *Smithsonian,* January 1988, 145–156.

Phillips, Claude S. "Some Forces Behind the Opening of Japan." *Contemporary Japan* 24 (1956): 431–459.

*Pineau, Roger. *The Japan Expedition of Commodore Matthew Calbraith Perry.* Washington, D.C.: Smithsonian Institution, 1968.

Plath, David W. "Pictures from an Exploration." Review of *The Art of Captain Cook's Voyages,* by Rüdiger Joppien and Bernard Smith. *New York Times Book Review,* 24 Apr. 1988, 13–14.

Polo, Marco. *The Book of Ser Marco Polo* . . . Translated and edited by Henry Yule. 3d ed. London: Murray, 1908.

Powell, Mary M. "Three Artists of the Frontier [Frederick Piercy, Paulus Roetter, Julius Kummer]." *Missouri Historical Society Bulletin* 5 (1948): 34–43.

*Preble, George Henry. *The Opening of Japan: A Diary of Discovery in the Far East, 1853–1856.* Edited by Boleslaw Szczesniak. Norman: University of Oklahoma Press, 1962.

Rayback, Robert J. *Millard Fillmore: Biography of a President.* Buffalo, N.Y.: Buffalo Historical Society, 1959.

Reader's Encyclopedia of the American West, s.v. "Artists of the Western Surveys."

Redman, Ben Ray. "New Editions." Review of *Narrative of the Expedition of an American Squadron,* by M. C. Perry and F. L. Hawks, edited by Sidney Wallach. *Saturday Review* 36, 11 Apr. 1953, 63.

Review of related works including *Narrative of the Expedition of an American Squadron,* by M. C. Perry and Francis L. Hawks. *North American Review* 83 (July 1856): 233–260.

*Reynolds, Robert L. *Commodore Perry in Japan.* 2d ed. New York: American Heritage, 1963.

Riesenberg, Felix. *The Pacific Ocean.* New York: McGraw-Hill, 1940.

Rodgers, John; Stevens, Henry; Gibson, William; and Brooke, John. *Yankee Surveyors in the Shogun's Seas: Records of the United States Surveying Expedition to the North Pacific Ocean, 1853–1856.* Edited by Allan B. Cole. Princeton: Princeton University Press, 1947.

Rohan, Jack. *Yankee Arms Maker: The Story of Sam Colt and His Six-Shot Peacemaker.* Rev. ed. New York: Harper, 1948.

Sakamaki, Shunzo. "Western Concepts of Japan and the Japanese, 1800–1854." *Pacific Historical Review* 6 (1937): 1–14.

———. *Japan and the United States, 1790–1853.* Tokyo, Asiatic Society of Japan, 1939.

Sansom, G. B. *The Western World and Japan.* New York: Knopf, 1950.

Schiff, Bennett. "It Took More than 200 Years to Get *This* Work Printed [Joseph Banks' Botanical Drawings of Cook's First Voyage]." *Smithsonian,* March 1983, 76–85.

Schwartz, William L. "Commodore Perry at Okinawa, from the Unpublished

Diary of a British Missionary [Bernard Bettelheim]." *American Historical Review* 51 (1946): 262–276.

Seubert, A[dolf Friedrich], ed. *Allgemeines Künstler-Lexikon oder Leben und Werke der berühmtesten bildenden Künstler.* 3 vols. 2d ed. Stuttgart: Ebner & Seubert, 1878–1879. s.v. "Heine, Wilhelm."

Sewall, John Smith. *The Logbook of the Captain's Clerk: Adventures in the China Seas.* Bangor, Maine: Glass, 1905.

Shao, Paul. *The Origin of Ancient American Cultures.* Ames: Iowa State University Press, 1983.

Shaw, Renata. "Japanese Picture Scrolls of the First Americans in Japan." *Quarterly Journal of the Library of Congress* 25 (April 1968): 134–153.

Shimazaki Tōson. *Before the Dawn.* Translated, and with an introduction and glossary, by William E. Naff. Honolulu: University of Hawaii Press, 1987.

Simons, Lewis M. "Why So Many Treasures of Western Art Are Going East." *Philadelphia Inquirer,* 28 Nov. 1987.

Smith, George. *Lewchew and the Lewchewans: Being a Narrative of a Visit to Lewchew or Loo Choo, in October, 1850.* London: Hatchard, 1853.

———. *Ten Weeks in Japan.* London: Longman, Green, Longman & Roberts, 1861.

Smith, Roberta. "When Japan Captured the French Imagination." *New York Times,* 7 Aug. 1988.

Sozanski, Edward J. "Japan's Debt to the West." *Philadelphia Inquirer,* 10 Jan. 1988.

Spalding, J. W[illet]. *Japan and around the World.* New York: Redfield, 1855.

Sproston, John Glendy. *A Private Journal of John Glendy Sproston.* Edited by Shio Sakanishi. Tokyo: Sophia University, 1940.

Statler, Oliver. *The Black Ship Scroll: An Account of the Perry Expedition at Shimoda in 1854.* 2d ed. Rutland, Vt.: Tuttle, 1964.

Stearns, Foster. "Edward Everett." In vol. 6 of *American Secretaries of State and Their Diplomacy,* 117–141. Edited by Samuel Flagg Bemis. New York: Knopf (later Cooper Square), 1928.

Stuart, Charles B. *The Naval Dry Docks of the United States.* New York: Norton, 1852.

———. *The Naval and Mail Steamers of the United States.* New York: Norton, 1853.

Taylor, Bayard. In "Editorial Correspondence," *New York Tribune,* 1853: "Report on the Japan Expedition" (5 Nov.); "Visit of Commodore Perry to the Regent of Loo-Choo" (8 Nov.); "Voyage to the Bonin or Arzobispo Iles" (9 Nov.); and "An Exploring Trip through Peel Island" (10 Nov.).

———. *A Visit to India, China and Japan.* 1855. Caxton edition, vol. 6 of *The Complete Works of Bayard Taylor.* New York: Putnam's, 1862.

———. *Life and Letters of Bayard Taylor.* See Hansen-Taylor and Scudder.

———. *Japan in Our Day.* 1871. New York: Scribner's, 1892.

Thieme, Ulrich, and Becker, Felix, eds. *Allgemeines Lexikon der bildenden Künstler.* 37 vols. Leipzig: Engelmann (later Seemann), 1907–1950. s.v. "Heine, Wilhelm."

Thunberg, Karl Peter. "Of Japan." Royal Society of London *Philosophical Transactions* 70 (1780): 143–156; Appendix, i–viii.

———. *Travels in Europe, Africa, and Asia*. 4 vols. London: Richardson, 1793–1795.

*Vagts, Alfred. "Wilhelm Heine: Traveler-Artist." *American-German Review* 22 (Oct.–Nov. 1955): 9–13.

Vernon, Manfred C. "The Dutch and the Opening of Japan by the United States." *Pacific Historical Review* 28 (February 1959): 39–48.

Walworth, Arthur. *Black Ships off Japan: The Story of Commodore Perry's Expedition*. 1946. Reprint. Hamden, Conn.: Archon, 1966.

War Records Office. *War of the Rebellion: A Compilation of the Official Records of the Union and Confederate Armies*. S.v. "Heine, William": ser. 1, vols. 11, 18, 27, 28, 35, 42, 43, 46, 51. Washington, D.C.: Government Printing Office.

Williams, Frederick Wells. *Life and Letters of Samuel Wells Williams*. New York: Putnam's, 1889.

Williams, S[amuel] Wells. *A Journal of the Perry Expedition to Japan*. Edited by F. W. Williams. Part 2 of *Transactions of the Asiatic Society of Japan* 37 (1910). Reprint. Wilmington, Del.: Scholarly Resources, 1973.

Writers' Program, Work Projects Administration. *Maryland: A Guide to the Old Line State*. American Guide Series. New York: Oxford University Press, 1940.

Zucker, Adolf Eduard. *The Forty-Eighters: Political Refugees of the German Revolution of 1848*. New York: Columbia University Press, 1950.

INDEX

ABOUT THE TRANSLATOR

Frederic Trautmann, associate professor of rhetoric and communication at Temple University, has published reviews and articles in many historical and other professional journals. He is the editor and translator of *Oregon East, Oregon West: Travels and Memoirs* by Theodore Kirchhof; *"We Were the Ninth": The History of the Ninth Regiment Ohio Volunteer Infantry* by Constantin Grebner; and *Twenty Months in Captivity: Memoirs of a Union Officer in Confederate Prisons* by Bernhard Domschcke.

Production Notes

This book was designed by Roger Eggers.
Composition and paging were done on the
Quadex Composing System and typesetting
on the Compugraphic 8400 by the design
and production staff of University of
Hawaii Press.

The text and display typeface is Galliard.

Offset presswork and binding were done by
Vail-Ballou Press, Inc. Text paper is
Writers RR Offset, basis 50.